LIVE
NOW

INSPIRING ACCOUNTS
OF OVERCOMING
ADVERSITY

LIVE NOW

GEORGE KLEIN

TRANSLATED BY CLAS VON SYDOW
PREFACE BY MIHÁLY CSIKSZENTMIHÁLYI
AUTHOR OF FLOW: THE PSYCHOLOGY
OF OPTIMAL EXPERIENCE

Prometheus Books

59 John Glenn Drive

Published 1997 by Prometheus Books

01 00 99 98 97   5 4 3 2 1

Library of Congress Cataloging-in-Publication Data

Klein, George, 1925–
    [Utvägen. English]
    Live now : inspiring accounts of overcoming adversity / George Klein ; translated by Clas von Sydow ; preface by Mihály Csikszentmihályi.
        p.   cm.
    Includes bibliographical references.
    ISBN 1–57392–154–8 (cloth : alk. paper)
    1. Courage. 2. Perseverance (Ethics). 3. Humanistic ethics. I. Title.
BJ1533.C8K5413   1997
179'.6—dc21   97–11796
                                                                                            CIP

Printed in the United States of America on acid-free paper

To Annika, Jonathan, Ester,
Miriam, Erik, Tom, and Olga,
our grandchildren

CONTENTS

PREFACE

Mihály Csikszentmihályi

We live in strange times. Space probes bring back beautiful pictures of billion-miles-long gas plumes swirling at the center of the galaxy; astrophysicists describe exactly what happened during the first few nanoseconds after the universe was formed billions of years ago. But—what should I do tomorrow? Is it worth it to go on living, or not? And what is a good life? Answers to such simple questions are just as elusive as they have ever been. Of course, there are many religious or ideological answers to the meaning of existence, but the leap of faith they require is not to everyone's taste.

It is certainly not to George Klein's, who gleefully describes himself as "religiously atheistic." History has made it difficult for him to accept easy solutions, and his training as an experimental scientist adds another layer of skepticism—as if the brutal barbarism he barely survived during World War II was not enough to raise questions about any pleasant myths regarding the role of humankind in the universe.

Yet Klein has taken on the burden of the survivor, the ancient prophetic task of wrestling with the meaning of life and death. As a wit-

9

ness to the worst pathology of the human species, he tries to understand the roots of evil, tries to interpret the signs of hope, and shares with us the result of his reflections.

Why should he, a world-renowned researcher of the causes of tumors and cancers, have anything new to say about these oldest of metaphysical issues? After all, in this age of specialization, we expect the expert to stick to the narrow area of his expertise. Wisdom, or even common sense, is supposed to have little general currency.

The way Klein contradicts these expectations is simple: in the first place, he holds on to his concrete experiences as a man—as a biological and cultural being who made it through the last two-thirds of this century in the maelstrom of Central Europe. A sensitive, clinically honest grasp of lived life is the first ingredient that makes this book, as his earlier ones—*The Atheist and the Holy City* and *Pietá**—so true, so thought-provoking. It could be objected that the experiences Klein draws on are too unique, that the tragic characters whose deeds he chronicles are irrelevant to the sane world in which we are privileged to live. But if, as some claim, the best truth is found in the scribbles of the shipwrecked, then we must pay close attention to what Klein writes. He has been in one of the worst wrecks our kind has ever engineered, and even if we were to have smooth sailing from here on out, his insights would still be indispensable.

The second strength of the book is that Klein does not embark on his quest alone. As Dante needed Virgil to lead him through hell, Klein seeks the help of humanists on his intellectual journey. Poets and philosophers help to avoid the twin chasms of denial and despair. The verses of Rainer Maria Rilke, Arthur Rimbaud, or Miklós Radnóti he quotes are no window-dressing, but an essential key for interpreting experience. When scientists follow Newton's lead in saying that they see farther because they are standing on the shoulders of giants, they rarely include nonscientists in their platform. Klein is an exception to this

---

*(Cambridge: MIT Press, 1990 and 1992, respectively).

rule. His perspective as a scientist is greatly expanded by the fact that he takes poets' words seriously and finds delight in them.

But finally, *Live Now* succeeds because of the characters it contains. These exceptional individuals Klein has known are so vividly described that it is impossible to forget them. What their stories show is a way of living that seems to be its own justification. Camus once wrote that the most concrete problem of our age is how to be a saint without believing in God. The characters in *Live Now* are no saints in the traditional mold, but they are striving to find ways of being that justify their existence without the safety-net of an external faith. They do this through intense concentration on the moment and the task at hand; through selflessness; through a genuine caring for other people, while remaining aloof from everyone else's opinions. In so doing they accomplish feats that seem beyond the reach of mere mortals.

So has Klein resolved Camus's problem? Yes and no. In one sense, the biographies he shares with us provide some of the best blueprints for living a life that is full, meaningful, and one that contributes to the well-being of others. Yet Klein is aware of the danger implicit in the tremendous energy that these remarkable individuals generate. Their hunger for stimulation, their uncompromising self-discipline, and their constant restlessness are only a step away from a fanatical drive that could trample every obstacle in its way. It is for this reason that Klein occasionally refers to them as "addicts," recognizing that their power is not always under control.

But what choices do we have? The alternatives are to find solace either in material comfort, or in the spiritual comfort of traditional belief. For those suspicious of the viability of these options Klein provides a glimpse of another choice: difficult, yes; dangerous, yes; but one that may yet provide a model for how to be a human in the next millennium.

INTRODUCTION

However one regards the issue, it must be agreed that *Homo sapiens* presently appears to be a successful biological species and will probably remain so for the foreseeable future. Exactly how far into the future we can see is a matter for discussion. James Michener has reminded us that we should be careful to rejoice at our evolutionary success since we've only been here for two, or at the most, three million years, depending upon from when we trace our origin. The dinosaurs, which we regard as failed species, ruled the planet for 150 million years. But we cannot deny that at this moment we dominate Tellus, or, in the words of the Swedish poet Harry Martinson, "the land of Doris," the gem of our solar system, even if the belief in our complete domination seems exaggerated. But our lust for life and our correlated ability to reproduce requires a certain optimism. The libido disappears and ovulation ceases in concentration camps, and many species of mammals stop reproducing in captivity. The humiliation of Native Americans in North and South America has led to the extinction of entire tribes.

Are we satisfied with our world and our place in it at this point in evolutionary history? Only a brief moment has passed, on the evolutionary scale, since our modern technology began transforming our conditions of life beyond recognition. The span of time that our technological development has claimed as compared to the total span of our evolution is briefer than the wink of an eye as compared to an entire day. But we haven't changed as biological creatures. Our heart and liver, our kidneys and brain, our chemical and physiological processes function in exactly the same way as they did in prehistoric man. If we liken the duration of our modern technological development to the wink of an eye, then we can regard our recorded history from the time of the most ancient pharaohs as perhaps half a minute.

Even at the turn of the last century, the poet, our most perceptive surveyor, knew where our civilization was heading:

> *Die Städte aber wollen nur das Ihre*
> *und reissen alles mit in ihrem Lauf.*
> *Wie hohles Holz zerbrechen sie die Tiere*
> *und brauchen viele Völker brennend auf.*
> *Und ihre Menschen dienen in Kulturen*
> *und fallen tief aus Gleichgewicht und Mass,*
> *und nennen Fortschritt ihre Schneckenspuren*
> *und fahren rascher, wo sie langsam fuhren,*
> *und fühlen sich und funkeln wie die Huren*
> *und lärmen lauter mit Metall und Glas.*

Rainer Maria Rilke, "Das Stundenbuch"

The cities, though, want only what will speed them,
and drag all with them on their headlong course.
They smash the beasts like rotten wood to feed them
and use whole nations up without remorse.
Their people serve some culture's domination
and fall afar from measure and from poise
and give the name of progress to gyration,
and travel with a growing acceleration
and have a harlot's soul and scintillation
and louder rings their glass and metal noise.

(Translation by J. B. Leishman)

The course was already set as the nineteenth century was drawing to a close. Since then things have continued in the same direction, still at a snail's pace. Our snail souls haven't increased their pace. Instead, they may even have slowed down to a complete stop, hidden in their shells, and then in some cases turned back. We're louder and more scintillating than ever, but we understand nothing. We haven't had the time to consider our new situation, much less adapt to it. The mind of Stone Age man is in our brain; we're pursued by his instincts and egged on by his way of making war. The rattling of sabers between peoples has to a large extent been muted by the threat of nuclear annihilation, but as soon as this threat is reduced to "conventional" levels—what a concept!—age-old ethnic hatreds burst forth anew. Our social relations haven't improved, and within the family they're often in much worse shape than during the Stone Age. We retain our ancestors' excellent biochemical reserve mechanisms enabling us to survive long-term starvation, but we almost never use them. Instead we store fat in our bodies in anticipation of famines that never arrive. We don't need to spend many hours gathering water, and have learned to protect ourselves from the rain and wind, the cold and the heat. Our demanding physical tasks and even many of our simpler tasks are performed by machines, while we have increasingly more leisure time to relax, rest, "enjoy ourselves," travel, or watch TV.

We're actually quite comfortable. Or are we?

According to Paul Verlaine's poetic vision our souls are inhabited by wandering, charming, masked figures who play the lute, sing, dance, or whisper to one another, but seem *"quasi tristes sous leurs déguisements fantasques"* (almost sad behind their fantastic masks). The poet's searching gaze and listening ear is not deceived by the pleasant facade:

> *Tout en chantant sur le mode mineur*
> *L'amour vainqueur et la vie opportune,*
> *Ils n'ont pas l'air de croire à leur bonheur . . .*
>
> *"Clair de lune"*

In minor key they sing artistic airs
Of gracious living, of triumphant love,
But seem to doubt this joy is truly theirs . . .

(Translation by Peter Zollman)

When everything is "under control" and we're carefree and compla-
cent, we tend to succumb to passivity. Pleasant relaxation can turn to
boredom and apathy as gradually and imperceptibly as day turns into
night. In his introductory poem to *Les fleurs du mal* titled *"Au lecteur"*
(To the Reader), Charles-Pierre Baudelaire lists the crimes and mistakes that we may commit and the misfortunes, diseases, and disfigure-
ments that we may encounter:

La sottise, l'erreur, le péché, la lésine,
occupent nos esprits et travaillent nos corps,
et nous alimentons nos aimables remords,
comme les mendiants nourissent leus vermine.

Our follies and omissions, our stinginess and sin
Possess our souls and sap our vital forces
And we nourish our favorite remorses
The way that beggars fatten vermin on their skin.

(Translation by Peter Zollman)

We try to squeeze all the pleasures out of life as we squeeze the juice
from an orange. If we haven't committed murder and arson, if we haven't
poisoned someone in order to enliven our day, if we haven't realized all
our perverse desires, it's only because of our weakness and inability to
act. But beyond all the wild beasts, hyenas, panthers, vultures, scor-
pions, apes, and snakes that howl, whimper, crawl, and roar, is yet another monster: the meanest, ugliest, and filthiest of them all. It hardly
moves and is too slothful to roar, but it's constantly about to lay the entire world to waste or swallow it in its yawning cavity:

C'est l'Ennui!—l'oeil chargé d'un pleur involontaire.
Il reve d'échafauds en fumant son houka.
Tu le connais, lecteur, ce monstre délicat,
—Hypocrite lecteur,—mon semblable,—mon frère!

He is the deadly Boredom—his tears flood in full spate,
He dreams of scaffolds, smokes his water-pipe.
Reader, you know this fiend, the dainty type:
—You hypocrite—my reader—my fellow man—my mate!

(Translation by Peter Zollman)

How does one escape Baudelaire's filthiest, most terrifying beast?

There are many ways out that are either useful or hurtful, creative or destructive, moral, immoral, or amoral. In Akira Kurosawa's early masterpiece *Rashomon—Port of Demons,* a rich merchant is traveling through the forest with his young, beautiful wife. A robber lies half asleep under a tree. The day is very hot. The robber sees the couple but is tired and apathetic and doesn't feel like doing anything. But suddenly a cool breeze revives him. He rapes the woman and kills the man. Without the cool breeze he wouldn't have had the urge or the energy to seek what is his natural way out of boredom.

Boredom, yes. Boredom is seldom mentioned as a cause of violent acts, meaningless vandalism, racist fights, or incomprehensible Nazi sympathies among teenage students. But boredom can play a more important role than many other suspected causes. Intelligent safe-crackers and other qualified criminals often answer the question "with your intelligence, can't you find an honest occupation?" with a blatant "it wouldn't be as exciting." Among the most excessive extremists we find the seemingly totally unfeeling American mass murderer who explained that the one thing that could give him a sense of being truly alive was committing murder. Adolf Eichmann, the most monstrous of them all, explained during World War II's last phase that he "will be jumping in his grave laughing" in the knowledge of the five million Jews that he murdered.*

---

*A. Tusa and J. Tusa, *The Nuremberg Trial* (New York: McGraw-Hill, 1985).

..ave chosen to mention the most horrifying examples first. But there is another side to the issue.

In the middle of his life's journey, Dante at the age of thirty-five discovered that he'd lost his way in the dark forest. He was too drowsy (*pien di sonno*) to notice when and how this had happened, he only knew that he'd lost the right way (*la diritta via*). After having continued in anguish further into the deep valley he arrived at the foot of a mountain. He looked up and saw the mountain's ridge bathed in starlight. Then his courage, which had disappeared during the anguished night, returned:

> *Allor fu la paura un poco queta*
> *che nel lago del cor m'era durata*
> *la notte, ch'i'passai con tanta pietà.*

> Then I could feel the terror begin to ease
> That churned in heart's lake all through the night . . .

(Translation by Robert Pinsky)

He rested for a moment and then began to climb the mountain, alone in the wilderness (*per la piaggia diserta*). He was now in good enough spirits to make a point to mention how he constantly placed the weight of his body on the lower foot during the ascent (*si che 'l piè fermo sempre era 'l più basso*).

But when the path became steeper, his way was blocked by three wild beasts that symbolized the dark side of his own soul but also the dark side of Florentine society: the envious and quarrelsome panther of pleasure, the angry lion of violence and pride, and the lean, lecherous she-wolf of greed. This symbolic bestiary has been interpreted thousands of times by the Dantologists of many centuries. The panther can be seen as the lax and artistically degenerate city of Florence, while the lion represents the French monarchy. The immoral and insatiable she-wolf, which mates with many animals and devours land and money instead of love, virtue, and wisdom, symbolizes the hypocritical papacy craving worldly power. The wild beasts forced the poet back down into the dark valley. He lost hope of being able to climb the mountain (*ch'io perdei la speranza de l'altezza*) because he was frightened away by carnal lust, the temptations of vanity, and the political intrigues between the burghers, the nobility, the church, and their internally quarreling factions. He felt like an eager gambler who at first is full of assurance but then suddenly loses, and weeps with his entire being.

When the poet again found himself in the deep valley "where the sun is silent" (*dove l'sol tace*) he suddenly encountered someone who seemed as if he was hoarse from a long silence (*chi per lungo silenzio parea fioco*) even before he had said anything. It was Virgil, Dante's admired spiritual mentor, who represented poetry, rationality, and humanism, and was the main source for "the beautiful style" which had won him glory and recognition (*da cui io tolsi lo bello stile che m'ha fatto onore*). Dante asked for his help against the beasts. Virgil's answer is the key to the eternally relevant *Divine Comedy* which is about us all:

A te convien tenere altro viaggio—You must choose another way.

What is this other way? The poet constantly returns to *le stelle* which he regards as his goal. The star-spangled mountain ridge drew him heavenward when he was in the forest. It was the stars that he first saw when he had climbed up the infernal funnel and viewed the sky through its narrow opening. When he was about to lift off from the mountaintop of Purgatory to fly to Paradise together with Beatrice, his soul was ready to "ascend to the stars." In the final divine vision of Paradise he saw Love, which moves the sun "and the other stars."

For most of us the stars have long since become cold, indifferent astronomical orbs that disregard us while blinking at a distance of many light years. They no longer lead our paths toward good or evil, their geometrical configurations at the time of our birth are no longer believed to determine our personality, and no wise prophet can ward off threatening dangers or foretell the future by studying them. We neither can nor want to reach Dante's goal, neither directly nor in a roundabout way. I myself am rather indignant at the heavenly injustice of Dante's world. Virgil can only take him to the top of the Purgatory mountain. Then this guide and Master, Dante's most beloved, must return to the bleak vestibule of hell, where he's doomed to spend all eternity in grey monotony simply because he was born too early to be baptized a Christian. Since Dante was born at the right time and baptized according to ritual he is allowed to follow Beatrice to Paradise. He accepts this as the natural, inevitable order of the universe.

Thus the feelings and the common sense of this most sensitive and rational poet are defeated by irrational mysticism and dogmatic frigidity.

Was this absurdity merely the result of medieval religious faith? Or could the poet not escape his wild beasts without regarding himself as the chosen one who is loved and protected by a heavenly being? Or was it primarily a sublimation of his yearning for Beatrice, who had died at a young age and whom he'd secretly admired and desired from a distance?

Or should everything be regarded as symbolism and allegory?

Whichever way we view the matter with our "modern" eyes, it's clear that Dante has managed to take "the other way." He could escape the interminable quarrel of politics and he didn't succumb to vanity, frivolity, or lust for power or greed. His way out was to create an immortal masterpiece.

Do the same beasts threaten us?

Yes, to a certain degree, but in a different way. Facing Dante's beasts can be disastrous for us as well, but in our protected reserves the beasts are less spectacular. We're probably more often threatened by Baudelaire's pipe-smoking monster: the lazy, indulgent, houka-puffing beast Ennui and his aimlessness. He robs us of the sense of being needed, and he paralyzes our capacity to use our skills. We're forced into the jungle of alienation by events beyond our control. We're rendered passive, despondent, and apathetic by socially sanctioned, generally accepted entertainments that are more or less empty.

This book is about a few individuals who've been able to escape their internal or external beasts by finding their own remarkable solutions. They're not my inventions, nor are their unusual actions the products of my fantasy—I've only observed them through the glasses of my own subjectivity. My ambition is to tell their stories as truthfully as I can, despite the risk of not being believed. (Reality is often more unbelievable than the most fantastic novels.) I don't claim to have completely understood them or their motives. Who can fully enter another human being who is or has once been alive? Only writers of fiction can create believable characters since they're allowed to assemble them from scratch.

One of my two Protean characters, Ali, tried to escape from deep disappointments and grievous personal loss. The second, Carleton, has used his exceptional gifts to escape from the incumbent dullness of conventional life. The third person, Miska, confronted the incurable pain caused by the annihilation of his family and his entire culture by immersing himself in meaningful work for others. If you don't understand their motives, you may easily brand them "obsessives" or "workaholics." But these conventional labels tell us nothing. Suffice it to say that they've found their own escape route, a way out.

I neither wish to praise nor recommend their methods. But I feel that their stories convey a message, although it is one which may say more about myself than about them. Each of us possesses an unsuspected reserve of skills and talents. One of the greatest dangers of our protected and organized way of life is our unwillingness or slothful inability to draw upon this reserve. It comes from our frequent, defective realization that we have a primary need to be active, to be involved. We tend to accept the conventional stereotypes of how life should be lived, inherited from the times of shortage and need and slyly exploited by the forces of commercialism. We don't listen enough to our own signals. Or is it that we lack the self-confidence to trust them?

The Hungarian-American psychologist Mihály Csikszentmihályi has devoted his work to this problem. My essay "When Time Stops," the last chapter of this book, examines his concept of "flow." Our experience of using our own skills when we're faced with a challenging task can transform our consciousness from trivial rambling to intense concentration. It can suspend our sense of time so that we live fully in the present instead of constantly planning for the future or mulling over the sorrows of yesterday. It grants us a rewarding sense of inner joy which we perceive as being truer and more satisfying than the rewards of the outer world.

PROTEUS—
PRELUDE

The works of great composers continue to live within us, somewhere on the cusp between the conscious and the unconscious. We remember them suddenly in the most unexpected situations. Sometimes they color our moods without us being able to identify the composer or the opus number. At other times they emerge openly and in their full glory. Sometimes you hear a piece you haven't heard in decades and know that a certain passage is approaching long before it arrives. You know that it's there and has always been there, but you haven't been able to conjure up its melody on your own. The words of great poets can act in a similar way. Suddenly scattered lines or entire stanzas can emerge out of our unconscious in a more or less hazy or articulate manner. Sometimes they speed by like a gust of wind. At other times they can occupy your entire being for a long period of time.

The Hungarian poet Mihály Babits introduces his collection of poems *The Gods Die, Man Lives* from 1928 with the sonnet "Memorial," here translated by Peter Zollman:

Memorial

No one has ever seen me. And the seasons
sail by. Each year I shed another veil
and still my soul is: veils within a veil
amid retreating melancholy seasons.

Slick like a fish, they never catch me live.
I'm Proteus, I change and melt away
like sea foam. Oh, I change, I melt away
and slip their grasp as long as I'm alive.

But when I die I leave my coffin, naked
to stand erect upon my grave forever.
I shall remain a monument forever
for all to see me motionless and naked.

The birds come, fly around me: I'm just standing.
The sun comes out, I smile and then a great cloud
looms over me, I darken with the grey cloud;
the rain turns heavier where I'm standing.

One day while walking on the beach I was reminded of Babits's sonnet. The first word I thought of was Proteus. Then the entire poem came to me, popping up like a cork that's been released from the bottom of a water tank.

Proteus. Have I met him? Yes, in two completely different yet equally authentic reincarnations. I had to look again and again, for I could not believe what I saw. But I was forced to recognize him. It was Proteus. I am no longer surprised when I look at him.

PROTEUS I—ALI

During the summer of 1965, my wife, Eva, and I were invited to a conference at the Weizmann Institute in Israel. The following week a large international congress would be held in Stockholm. I had no desire to stay at home, since we'd receive many visitors and there wouldn't be time for useful work. Wouldn't this be a good opportunity to bring one of our daughters, who was on vacation, to spend an extra week in Israel?

I wrote to an old friend, Feri Izsak, the chief surgeon in Yafo. Feri was born and raised in Beregszász, at the foot of the east Carpathians, not far from my father's village. Could he help us find a small place, preferably by the sea, perhaps in some fishing village? We wanted some peace and quiet to go swimming and sight-seeing, and I hoped to catch up on my writing.

Feri replied that there weren't any fishing villages in Israel. The only thing fishable during the summer would be compact groups of people cavorting in the surf. Despite my misguided idea, he promised, in somewhat cryptic words, to arrange a pleasant week for us. "It won't cost you any more than your envisioned fishing village." Our need for

25

sun, sand, and peace and quiet would be fully satisfied. We thanked him
and said we'd come.

After the Weizmann conference we rented a Volkswagen, drove
through the Negev desert to Eilat in the south to get a glimpse of the Red
Sea, went swimming, admired the underwater fauna, and then continued
north to find the address that Feri had recommended. The location
sounded strange: The Golf Hotel, Caesarea—nothing more. Wasn't Caesarea, the old harbor town of King Herod, an important archaeological
site? But naturally Feri knew what he was doing.

We drove from Eilat to Caesarea on a scorching Sunday and arrived
at dusk dirty, sweaty, and tired. I couldn't see the slightest glimpse of
any city or village, only Herod's ancient ruins (which were now accessible for a fee), sand dunes, the sea, and cultivated fields that alternated
with arid stretches of land. In the distance was a large, mirage-like
aquarium of a hotel. Where was my longed-for quiet retreat? There had
to be some city or village named Caesarea—why else would we've been
given the address? Perhaps it was somewhere else? I asked a passing
motorist, who laughed: "The city of Caesarea? It was leveled at least a
thousand years ago."

But it has to be here! I showed him the address of the hotel where
we were booked. He looked at me in surprise and pointed to the large
luxury aquarium. Its silhouette now loomed less improbably but more
threateningly on the horizon.

Was Feri insane? Had he forgotten that our budget was limited?
After a rather agitated discussion we concluded that Feri had indeed
sent us to a luxury hotel. I trembled in anticipation of the costs we would
most likely incur.

The porter inquired about my name. As soon as I replied, he yelled
at the top of his lungs and four members of the hotel staff came rushing
to collect our scant luggage. We were escorted to a magnificent suite on
the second floor filled with flowers and a complimentary bowl of fruit.
My heart sank and I suggested that they must have made a mistake. No,
everything was as it should be; we've been expected.

As soon as the staff left the room I feverishly searched for the small listing of the hotel's fees, but could not find it. Filled with dread, I called Feri in Yafo.

"Where have you put us? Are you out of your mind?"

"No, don't worry. You're the personal guests of the hotel's general manager who's one of my best friends."

"No, I can't accept such a favor. Why would he treat me to this luxury? I don't know even know the man."

"Calm down. Just enjoy your dinner in peace and quiet. I'll come by later and tell you about him. But be prepared for an incredible story. I hope you're not planning to retire early, because I've much to tell you before he returns from the United States and visits you tomorrow."

Two bands were at opposite ends of the enormous dining room playing both Israeli and South American music. There were very few guests, only some elderly American couples and a sprinkling of diplomats and businessmen, but no young people. My ten-year-old daughter was the only child present. Fortunately she became totally engrossed in the singing trio Los Paraguayos and didn't notice the absurdity of the situation or her parents' concern.

The staff was polite but aloof with a distant look in their eyes. During my earlier visits to Israel I'd become accustomed to a spontaneous informality which at times seemed nearly rude, yet was always friendly. Now this formal and insincere courtesy annoyed me. We ate our dinner in tense silence. Gone was our cozy "Israel mood."

Feri arrived in time for coffee. He laughed at my concern. Hadn't I noticed that there were three swimming pools to choose from? On weekdays they were almost abandoned. If I couldn't work here, I couldn't work anywhere.

I answered that I hated the place. But Eva liked it. And Margareta loved the Los Paraguayos.

"Wait until you've met the hotel manager. He was very eager to invite you as his first personal guests since taking charge a few months ago," Feri said. "As you can see, the hotel is about to go bankrupt. If anyone can turn it around, it's him. But now let's go up to your suite so that Margareta can go to bed. Then Eva and you can listen to my story until dawn."

I still felt uncomfortable. But the Los Paraguayos saluted Margareta when we left and she blushed. She went to bed with a contented weariness in her eyes which soothed the trivial worries of her parents. We sat down with Feri and I wondered if he'd tell us a story from the Arabian Nights. Feri began his tale.

FERI'S TALE

Ali Elovic comes from the same small country town as I do, Feri said, called Beregszász in Hungarian, Berehovo in Czech. The town is only about twenty miles from Kaszony, your father's village. Wasn't Beregszász the first "city" of your childhood? You remember that the town belonged to Hungary until the First World War, then to Czechoslovakia, then to Hungary again, and that it's now part of the Soviet Union. When we were young practically all of Beregszász's inhabitants, about 40 percent of which were Jews, spoke Hungarian. The large Jewish "metropolis" Munkács, with its 50 to 60 percent Jewish population and the only Hebrew senior high school in Central Europe, was only an hour's drive away. Practically all Jews from the area perished in Auschwitz; Ali's and my families, as well as yours. Hardly any Jews remain there today.

Ali and I belonged to the assimilated, Hungarian-speaking Jewish bourgeoisie. We went to the only Hungarian-speaking senior high school in Czechoslovakia. Since Ali had attended a Czech elementary school, he also spoke perfect Czech, unlike most other students. Although Ali came from a much more prominent family than I did, we were good friends. His father had an unusual position for a Jew: he was a court president. He'd been a judge during the Hungarian-Austrian monarchy and continued during the Czech regime. Compared to other bourgeois homes, Ali's was a castle. Their household was attended by four servants.

Our school was unusually good. Most of the teachers were university professors and senior lecturers from Hungary who'd "compromised" themselves politically during Bela Kun's short-lived Communist regime.*

*March 21 through August 1, 1919.

Ali was the school's best student. He was one or several years ahead of the rest of us in the class, especially in languages and foreign literature, and he didn't care much for the educational material. But he was quite the opposite of a stereotypical intellectual introvert. He was only twelve when he began earning an income, being quite successful at tutoring the less gifted children of the school. He instinctively knew how to inspire every slow or ungifted student: if the boy loved soccer, Ali would let him play as much soccer as possible as long as he followed Ali's individually prepared curriculum. Remarkably, Ali did this in a completely natural, spontaneous manner so that neither the student nor anyone else felt that he was domineering. He remained the student's friend and was never regarded as a representative of either the school or the student's often stern and over-ambitious parents.

Another of Ali's remarkable qualities, evident even in his teens, was his unusual appeal to women of all ages. They've always loved him, and still do, as you'll see. I don't really know why. We should probably ask a woman. Ali likes to say that he loves all women. He certainly seems to have convinced a great many of his devotion. I guess it could be true to a certain degree. He stood apart from the rest of us in high school even in this regard. He never cared about making real or imagined conquests merely to boast about it afterward. No, he really did love women; sometimes two or three at the same time, and with equal passion. He never could understand why love for one should exclude love for another. He preached his special gospel of love to all of us: You should love your fellow human beings. Ali regarded this as a fundamental condition for being able to live. As for women, he viewed sexual contact as the most obvious expression of this love.

"Have you seen Pasolini's film *Teorema*?" Eva asked Feri while I ordered more coffee. "It has a similar message of love. Consequently, the film's modern Christ-like protagonist is bisexual."

"That would be quite alien to Ali," answered Feri. "But let us return to Beregszász."

Since Ali was several years ahead of his class he had plenty of spare time. He read everything he could find and had a phenomenal memory.

Quite early he came across the writings of Marx, Engels, Lenin, and other revolutionaries. He was troubled by the rigid social structure of school and society, and was ashamed of his bourgeois family. He couldn't have been more than thirteen when he persuaded other middle-class boys to ask for a more substantial lunch bag at home. Ali instructed them to tell their worried mothers that they became very hungry during the long school hours. Didn't the mothers know that teenage boys need plenty of food? The strategy was successful. The boys shared their double lunch rations with their poorer classmates. Ali spearheaded the action through his own good example. But he was later to realize that charity doesn't solve any social problems but rather carries with it some less desirable psychological effects.

Ali also socialized with many adults. He had especially many friends among those ten years older than himself. With their help he sought contact with the town's relatively small but strictly disciplined Communist party. He was allowed to attend their meetings, which were held in a narrow room behind a tobacco shop. At first he was suspected of being a bourgeois spy, but Ali wasn't deterred. He stubbornly attended all meetings and energetically participated in the discussions. Soon after turning fifteen he caused a sensation by taking a summer job at a construction site. This had never before happened to a middle-class family in the area as far as anyone could remember. The judge's son was severely reprimanded at home and by friends, but he shrugged off the criticism.

At first the workers weren't impressed. Their obscene insults turned to derision when Ali's mother brought him a sumptuous lunch on his first day. Ali refused to touch it. He worked as hard as he could even though he wasn't used to it and although he suffered from a bad back and developed sores on his hands. The workers stopped criticizing him after a few days. Ali ate with them and during breaks he recounted what he had read in the Communist papers at the tobacco shop. He spoke the language of the workers with as much ease as he spoke the language of his bourgeois background.

A few years after Hitler's rise to power in Germany, Ali's father made an unexpected announcement at the dinner table. He had never before

in any way stressed his or his family's Jewishness. He had instead identified himself as a Hungarian-speaking citizen of the Czech democracy.
He belonged to a Jewish congregation, but wasn't religious. His sons
weren't even circumcised, which was the ultimate sign of their assimilation. Therefore the family was quite surprised when the father announced that henceforth they would have to regard themselves as Jews.
The Nuremberg laws were in effect, with predictable consequences.
Pogroms on an unforeseen scale could start at any moment, not because
they were capitalists or Communists, but simply because they happened
to be Jews. Ali's father realized right away that Hitler was a paranoid
maniac who wouldn't let himself be stopped.

Despite the fact that Ali had already chosen to go his own way and
only seldom spoke with his father, he was greatly moved by the judge's
measured words. He decided to fight anti-Semitism wherever he encountered it. An opportunity soon arose when one of his previous girlfriends in a fit of jealousy in the schoolyard called him "dirty, stinking
Jew." Ali slapped her as well as a boy who came to her defense. The
principal's investigation of the incident proved that the girl had reason
for her jealousy. She could prove that Ali was having an affair with the
beautiful French teacher. The teacher was fired and Ali's father was
asked to withdraw his son from the school. But Ali was allowed to continue as a private student.

When things calmed down, the change proved very positive for Ali. It
took him just a month or two to learn everything that was taught during the
course of a regular school year. The rest of his time he used for his own
activities. The effect was soon evident. A long bicycle tour on his own
through the poverty-stricken countryside made him familiar with the
meager conditions under which many people lived. Shortly thereafter, sixteen-year-old Ali organized the first workers' strike in the region's history.

I don't think you can imagine what a feat this was. A strike was
simply an unheard-of concept. Ali was driven by heartfelt anger over the
indescribable poverty he had seen during his wanderings. He picked a
strategic moment for his action, just before the grape harvest. A large
number of casual laborers lined up each morning for a hard day's work,

for which they were paid a pitiful salary that they regarded as a great privilege. Many had large families, and their children were constantly starving. Ali was well aware of the great profits that the wine-growers made on the laborers' account. He was certain that a strike would have an immediate impact, since he knew that any delay in the harvest would be catastrophic for the owners.

Ali presented his plans to the Communists and the Social Democrats without gaining their support. But he was so convinced of his cause that he went ahead with it anyway. He gave speeches to the laborers when they lined up in the mornings. After some hesitation, they began to listen to him. When Ali set up a strike fund with the money he had saved from tutoring, they understood that he was serious. A growing number were convinced that they actually had a real chance of winning better conditions. The action was successful. Ali's construction worker friends signed up as voluntary strike guards. A special police force appeared, making threatening moves, but Ali knew that it had no right to intervene. The wine growers tried to harvest with the help of their own families, but gave in after a few days. They had no choice if they wanted to save the grapes. The laborers' salaries were increased by 150 percent. Ali became something of a people's hero in his home town. Even the wine growers viewed him with grudging respect. Several of them were close friends of his parents.

After his graduation Ali studied law in the remote capital of Prague. In a few months he had made hundreds of new contacts, mostly within Socialist and Communist circles. He wrote articles for several leftist papers and founded a new Socialist youth club. He wrote home to his family in Beregszász, but avoided visiting for several years. After finishing his degree he began his military service in the Czech army. It was 1937, the year before the Munich agreement.

He became as intensely involved in the military as in his earlier commitments, and his skills were soon noticed by his superiors. He was appointed to a special unit in the Sudetes assigned with the task of fighting the paramilitary Nazi organizations that operated with German support. Once there he advanced to lieutenant's rank in record time, and participated in the increasingly frequent armed skirmishes with the

Nazi organizations. Soon he was in charge of the whole unit. The young Socialist who wanted to save the world had been transformed into a loyal soldier determined to combat "the cancer of Europe."

Events didn't turn out the way he had hoped. Instead of a "cure for cancer" came Munich and the partitioning of Czechoslovakia. According to the agreement, Czech troops that remained within the areas annexed by Germany would be allowed to leave. But the German commander presented a list of thirty-two officers who would be detained, and Ali was one of them. The impotent Czech government settled for a weak protest. The thirty-two officers were severely tortured and put on a sealed train destined for Dachau. Ali had hidden a knife in his shoe. After many hours of persistent work he was able to force an opening in the damaged door to the aged cattle transport car and escaped along with a few fellow officers. He then walked for two months through the mountains before reaching our home town of Beregszász. At this time the entire Subcarpathian region had been reclaimed by the half-fascistic Hungarian state. Anyone who had been a member of the Czech army was regarded as an enemy.

Ali was arrested the day after his return. A police dossier turned up with information about his Communist contacts and the laborers' strike. In jail he met several of his earlier Communist comrades. Twice a week he was questioned under torture, but after a few weeks he was freed and allowed to return to his parents' home. His father and brother were at home when he arrived. They had been fired from their positions as a result of the anti-Jewish laws. They were without work and the family was in dire economic straits.

Ali found a job at the town hotel as a waiter. It was degrading work to serve the arrogant and often drunk Hungarian officers, who took every opportunity to express contempt for Jews and other "inferiors." But Ali ignored them. He was happy to be able to support his family. Disaster struck one night, however, when the same girl that Ali had slapped in school arrived in the company of an army captain. She was now a well-dressed, haughty lady and did her best to humiliate Ali, whom she pretended not to recognize. Ali took this in stride. Around midnight the

army captain took command of the Gypsy musicians and began dancing
to their accompaniment. Suddenly he started singing an infamous anti-
Semitic song. Ali grabbed a wine-bottle, walked up to him and smashed
it against his head. The captain collapsed, unconscious. Ali was immediately arrested and taken to the most dreaded police station in De-
brecen, where he was beaten and tortured daily. The interrogation leader
accused him of having killed the captain. It was a lie, but Ali had
cracked the captain's skull. Of course, this was not the crux of the
matter. In the eyes of the military the much worse crime was that a Jew
had struck down a Hungarian officer. It was imperative to demonstrate
the severity of this offense. The charges against Ali mounted. They tried
to force him to confess to being a spy. He was kept in solitary confinement between his increasingly severe "treatments," but he refused to
sign the documents that were placed before him. The court sentenced
him to death anyway. After the sentence had been announced, the torture stopped and Ali was allowed to get some sleep in his solitary cell.
The days went by and Ali waited for his execution, full of fear. He had
no wish to die; he loved life more than ever. Ali's fighting spirit returned
when the Catholic priest, who knew that Ali was a Jew, came to his cell
to obtain a last confession before the execution. Ali kicked the priest in
his backside and threw a chair at him. He didn't rough up the rabbi who
arrived after the priest, but also sent him packing.

Late that evening before Ali was to be shot, an older guard came to
him. The guard had earlier been relatively kind to the convicted youth,
and now came to tell him that dying wasn't hard. It's a quick process;
your eyes are covered and you're snuffed out like a candle. Dying of
cancer was much worse. The guard offered to carry out Ali's last wish.
Did he want a good meal or a bottle of wine? If he so desired, the guard
could even find him a woman. But Ali wasn't interested. He asked to be
allowed to breathe some fresh air and to look at the moon and the stars
one last time from the prison yard. Ali's wish was granted. In the relaxed
presence of the guard he drank a glass of wine and admired the con-
stellation of Cassiopeia.

The rectangular yard had the prison on one side and was surrounded by a thick wall. There were two watchtowers at the far corners of the wall. Ali doesn't know if it was the wine or the knowledge that he would be shot in a few hours which made the walls seem less high than before. What did it matter if he was shot now rather than later? A sudden impulse made him dart off and climb the wall with a strength he didn't know he possessed. He jumped down on the other side chased by shouts, shots, and searchlights. He stopped and pressed tightly against the exterior of the wall beyond the reach of the searchlights. When the lights searched in another direction he ran off as fast as he could.

Ali found himself in a large park among bushes and trees. In the moonlight he caught sight of a man on a park bench. Ali was prepared to strangle the man if he turned out to be a guard or a policeman, but he was an old Jew. Ali approached him and quickly but silently identified himself as a Jew who had escaped and was in need of help. The old man stood up without a word, looked about cautiously, removed his coat and draped it over Ali's prison clothes. They then walked through the sleeping city, as if out for an evening stroll. They arrived at the man's house without having met anyone.

The old man hid Ali for several months. Large wanted posters with Ali's picture were displayed everywhere in town describing the runaway as a dangerous criminal who'd been sentenced to death for his violent acts. A substantial reward was promised to anyone who could provide information regarding Ali's whereabouts, and anyone who hid him risked execution by firing squad. But the old man ignored all of this. He'd lost his wife and only son in a boating accident a few years earlier and now lived alone. He experienced Ali's presence as if his own son had returned to him. Ali grew very fond of the man but felt restless after a few months. He'd grown a long beard, shaved his hair and wore dark glasses. Ali wanted to venture out into the world again!

After bidding a painful farewell, Ali took the train to Budapest, where he hoped to be able to disappear among the city crowds. When he arrived at the railroad station he encountered soldiers everywhere. Because of his isolation he knew nothing of the cause: while he'd been hiding, the war had broken out. The old man was uninterested in world

events and had said nothing about the war. During his journey Ali had
not dared speak to anyone, much less reveal his ignorance of the political turn of events. Worried by the apparent mobilization, he decided to
continue toward Poland. Ali hoped to get in touch with some Communist
journalists in Warsaw, and took the train to a village up north in the
mountains where he would try to walk across the border. When he arrived he was so tired that despite lacking the proper identification documents, he took a room in a small hotel. The owner was in the army, and
his wife ran the hotel on her own. As soon as Ali saw her he felt safe. He
was not mistaken. Despite his tired and disheveled condition and long
beard they were immediately attracted to each other. Without asking,
the woman knew that Ali was a refugee. After two intense days and
nights she simply said that her brother, who knew the mountains better
than anyone else, was prepared to help him across the border.

Ali's voluntary imprisonment in the small hotel room and his passionate affair left no room for political discussions. The silent brother
who led him across the mountains with unfailing precision turned out to
be a deaf-mute. Ali crossed the border in a euphoric mood, still completely ignorant of the war, the Molotov-Ribbentrop Pact,* and—most
important—the partitioning of Poland between Hitler's Germany and
Stalin's Soviet Union. Ali believed that he was entering a free country
where his Socialist friends would welcome him with open arms. But after
just a few kilometers he came upon a Russian patrol that took him
straight to the military police. Only now did he realize his mistake. Still,
he remained confident. He'd been persecuted as both a Communist
sympathizer and a Jew. He would certainly be treated as a friend and
would perhaps not even have to contact anyone in Warsaw.

But his welcome at the police station was anything but friendly. He
was forced to stand with his face against the wall and his arms above his

---

*In 1939 Soviet Premier Vyacheslav Molotov (1890–1986) and Nazi German Min-
ister of Foreign Affairs Joachim von Ribbentrop (1893–1946) signed what is also known
as the Russo-German Nonaggression Pact. This agreement allowed the Soviets to seize
eastern Poland, attack Finland, and absorb two Romanian provinces without opposition
from Germany, subsequent to that country's September 1939 invasion of Poland.

head for several hours. He understood only one recurring word of the conversation behind his back: "spy." Ali's explanation during his interrogation fell upon deaf ears. He was accused of spying regardless of what he said. Then he was thrown into a military prison with several hundred Polish, Hungarian, Jewish, Czech, Russian, and Ukrainian prisoners. The Russians and Ukrainians had tried to flee to the west. The others were on their way eastward, attempting to flee the Nazis. It made no difference; they were all caught in the same trap.

In prison Ali was subjected to new interrogations that continued for three days and nights. The interrogating officers tried to convince Ali to confess to being a spy, but he refused. He was then transferred to a prison in Poltava, where he was kept in solitary confinement for a long period, with little access to food and water, constant interrogations, little sleep, and a persistent lamp burning in his face. The interrogations consisted of mechanically repeated demands to sign a confession that he was a spy. Every now and then he was roughed up, but the long, mostly sleepless nights and the strong lamplight were worse torture. This carefully rehearsed procedure got most prisoners to sign anything. Ali cannot say for how long he was held in Poltava. He lost all sense of time during this period. It could have been weeks or months.

One day Ali was denied food or water. Three days later, when he could hardly stand on his own two legs, he was led in to the officer who had conducted all earlier interrogations and who used to laugh at Ali or spit in his face. This time he greeted Ali with warm, delicious-smelling chicken soup. Next to the soup was the prepared confession. Ali was asked to sign as a condition for being allowed to eat. But he refused to take a seat and asked to be returned to his cell.

After a while he received tea and bread and a note that he was to be shot the next day. But he was now too weak and tired to worry about death. The lamp was turned off and he slept like a log through the night. The next day he was taken by heavily armed soldiers to a quarry, where he was handed a shovel and ordered to dig his own grave. When he was finished, he was blindfolded. An officer read his death sentence: execution by firing squad for spying. The order to fire was given and Ali heard

the shots. But instead of being cut down dead he suddenly heard the
voice of the interrogating officer: "Will you sign now?"

This was too much and Ali fainted. He woke up in his old cell. The
next morning he once again faced the interrogation officer, who now
seemed uninterested and factual, and merely read out the military
court's verdict. Ali was convicted of crossing the border illegally in an
attempt at spying, and was sentenced to five years of hard labor.

After having read the verdict, the officer suddenly turned amicable,
and even joked with Ali. Ali then asked: "Comrade officer, can you please
tell me what hard labor means? Will I die from exhaustion or starvation?"

The officer's face was now gentle and mild. In a friendly tone of
voice he said: "You'll eat, you'll live, but you won't long to sleep with a
woman." He then laughed out loud and continued: "No, my friend, that
thought'll never cross your mind while you're doing hard labor."

The case was closed. Ali was herded together with about sixty other
condemned prisoners in a tightly packed cattle railway car, and the long
train began rolling toward an unknown destination. Ali was lucky to be
near the door and could look out at the sky and at passing trains. Sometimes he stood, sometimes he could sit.

If you ask Ali about the most important moment of his life, he'll tell
you of the instant during this infinitely long train ride when he happened
to look out through the iron bars of the door during a short stop at an unknown station. In the motley crowd of people jostling about like at most
train stations, he suddenly spotted a familiar face. For a moment he
couldn't believe his eyes, but the young woman in a Russian military
nurse's uniform was Adi, the tobacconist's daughter from Beregszász
who used to make tea and sometimes join in the passionate political discussions that were held during the Communist meetings behind the
shop. At first she'd been very suspicious of the judge's son, but her suspicion turned to admiration after Ali's successful strike.

Ali called out her name as loudly as he could through the bars. She
immediately recognized him. When she realized that he was a prisoner
she began a desperate search for some official. But the train rolled off
before she could find anyone.

The train ride took countless days and nights. The crowded prisoners were given tea, water, and bread at irregular intervals, and a couple of latrine buckets. When the train made a longer stop at a station, the dead were carted off. The temperature became progressively colder. A prisoner versed in geography kept track of the station signs. He observed that the train was on its way to the Arkhangelsk area in the northwest Soviet Union.

Feri looked at me. "Do you want me to continue?" Margareta and Eva had gone to bed a long time ago.

"Yes, even if it takes all night," I answered. "I don't want to meet Ali until you've told me everything you know."

After traveling for several more days, they were taken off the train at a station called Yercovo. After a strenuous march Ali and his unfortunate companions arrived at a labor camp that was part of a several-miles-long belt of similar camps. The prisoners were each given a number and were divided up into work groups of fifty led by a foreman. Their task was to chop down and process trees and they were forced to produce a proscribed quantity of timber each week.

Ali's group consisted of criminals, political prisoners, fugitives, and innocent people like Ali who'd fallen into the hands of the patrol. The professional criminals were the appointed leaders. Ali's foreman, a convicted murderer, behaved in an exceptionally cruel manner toward the prisoners and took a particular dislike to Ali.

The prisoners worked sixteen-hour days. When Ali collapsed of exhaustion on his wooden cot in the evenings he often remembered what the officer in Poltava had told him. Ali worked and ate but never felt the desire for a woman.

But the Arkhangelsk camp was not the most punishing. After some time he was moved to a labor camp in Kamchatka, where he arrived after a trip of several weeks. Here, 36,000 prisoners worked twelve hours a day in a coal mine underground. No one had ever left the place alive. Among the prisoners were criminals, deserters, juvenile offenders, bankers, beggars, waiters, policemen, generals, political prisoners, and murderers— all of many nationalities. The larger groups were Russians, Jews,

Ukrainians, Tartars, Slovaks, and Hungarians. The camp also featured an "intellectual elite," that included the prominent Communist ideologue Karl Radek. Radek's revolutionary faith was unbroken. He insisted that the party had the right to imprison everyone in the camp including himself, regardless of the great personal injustice done. Individual tragedies were of no importance as long as the revolution persevered. Radek held endless discussions with a general who maintained that the party leadership consisted of liars and criminals. A favorite remark of Radek's was that a river is important, not its individual drops of water.

The outbreak of the Finnish Winter War (1939–1940) between Finland and the Soviet Union caused a complete breakdown of transportation. Food rations dwindled disastrously and eventually disappeared. The prisoners died like flies. They fried pine cones, rats, and mice— anything they could find. There were instances of cannibalism. Ali found a place were mushrooms grew on dead trees and managed to subsist on these for a while. He quickly lost weight. Even the guards and officers starved. The work dropped to sham levels. Sometimes only half of the work force returned in the evening, the other half having died during the day. Ali lost all sense of time. The fellow prisoner who upon their arrival had informed him of the total number of prisoners now told him that seven months had passed and only four thousand were still alive. After two weeks and an additional dysentery epidemic only 1,600 remained. Ali knew that he could survive for a few more weeks at the most.

The night after Ali became aware of his numbered days and had abandoned all hope, he was told to report immediately to the camp commander. He could no longer walk without support and was assisted by two guards while he kept mumbling that he was innocent of committing any crime. Against all hope he pleaded for his life. But the commander gave him a different message than he'd expected. Ali would be freed the next day in order to be drafted into the Czech army which had been reconstituted in the western Soviet Union. He fainted.

Only much later did Ali find out what had happened. The Germans were on the outskirts of Moscow while Leningrad was under siege. In early 1942 a Czech exile government had agreed with the Soviet government to gather all available Czech soldiers and found a new Czech army. This was the official grounds for Ali's release after two and a half years of imprisonment. But no one would ever have found him had not Adi from Beregszász raised hell and high water. She approached Russians and Czechs, party representatives and military brass, but was snubbed everywhere. Her tale of Ali's work for the party was ignored. There was a war on and no time to look into the whereabouts of an individual person. But Adi never gave up. She signed up with the Czech army as soon as possible. It then consisted only of some ten officers and a hundred men who were housed in an old school. They didn't want a woman at first, but Adi persisted and was eventually accepted.

She then continued her campaign for Ali's release. She insisted that it was an obligation of the Czech army to secure his freedom since he must still be regarded as a Czech officer. The provisional Czech embassy looked into it, but the Soviet authorities answered that no one with Ali's name had entered the Soviet Union. Adi knew this was incorrect. She continued to explore all available channels. Finally Ali was found, literally at the last moment. He weighed only sixty-five pounds and was taken directly to the military hospital at the Czech army headquarters in Kuybyshev.

Ali spent three months in the hospital. Not even the stubborn Adi believed that he'd survive, but after three weeks his prognosis improved and he began to gain weight. And as a result he regained his lust for life. His curiosity about the people around him and his natural cheerfulness burst forth anew. He wanted to learn about everything that had happened in the world during his imprisonment. He also quickly regained his lust for women. A beautiful Russian nurse in the hospital was his first conquest. Three months after being admitted, he left the hospital as strong and full of life as before his hellish journey.

Like Adi and her companion, a Moravian teacher, Ali immersed himself in restless preparations with the Czech army. There was little time. Czech soldiers were arriving from everywhere and it was increasingly difficult to find barracks for them all. Ali was appointed training officer for a mixed group of young men. Runaways from Jewish religious schools who'd never held a weapon in their hands were thrown together with Ruthenian peasant sons from the Carpathian mountains who didn't know left from right and had difficulty reading or writing. Still, this wasn't a sufficient outlet for Ali's energy, and so he took up soccer. His youthful athleticism remained, and he was soon the star of the Czech soccer team. Every Sunday they played against Russian soccer clubs. Ali also sang in the army choir, wrote comic sketches and short plays for the army's Saturday soirées, and developed close friendships with both Czech and Russian officers. Everyone liked his constant good humor, his ability to take life for what it is, to joke and talk about serious things, to chase girls and, if need be, to drink with his buddies.

One day Ali met the daughter of a Russian general who was a leading member of the regional hierarchy. Zora was slender and beautiful, unlike most stout Russian women. She spoke French and German and loved western literature. She and Ali took long walks together and discussed poetry. Though they were careful to hide it from the prudish official world, they soon moved in together. Barely a month had passed before Zora brought Ali into the general's home to introduce him as her future husband. But the thought of marriage was alien to Ali. He'll tell you himself that he has pretty much the same ideas as he had in his youth: he loves all women, and he'd betray the female sex if he were to tether himself to just one of them for life. He claims that married men are like chained prisoners. But Ali's situation in Russia was complicated. His imprisonment had extinguished his romantic dream of a Communist world revolution and he now viewed Stalinist reality exactly as it was. The Soviet Union was in the middle of a devastating war. Ali wanted to fight against the Nazis who held his family and hometown in their grip. He needed a kind of foothold, and consequently marrying Zora was not an unthinkable prospect.

Despite their mutual courteousness, Ali was not well-received by Zora's parents. The general was polite but stern, and rejected the thought that the Soviet justice system could make a mistake. Ali was a Jew, a foreigner, and had been convicted by a Soviet court. Zora was the general's only daughter. He and his wife advised strongly against the planned marriage. For a while Zora was sent off to live with an uncle in Tashkent to study, but she returned after three weeks and lived openly with Ali. Soon thereafter Ali was ordered to take charge of the so-called punishment unit, which consisted of Czech citizens who had served time in Russian jails for criminal offenses. These were very hardened men. According to rumor they would fight the Germans on the western front. After a few months of training in 1943, Ali and his troops were sent to the front. A high-ranking Czech officer told Ali in confidence that Zora's father had asked for the transfer "in order to test the courage of my possible son-in-law."

By now the Germans had lost the battle of Stalingrad and were under heavy pressure along the entire front. They made desperate attempts to regain the initiative and, in order to reconfirm the myth of the invincibility of the German army, mounted a large counteroffensive in the Kharkov area, about 250 miles east of Kiev. Ali's unit was part of a force of about a thousand men who were thrown into the fighting. They found themselves in a frozen wasteland that had suffered severely during the war's earlier period. Because of the quick advance after Stalingrad, the Russian supply lines had been stretched dangerously thin. Every soldier was needed, and the inexperienced but rested Czechs were more than welcome.

Ali's unit was assigned to defend a stretch along the river by the village Sokolovo. This was sheer madness. Three hundred and fifty inexperienced soldiers were to hold a two-and-a-half-mile-long stretch against several dozen German tanks until the spring flood began a few months later. They mounted their machine guns in a half circle in front of the frozen river in order to prevent the Germans from crossing. Ali was responsible for one of these posts. The nearby villages had already been recaptured by the Germans. Gunfire was heard close-by when a dozen German tanks rolled out of the little forest opposite Ali's position. They spread out in both directions under heavy fire. Ali saw his men abandon their machine-gun posts and try to flee across the frozen river. Several of his friends and comrades-in-arms, including Adi's Moravian companion, fell. Through his binoculars Ali saw that he was badly wounded but alive. Ali carefully crept up to him and pulled him into his own bunker. He then threw himself behind his machine gun and, shaking with fear and anger, began firing at a group of German soldiers who were approaching behind a tank. Believing that the Russian resistance was broken, the Germans advanced fairly carelessly. Ali was convinced that the end was near, but he wanted to die in battle rather than once again be taken prisoner. Let them come and try to take me, he thought.

They tried. Wave after wave moved toward Ali's machine-gun nest. He mowed them down, all alone, with two severely wounded men and a corpse for company in the bunker. The sun was descending and he was running out of ammunition. He had just loaded his gun to shoot the wounded and kill himself when a violent barrage of blasts opened from the other side of the river. Suddenly the Russian artillery got going. This was an unexpected surprise for the German tanks; they turned around and retreated in panic. Ali kept firing at any Germans he could see, but now Russian shrapnel began to fall on his position. The artillery obviously didn't know that one of their own posts that far up still held on.

Suddenly the explosions ceased and Ali saw his own forces advancing on both sides, pursuing the fleeing Germans. Ali began to walk back toward the river with his badly wounded friend on his back. When the front had calmed down, a patrol was sent up from the Russian positions to see what had happened to Ali and his bunker. The bunker was empty, but ninety-six dead Germans were strewn in a half circle in front of it. Soon Ali was found near the river. He was staggering along carrying his wounded friend. They hailed him as a hero and asked if he knew how many Germans he'd killed. He didn't know, and he wasn't interested. His only thought was to repay his debt to Adi. Her friend was unconscious but alive. Ali took him to the field hospital and then looked for Adi, who was the hospital's head nurse. But Adi was dead. A German grenade had torn her to pieces when she tried to bring wounded soldiers to the hospital. Her friend died an hour later. Ali drank an entire bottle of vodka and slept for two days and nights. When he awoke, he was told that he was up for promotion and a high medal of distinction. But he wasn't interested. He wanted more vodka and to keep sleeping. They kept him in the hospital where he was treated for shell shock and given tranquilizers. But Ali stole the liquor from the surgery and stayed drunk. Finally, at his insistence, he was sent back to his own unit to continue fighting, drunk as he was. Ali drank and fought, drank and fought. He tried not to think of anything at all.

I shuddered. Feri looked at me, perplexed. "It was nothing," I said. "I was just reminded of my own experiences with the Russian soldiers who conquered Budapest. They fought from house to house. They saved our lives. They raped the women, stole watches and other valuables. Many were drunk. Was Ali one of them? Could he have been one of them? Is that what you become when you're hunted, homeless, armed, and driven against a mighty enemy, day after day, week after week, month after month—or, as with the Russian soldiers I had seen—for up to six long years? But don't try to answer my impossible question; I know the answer. Continue telling me about Ali."

The Germans amassed their entire force in the area to recapture Kharkov, but without success. They were forced to withdraw and in doing so opened the route toward the Ukraine. Before the Czech unit began moving west again, Ali received his first medal of distinction: The Order of the Red Star. Soon thereafter a congratulatory telegram arrived from Zora's father, the general. Ali was welcome to marry Zora. The general offered to get him a few days leave and to prepare a grand wedding. Ali threw the telegram in the wastepaper basket and looked for more vodka.

The westward advance continued. Ali kept drinking and fighting. Sometimes the Czech unit was granted R & R periods of several days or weeks when they regrouped and recovered behind the front. Vodka was not difficult to find, and many liked drinking with Ali. His well-honed skill at cheering up depressed people by clowning around now came in handy. Everyone liked him, no matter how drunk he was, and he was seldom sober. He also had no problems finding women. He made love to Czech girls from his own unit and Ukrainian women whose men were at the front, and he often woke up in a different bed each morning. Often he wouldn't remember what had happened the night before or during the previous weeks. Only when he was given important assignments that demanded his full concentration did he snap out of his drunken state. Then, after having completed his task in exemplary manner, he would throw himself into an alcoholic stupor again. Ali was constantly awarded new medals. He pinned them on his chest but viewed them as part of his clown's costume.

If you meet Czechs who served at the same part of the front as Ali, they'll tell you lots of stories about him. There are legends about his quick reactions, his talent for planning and coordination, and especially his ability to relate to anyone. He's still able to get very different types of people or groups of people to cooperate. His language abilities came in handy. For a while he worked as interpreter and translator to the Czech supreme commander, and thereby got to know the Russian army leadership. Ali easily charmed the Russian staff officers, behaving as naturally with them as with anyone else. He drank and joked with them—they loved his raunchy stories—and for a moment now and then he was able to help them forget the war.

Ali's reputation reached General Konjev, who was in charge of the Ukrainian front. After a meeting when Konjev, according to what Ali says, laughed so hard at one of his ribald stories that the next visiting group had to wait for several minutes, Ali received a new medal and was appointed communication officer and liaison between the Czech and Soviet armies. According to Ali his fellow Czech officers insisted that Ali won the award for his ability to drink with the Russian officers. But he prefers to think that he was rewarded for his devotion to the patriotic Russian and Ukrainian women.

The Russian winter was again approaching. After a twelve-day train ride, which was constantly interrupted by German air strikes, the Czech unit was employed in the battle of Kiev. Ali was dispirited when he marched into the city with the Red Army. Over a hundred of his soldiers and fellow officers had been killed in battle. Besides the obligatory rounds with the Russian officers, Ali hadn't touched alcohol in several weeks, and he hadn't chased any women. He fought his depression by working as hard as he could. Whenever possible, Ali volunteered to lead assaults on the enemy. He had no desire to rest. Against his nature he had stopped leaving the camp at night. He had had enough of waking up in new beds each morning with different women whose names he couldn't remember. The war was raging. It had to be won before he could focus on life again.

The year 1943 was drawing to its end. The war had been going on for almost four years. The Germans were in retreat on all fronts, but they were still strong and convinced that they'd win the war. They wanted to sit out the winter in the Ukraine while preparing their spring offensive. But when the Red Army suddenly crossed the Dnjepr River, the Germans were forced to flee along the entire Ukrainian front, retreating faster and in a wider sector than the Russians had expected. The Red Army pursued the Germans as well as they could, but it was often difficult to get quick information about the exact positions of the home troops.

At a certain sector of the front the Germans were approaching their prepared positions in the town of Biela Cerkev. The Czechs were ordered to take up positions south of the city and block off the Germans' probable escape route. In the town of Ruda they fought from building to building. The Germans put up a desperate resistance, despite a freezing temperature of thirty degrees below zero centigrade. The soldiers of both sides wore white snow camouflage, making it difficult to tell friend from foe. The situation was further complicated by the fact that strategically important locations could be captured and lost four or five times a day.

Marshal Vasily Chukov was in charge of the entire southern front. Ali was assistant and interpreter to his own Czech general. In this role he participated in Chukov's meetings with the commander-in-chief of the front sector and was well-known to the marshal. During one meeting a message arrived that the entire Russian army leadership of a certain front sector, including seven generals and two hundred officers and staff, were trapped in a pocket that was cut off from the home army. This came as a shock. Even worse, the trapped group carried several highly classified documents that under no conditions could be allowed to fall into the hands of the Germans. Chukov and his aides were forced to consider annihilating everybody and everything within the surrounded pocket. But first they decided to try a rescue mission. Chukov chose Ali for the desperate task. Ali was given an armored car and ten men plus a letter from Chukov which entitled him to order all Russian officers and soldiers whom he met along the way to join him if he so demanded. But Ali never used Chukov's letter. He felt it would be impractical to in-

crease the number of people in the commando unit assigned with the
task of stealing through the German lines unnoticed in order to reach the
surrounded Russian officers, who might not be fully aware of their vulnerable situation.

Ali and his men drove slowly with their headlights off. They saw and
heard the relentless artillery duel between the Russian and German bat-
teries. After determining the units' respective positions they left the armored car in the forest and hid during the day. Just before dark Ali observed through his binoculars the little village where the Germans had
concentrated some of their troops. There was intense activity. The Germans were obviously preparing an offensive. A German reconnaissance
plane began to mark the Russian positions with flares. Ali supplied four
of his men with similar flares, and ordered them to circle the village
under cover of darkness and mark the entire German-occupied village
with rockets that could be confused with the German markings. When
the men were on their way and Ali knew that their rockets would soon
be fired, he opened the hood of the armored car and raced the motor at
full throttle, making it sound like a tank. At the same time he began to
fire toward the village from the armored car. The remaining soldiers
were ordered to fire their assault rifles while constantly changing positions, making the Germans think that an entire tank battalion was approaching. When the Germans aimed their searchlights, Ali could easily
pick them off.

Ali's plan was based on his earlier experience of the Germans' style
of action. As long as they followed their carefully prepared plan, they
were unbeatable. But as soon as something didn't work according to
schedule, they were helpless. This was what was happening now. A
dozen German planes flew in over the area to bomb the Russian positions that should have been marked by the reconnaissance plane. Just
as Ali expected, they dropped their bombs on all of the marked positions, including the German troop concentration in the little village.
Total chaos broke out in the village, and Ali could easily reach the surrounded Russian pocket of resistance with his armored car without
firing a single shot. Quickly he explained the situation to the surprised

Russian generals, who didn't know that they were surrounded. They immediately destroyed all sensitive documents.

A few minutes after the papers were burned and while the Germans were still in an utter state of confusion, Ali got the generals into his armored car. The soldiers had to follow on their own. The entire force made their way unharmed through the jumbled German lines, whose defenders now had to take shelter both from their own planes and the Russian artillery. When they arrived at Chukov's headquarters, everyone was speechless. No one had expected Ali to return alive. He was promoted to the rank of major and awarded the Order of the First Degree in the Great Patriotic War, one of the highest decorations available. But now Ali wanted vodka again.

As you've noticed I've collected some pretty detailed information about what happened up to this point, partly through my talks with Ali and partly from other Czech friends who were in the Red Army. But it's difficult to find out what happened during the war's last phase. Ali fought, drank, and advanced with the army toward the west. He received yet another dozen medals, but now claims not to remember why he got them. His memory of town names is hazy, and he remembers even less about all the women he slept with along the way. He sometimes recalls their voices, but not their faces. Yet he still claims to have loved every one of them, for as long as it lasted.

Despite his often dazed state Ali continued to fulfill his military duties admirably. At Rovno the Czechs were reinforced by 12,000 new soldiers. At Kamenec Podolsk several thousand deserters who had escaped from the Slovakian fascist army joined up. Ali had to spend a large part of his time in training, which he hated. He also continued to serve as communication officer—and not just in terms of language—between the Czech and Russian headquarters. When the Czechs were ordered into battle to make it across the Carpathian mountains and into their homeland, Ali was in the first line of the advance. During the fighting in the mountains his left arm was severely wounded. The field surgeon told him it had to be amputated. Ali said nothing, but at the first unguarded moment he walked out of the hospital, got into his jeep and drove, using only his unharmed right arm, to the civilian hospital run by Catholic nuns in a nearby village. His injured arm was saved. I won't bore you with his many stories about what he did with the nuns during his convalescence.

Feri was thirsty. We ordered something to drink. I told him about my experience as a medical student in Szeged (Hungary) in 1945, shortly after the Russian Army had captured the town and the war was still in progress. The clinic was cramped and crowded. The Russian field surgeons were working at one operating table, the Hungarian surgeons at another. The Russians amputated limb after limb. Sometimes they had time for nothing else. They had to work quickly to save as many lives as possible. At other times it seemed like mere routine.

"Ali's good fortune was that he had no illusions as far as his own army was concerned," said Feri.

During the final period of the war an agreement was signed between Moscow and the Czech exile government in London regarding the areas in the Ruthenian Carpathian mountains that had been liberated by the Russian Army. A member of the London government was appointed administrator for the area. Ali became his liaison officer with the Russian army leadership. It was a difficult assignment. The Czech Communist leaders, who had spent the war years in Moscow, were conspiring against the exile government London. It was a very complicated gambit which ended with the entire region, including Beregszász, our hometown, being annexed by the Soviet Union. But Ali visited Beregszász long before that. As liaison officer he could travel freely throughout the liberated area, and he followed everywhere in the footsteps of the advancing army. He was the first Czech soldier to reach the town. But he didn't search for any family members. He knew that all Jews had been deported to Auschwitz six months earlier.

Ali first went to the vineyards outside the town. He found the elderly caretaker of the family's vineyard, who was overjoyed to see him. The caretaker told how Ali's parents and the rest of his family had been driven from their homes, pushed together in a brick factory under inhuman conditions and finally carted off in crowded, sealed cattle cars. No one returned from the journey.

Ali spent his first night in Beregszász in the caretaker's house. In the morning he put on his uniform with its long row of medals. He was now a lieutenant-colonel, the youngest in the Czech army. Dark, brooding, and bitter, he walked toward the center of the town. No one recognized him. The people were obviously frightened by the high officer from the infamous Red Army. They turned away, avoiding him. Ali walked the streets where we'd grown up, remembering relatives, friends, and women he'd loved. He passed the tobacco shop where he'd first met Adi, who had saved his life. He entered the ruined synagogue that he mostly had refused to attend as a child, and he visited the courtroom where his father had presided as judge. He entered the house where he'd grown up and recognized every corner, every tree. The peasant family who lived there was terrified to see him. When they understood who he was, they loudly pleaded for mercy and swore that they hadn't stolen anything from the Jews. Nothing was left when they moved in. The Jews had been taken away much earlier. Ali found a few of the family's books, a small magnifying glass which had belonged to his father, and a fan which had belonged to his mother. He then turned around and left.

When he emerged from the house a crowd was waiting for him outside. The rumor had spread quickly. A couple of workers who remembered the strike and Ali's youthful exploits stepped forth. Suddenly everyone wanted to greet him, touch him, embrace him. He recognized a few faces from school. One of the family's female cooks kissed him. Everyone shouted and spoke at the same time. Finally they lifted him up and carried him to his waiting jeep, which they then escorted in triumph to the marketplace. All windows were opened, people waved and threw flowers. Ali wondered if everyone had gone mad or if he'd lost his bearings. He gave a speech about victory, justice, a new order, and new life and acknowledged the applause. In all likelihood he was the only one present who realized how hollow the words were. Someone yelled that the marketplace should be named after Ali. But now he just wanted to leave. He knew that he'd seen the town of his birth for the last time. Contrary to his usual behavior, he didn't chat with the chauffeur. He just sat there, bitter and passive; nothing and no one could help him now. As soon as he made it back to his office, he asked to be moved to another post, as far away from his home region as possible.

Just after the end of the war and a few transitory assignments, he was appointed chief delegate to the Czech government at the United Nations Relief and Rehabilitation Administration (UNRRA) in Constanza, Rumania. The position demanded that he remain in uniform with an officer's rank. He was informed confidentially that he'd be appointed general if he applied to become a member of the Communist party. Ali remembered, not without bitterness, that party membership once was his highest ambition. But he no longer wanted to join Stalin's party. He had abandoned his ambition to "change the world." He wanted to live his own life and try to forget everything that he had experienced.

Ali claims that the demands of his work in Constanza were mainly twofold: to be able to drink whisky with the Americans and vodka with the Russians. His job also required administrative ability and a sense of psychology. Ali was as skillful a negotiator with corrupt politicians as he was with military brass and outright mafia leaders, whether or not these were part of the social establishment. Again, combining his natural charm with his firm authority and excellent organizational skill, he managed the impossible. In addition, the commanding Russian medals on his chest made a big impression on otherwise implacable nay-sayers. By combining whip and carrot in individually tailored proportions he managed to organize effective relief transports. I visited Ali myself several times during this period. For a few months I worked with him as medical advisor and was able to get a fairly accurate impression of his activities.

Ali cultivated contacts at all levels, from shipping magnates to dockworkers; from generals to foot soldiers and guards; corporate executives, workers, policemen, and customs officials. He spoke with them, remembered their families, knew their problems. This was the key to his success. These were uncertain times. Goods disappeared, transports were never delivered, suppliers and recipients suffered great losses. Ali's transports were the exception. Miraculously, they arrived intact. Soon more and more private businessmen turned to him and asked to be allowed to connect one of their own rail transport cars to his train. Ali obliged them when possible, for friendship or money. He collected quite a bit of money, but he's never really grasped the true value of money, except when buying presents. He spent his money on friends and a steady succession of new women. But there was an absolute limit to his helpfulness. If he found out that someone had been a Nazi or had collaborated with the Germans during the war, that person would find no mercy in Ali's eyes.

In Constanza Ali first came in contact with the stateless Jews who waited for a chance to travel to Palestine illegally. The British had practically stopped all legal immigration of Jews. The wait was long, and they lived in refugee camps, totally unsure of their future. Many were concentration camp survivors. Zionist representatives tried to boost their spirits, but with little success. These Jews hoped to hire Greek or Turkish boats to take them to Palestine despite the British ban, but they lacked the money. There were many captains willing to sail, but they all demanded a substantial fee. Ali invested everything he owned and managed to rent a boat. He also personally helped the refugees to sneak past the guards in the harbor. His scheme succeeded. He could now regard himself as the lone financier of an entire boat transport to Palestine of 280 souls.

After his stint in Constanza, Ali became Czechoslovakia's representative with the Allied control commission in Rijeka and Trieste. But after just a few months he was called to Prague, where the Czech government appointed him liaison with the Russians, since he was considered better able to communicate with them than anyone else. It was Ali who first introduced Ludwik Svoboda, later Czechoslovakia's president (1968–1975), to the representatives of the Soviet government. But one problem got worse after his return to Prague: his drinking. Apparently Ali's friends were too numerous or his memories of Prague too painful. The citizens of the capital had begun to notice the inebriated officer with the impressive war medals. Once, in a drunken but cheerful mood, he handed out ten-dollar bills to pedestrians in the street. Another time he sold his car for a pittance to the highest bidder offering cash, and then proceeded to hand out the bills to strollers passing by.

For the first time his drinking habits became a problem at work. He walked in and out of governmental buildings at his leisure, as if he lived there. He seemed to lack inhibitions preventing him from showing up inebriated. Because of his excellent Russian contacts he was treated gently, but his superiors wanted him out of Prague. So he was appointed deputy head of the Czech governmental commission in East Berlin.

Ali felt ill at ease arriving in Berlin in the uniform of one of the victorious powers only a few years after the war. He could not help but wonder what was behind each face. Who had been a Nazi? Where were Hitler's enthusiastic followers? Or his executioners? But sometimes Ali's sense of humor perked up. He likes to tell a story about an old man in a hunting cap with the typical German duelling scars on his cheek who was pushing a twin baby carriage with two attractive black three-year-olds on the Unter den Linden. Ali wondered if the man's daughter had transgressed against the Nazis' rigid racial code, selling herself for coffee and cigarettes after the American army's arrival in Germany.

Since he didn't want to aggravate the *Rassenschande* of the German women, Ali decided not to pursue them. He drank and played cards with Americans, Englishmen, Frenchmen, and Russians, and courted their secretaries. But mostly, he worked and stayed sober. He was in charge of trade contracts at the Czech trade commission. It was intricate work, since all imports and exports were regulated by licenses and carefully controlled. Once again Ali was in his element. He enjoyed the challenge and developed an efficient system which worked despite all restrictions. Instead of imitating others, he attacked the problem in his own way. He boldly ignored all diplomatic formalities and instead created his own form of social intercourse. After only a few months he was on a personal basis with anyone who was essential to his business activities. He quickly became very popular. Many owed him a debt of gratitude and were more than happy to be able to reciprocate his generous favors.

Ali was content as never before. He no longer needed alcohol in order to endure life, and he was usually in a state of euphoria. He empathized with his friends' often troubled lives; he knew their ambitions, their dislikes and jealousies. This remains one of Ali's most characteristic traits. He instinctively knows the measure of a person, even after just a short while. You'll soon see for yourself.

His work in Berlin was a great asset to the young Czechoslovakian state. The innumerable bureaucratic bottle-necks which hampered others did not trouble the Czechs, who seemed to enjoy a strange immunity. Czech textiles were traded for machines and chemicals almost as smoothly as in a capitalist system. License barriers were lifted as if touched by a magic wand. If you want to hear something funny tomorrow, ask Ali to tell you about when the entire staff at East Berlin's airport—except the air controllers—celebrated Ali's birthday, which actually fell on another date. While they consumed the drinks that Ali lavished upon them, some twenty Czech planes landed, unloaded their textiles and were reloaded with machinery without having any paperwork processed. Before the party was over, the planes were on their way back to Prague.

Despite his successes, Ali could read the writing on the wall. During a brief visit to Prague at the end of 1947 he sensed an atmosphere of general suspicion. Clearly great political changes were being prepared. A few months later the aging President Edvard Benesj (1935–1938 and 1945–1948) surrendered to Soviet pressure and was deposed in a bloodless Communist coup. Czechoslovakia became a one-party Stalinist satellite. Ali remained in East Berlin, but he was increasingly aware of the anti-liberal and anti-Semitic signals which soon led to the Slansky process, one of the infamous show trials of the post-war years. Ali knew that sooner or later he too would be charged. He had no desire to once again be subjected to Communist "justice." Unlike many others in similar positions who indulged in wishful thinking, Ali had abandoned all illusions about the system.

With his customary attention to detail, he prepared to flee to the west. This proved more difficult than he had expected since he was obviously under surveillance. Soon after the Communist seizure of power Ali's closest assistant was replaced by a person whose main task was to study Ali's movements. Ali decided to use his British contacts to organize his flight. On the decisive evening, Ali met with a couple of English officers and arranged a number of evasive maneuvers in order to delude his monitor into thinking that he was on a secret tryst. The English officers promised Ali that he'd be able to join an English military plane to West Germany.

On the day of his escape he arranged so that virtually the entire staff of the Czech delegation, including his monitor, was ordered to be present at the airport in East Berlin to deal with a bureaucratic tie-up regarding an important delivery to Prague. Only the general, Ali's boss, remained at the office. Ali knew that diplomats and civil servants who had defected were often charged with embezzlement. He placed all his official and private assets in the safe. Then he walked into his boss's room, drew his pistol and announced that he was about to defect. He ordered the general to go to the safe and inspect the assets, and then to draw up a list of everything he found and sign it. Ali tied the general's hands and feet, cut the telephone wire and locked the doors. Half an hour later he was on his way to Munich with a Royal Air Force plane. He finally reached the freedom that he had so longed for and so doggedly earned. He was poor as a church mouse, robbed of all pomp and circumstance, but full of confidence.

Ali began his new life by vowing never again to touch alcohol, a promise he kept without fail. He also decided to return to manual labor. A bit of the young Socialist was still alive in him. In the daytime he worked as a porter and at night he washed dishes. But he felt unsafe in Germany. He knew that the Czech government had contacts everywhere. He traveled to Italy and supported himself for several months as a dock worker in Genoa. He enjoyed the hard work until a slipped disc in his spine forced him to stop. He was taken to a poor people's hospital run by nuns. He was released only after several months, unable to perform manual labor.

While searching for less strenuous work work he by chance met a successful young Italian businessman with whom he had conducted business in Rijeka. The Italian welcomed him as a long-lost brother. Ali suggested that the two should embark on a project that had occurred to him while loading boats in Genoa. The free port in Tangier offered great opportunities and Ali wanted to start an export-import business based there. The Italian agreed to the project without really believing in it but regarding it as a way of helping Ali. But the business bloomed after just a few months. After six months Ali could repay the Italian the original amount he had invested as well as a tidy profit.

But now Ali faced a new problem. For the first time in his life, he was bored. He could amass huge sums by continuing his business. But, as he puts it, he was about to loose his vitality. He mainly socialized with people who were interested in business and money. He thought they resembled mass-produced automatons. One day was like the next, the conversations were predictable, and all challenges had disappeared. Ali felt increasingly drained of his lust for life. A beautiful Spanish-Arabian woman prevented him from once again taking to the bottle. When the Korean war began in 1950, Ali's business suddenly went bust and he lost most of his money. Savings and private investments are not Ali's strong points, even today. Perhaps it's the young Socialist in him which keeps him from enjoying money when he has it. With his remaining funds he bought a boat ticket to Canada. At the same time he observed—not without certain surprise—how his lust for life began to return as he faced the thrill of the unknown.

When Ali arrived in Montreal he had only twenty dollars left. He slept for six nights in the waiting hall at the central station. His meals consisted of tea and toast twice a day. During the days he looked for work, but lacking money, credentials, and personal references he was in fairly bad shape. Only after a week did he find a job washing dishes at a large hotel. He received twenty-seven dollars a week and a hot meal each day. The work was monotonous, but at least he didn't starve. In addition, he was able to observe everything happening around him. He was fascinated by the pecking order at the hotel and in the kitchen. After a short while he knew the entire staff, understood their problems and personal relations, and was familiar with their many methods of earning a few extra dollars.

Ali's obvious intelligence and honesty enabled him to quickly move up in the hotel's hierarchy. After a few months he was head cashier at the hotel night club. Whatever spare time he didn't spend with his newly acquired girlfriends he spent at the library. He read everything he could find about how to run and organize a hotel. He noted with surprise that he was already more experienced and knowledgeable in practical matters than many writers on the subject. If they could write, so could he, so he wrote two articles in rapid succession. The first was about selling food and drink at restaurants. The second and more important essay concerned the importance of interpersonal relations in the hospitality business. Both articles were accepted by respected trade journals. He began receiving letters and offers to give lectures on the subject. He continued to write texts that were simple and direct and displayed great insights about the system. At the same time he conducted several practical experiments in his daily work. He encountered practically no resistance since everyone knew that he was helpful but hard to deceive and incorruptible. But Ali's most important asset and the one most difficult to describe was his charismatic way of relating to those around him. He became a personal friend to every waiter and bellboy, and he had a good word or an interested question for everyone. He listened to their answers, remembered them, and showed concern for their problems. They felt that his interest was genuine rather than full of pretense as was the approach of most others in the business.

Within less than a year in Canada, Ali was appointed manager of the night club. His name was known in the business through his articles. Six months later he was promoted to manager of the large hotel. Ali had done it again! His rise in the North American hotel business was as rapid as his rise in the Red Army had been ten years before.

Even at his first job as manager of a hotel he succeeded in increasing the number of guests in a remarkable way. But suddenly Ali was bored again. As soon as he'd assembled an optimal organization which he could manage while working gradually less, the challenge and the joy were gone. Ali felt an irresistible urge to move on. However enviable his position seemed to others, he was as uninterested in being tied down to a place or a position as he was to being tied down to a woman.

Ali didn't have to wait long for his next opportunity. One day the president of the American Hotel Corporation, which specialized in luxury hotels worldwide, booked a suite at Ali's hotel and asked to see him for dinner. The man offered Ali a new job as a member of the American Hotel Corporation's management team. His task would be to travel the world and open new hotels, reorganize old ones, and take action whenever a hotel was in the red. He accepted the job and is now assistant president of the organization. This hotel, where we're now sitting, was about to go bankrupt when Ali took over three months ago. He's already had a great influence on the organization and I'm certain that within six months this hotel will be as great a success as his earlier ventures. But you'd better go to bed now. Ali will tell you the rest himself.

I looked at the clock. It was almost three in the morning, but I still had a few questions for Feri.

"How did you get Ali to invite us here, even though we're complete strangers? And how can we accept his hospitality?"

"Ali is my best friend," answered Feri. "I'm his doctor. He comes from the same region as you and I. He's curious about you. He's hoping that you'll go for a few walks with him, listen to his stories, and that the two of you'll be able to discuss the absurdities of life. But I must warn you of one thing: he usually has a new girlfriend every week, often a twenty-year-old. Don't be horrified; women love him."

"Does he have a family?"

"He's married to an Italian Catholic professor of biology. She lives in Venice, and Ali usually visits her every year for a few weeks around Christmas. He speaks of her with great respect. Wicked tongues claim that she resisted his attempts at seduction, forcing him to marry her. But I don't know if this is true. There are too many stories about Ali. His marriage appears to function quite smoothly."

"Does he have any children?"

"He has no children of his own, but he gives financial support to a number of children and pays for their education. He speaks of them as his "adopted" children, but I don't think he's adopted them legally. He met one girl when she stopped his car in Mexico and wanted to sell him her body for a few dollars. She was only twelve. Ali asked her to get in the car, drove her straight to the police, found out about her social background and has since then paid for her upbringing. There are supposedly at least seven more. But now I'll definitely bid you a good night. Enjoy yourself; I'm sure the hotel staff will treat you as their favorites."

SUNRISE IN CAESAREA

I lay down and immediately fell asleep, but woke up after half an hour, haunted by Feri's tale. My nerve cells and synapses wrestled with it; they tried to chew it up and break it down into its smaller components. That's how the specialized gluttonous cells in our immune system, the macrophages, dissolve bacteria, parasites, tumor cells, or simply cells that have died a normal death. But my nerve cells were not particularly successful. Many parts of Feri's tale were difficult to digest, thrown about erratically, disturbing my entire system. Sometimes they moved dangerously close to the carefully protected innermost chamber where anxiety dwells.

But my censor was on guard. Get up! Don't stay in bed; you won't fall asleep again. Go outside. Didn't you want to look at the sea?

It was just before dawn as I stood on the beach. As the sky brightened behind me, the birds begin their morning concerto. King Herod's great port of Caesarea, or Keisaria as it's called in Hebrew, rose impressively on the shore. Its walls and towers guarded the ruins within, the petrified messages from many epochs.

Yes, Herod. Wherever you travel in this small but varied country you'll encounter this still controversial Jewish king and his magnificent works of architecture. He's regarded with great ambivalence. Some say that he was rather anti-Jewish and, above all, wanted to be regarded as a champion and protector of Greco-Roman civilization. In our eyes he resembles an oriental despot capable of extraordinary cruelty. But everything is relative. He wasn't a Stalin or a Hitler, and he was relatively "mild" in comparison with the rulers of neighboring countries. A modern work on Jewish history* describes him as a brilliant, constructive, and highly efficient politician and statesman with long-term perspectives who was also superstitious, selfish, and self-pitying. Johnson claims that Herod was a borderline paranoiac, and perhaps well beyond that border.

---

*Paul Johnson, *A History of the Jews* (New York: Harper & Row, 1987).

Aided by Rome, Herod seized power in the year 37 before Christ was born. He remained on good terms with the successive rulers of Rome. He was a friend and confidant of Marcus Antonius, but as soon as Antonius's career was on the wane, Herod befriended Octavius. When Octavius became emperor and took the name Augustus, Herod became the most loyal of the empire's lesser oriental kings. He was rewarded by being allowed to extend and secure the borders of his kingdom. He treated his own family members with what we would regard as incomprehensible cruelty. He accused his beloved wife Mariamne of conspiracy and planning to have him poisoned. He conducted the trial which sentenced her to be executed. According to Josephus Flavius, he had Mariamne's brother Aristobulus drowned in one of Jericho's magnificent bathing pools, the ruins of which are admired by tourists today. According to another version, the drowning was an accident blamed on Herod by his scheming mother-in-law, Alexandra. He put his and Mariamne's two sons on trial and charged them with conspiracy. They were sentenced to death and strangled by the executioners. Alexandra, whose intrigues may have initiated much of this family drama, was also executed.

How can these contradictions exist within the same person? Are we all like this? Are Ali's experiences and Herod's exploits only different versions of the same story?

The sun was up. I sat down in the sand and thumbed through Josephus Flavius. This boastful truth-sayer, this faithful deceiver doesn't only chronicle Herod's cruelties. He also writes: "If there was ever a person who was fond of his family, it was Herod." This might well have been partly correct. Herod named several cities after his closest relatives. But he was also suspicious and brutal toward anyone who might demand part of his power or wealth. Was this not the same oriental despot's mentality, the absolute power which corrupts absolutely, that Ali met two thousand years later when, filled with the naive socialism of his youth, he sought refuge from the Nazis in Stalin's Soviet Union?

Herod's cruelties were in opposition to Jewish religious law. It's therefore hardly surprising that he treated religious institutions with equal brutality. Herod began his rule in Jerusalem by executing forty-six leading members of the Sanhedrin, the Jewish religious court, which had tried to uphold the law against him. He then transformed the court into a purely religious institution lacking secular power. He separated religion from the state and thus relinquished the possibility of appointing himself head priest. Yet he arbitrarily hired and fired high priests, preferring to import them from the Jewish diaspora in Egypt and Babylonia. At the same time he paradoxically showed great respect for Jewish history. He tried to shape his own image after King Solomon, to whose memory he erected enormous public buildings. He was as exorbitant in his wastefulness as in his acquisition of wealth. He severely taxed all commercial traffic through his realm, and he leased the copper mines on Cyprus from Emperor Augustus with whom he shared the mines' profits. But he gave away much more than he could acquire. He corrected the imbalance by confiscating the property of anyone who'd been declared an enemy of the state. Yet as a result of the domestic stability, external peace, and increased trade during his rule, standards of living rose considerably.

Herod viewed himself as a great renewer of Judaism. He formed his policies alone, with a peculiar mix of idealism, ambition, intelligence, cruelty, and paranoia. He wanted to be regarded as the leader of a modern nation devoted to spreading enlightenment and civilization among the barbarians of the Middle East. By giving the Jews a share in the golden age of Augustus during the Roman domination, Herod had, in his own opinion, saved them from Roman exploitation.

I closed the book by Josephus. After a sleepless night and Feri's long tale, history seemed strangely close. Caesarea, the city of ruins, seemed to have come to life. Herod ruled here exactly two thousand years ago. Caesarea was his capital and main port; this was where he received the emperor's envoys, and from here he traveled to Rome and to other capitals within the empire. I cannot relegate him to the history books or to the world of archaeology, no matter how hard I try. It's Caesarea the tourist attraction with its ticket counters and labels that are unreal, not Herod. Our usual conception of present and past reality, the clichés with which we automatically label everything that happened more than a hundred years ago, vanish without a trace. It wasn't "once upon a time," as we like to tell our children, by which we really mean that we've never met a living person who's talked to someone who was alive at that time. Our distinction between "us" and "them" isn't valid. We've no reason to feel secure. The depths of ancient history are actually quite shallow. My own existence is no more well-grounded than the rapid movements of the water insects on the surface of the still pool before my eyes. With their long legs they moved without a sound, the surface tension of the water their one fundament. Like them I'm totally ignorant of the depths under my much less sylph-like legs.

Are there any principal differences between the cruelties of Herod's time and those of Hitler and Stalin? Only technology separates the two. Today the veneer is more polished, but we haven't changed since then. What are two thousand years? Eighty human generations at the most. This is comparable to eight years for my laboratory mice. Which lab mouse would argue that he differs from his forefathers who inhabited my cages in the early 1980s?

I wished to leave Herod and return to my own century, but he wouldn't leave me alone. Why don't the Jews, Herod's own people, identify with him? Why this reluctance from a people who are so aware of their history? He's definitely not a part of the "us" concept as are most other Jewish kings; he belongs to "them," like the Swedish Vikings (and in contrast to Icelandic Vikings to Icelanders today). I turned to Josephus for answers but encountered only further paradoxes. You cannot say that Herod acted against the interests of the Jews—quite the contrary. Thanks to his friendship with Agrippa, one of Augustus's leading generals, Herod ensured that the vast Jewish diaspora would enjoy Rome's protection. At the time there were about eight million Jews in the world, of which only two and a half million lived in Palestine. The diaspora Jews who lived within the Roman Empire's sphere of influence regarded Herod as their closest ally and most important protector. He contributed generously to synagogues, Jewish libraries, ritual baths, and public institutions. Thanks to his support the Jews could build their first prosperous communities in Alexandria, Rome, and Babylon. These communities were the first to establish institutions that aided widows and orphans, the poor and the sick. They were also the first to introduce correctional treatment, and to pay for the interment of indigent citizens with public funds. Herod wanted to show the world that the Jews were a talented, advanced civilization, but he was broad-minded enough not to limit his protection to Jewish organizations and communities. Partly because of his interest in sports, he also supported many Greek institutions. He was known as an avid hunter, a skillful rider, archer, and discus thrower. It was believed that Herod had saved the Olympic games from degeneration with his money, energy, and organizational skills. He built the temple of Apollo on Ródhos, as well as libraries, roads, aqueducts, fountains, and public baths in Syria and Greece. In Antioch, the largest city in the Middle East, he paved the city's one-and-a-half-mile-long main street and built a marble colonnade as protection against the rain.

The majority of his buildings, the largest ones, are here in Caesarea. Josephus Flavius calls the city's manmade harbor a masterpiece of engineering, "greater than Pireus." It must have cost enormous investments in material and labor. This area contained governmental buildings, theaters, marketplaces, and a large stadium where athletic celebrations were held every four years. Herod erected a statue of the emperor which was as large as the Olympian Zeus and was counted among the seven wonders of the ancient world. When the realm was dismantled after Herod's death, Caesarea became the natural Roman administrative capital for Judea and remained the seat of the procurator for a long time. Pontius Pilate ruled here. In fact, the only archaeological proof of Pilate's existence that has been recovered was found carved into a stone here.

Herod also helped develop Jerusalem, which was not only one of the most beautiful cities in the world even then, but also one of the most tense and suspicious. Herod wanted to give the city more of an international character. He brought in Jews from the diaspora who were better educated and more broad-minded than the rather provincial local inhabitants. They were also more open to Greek and Roman ideas and prepared to reform Judaism so that it would better adapt to the modern world. Herod appointed several diaspora Jews to high positions in the city. He wanted to provide them with everything the modern Greco-Roman culture had to offer. But his most important goal was to rebuild the temple to spectacular effect. He understood the public's need for drama and overwhelming experiences. By manipulating and satisfying this need he increased his power, which he then used to further his personal vision of Judaism.

One may wonder where Herod found the time for all his undertakings. Josephus in particular provides the answer. Herod's restlessness from early morning until late evening left him no peace. He shunned idleness by traveling, studying, remarrying, sporting, hunting, and constructing. Herod's restive industriousness was apparently his way of satisfying his own mental needs.

In 22 B.C.E., Herod proclaimed that he would rebuild the temple in Jerusalem on such a glorious scale that it would overshadow the first temple of Solomon. Over the next two years a force of 10,000 construction workers and a thousand priests were recruited. The priests were not just supervisors. Herod tried not to offend the orthodox unless it was absolutely unavoidable, so some of the priests served as construction workers within those temple areas where laymen were forbidden to enter. Like the present-day Israeli government, Herod conceded to religious demands. Even the most minute, often wholly irrational, religious proscriptions were followed rigorously. The completed building was magnificent. According to Josephus the stone was "exceedingly white," and rich gold decorations of the facade reflected the sunlight. On major holidays hundreds of thousands of pilgrims arrived from Palestine and the diaspora. As they ascended the hills of Jerusalem a few miles away they were met by an overwhelming sight. They approached the temple via an imposing staircase and a broad bridge. Money-changers conducted their business in the outer perimeter. Here visitors exchanged their moneys for "holy shekel," the prescribed currency for the entrance fee to the temple. Signs in Greek and Latin forbade gentiles from entering the temple. Those who disobeyed were punished by death.

The temple was extremely wealthy. Jews from the entire diaspora contributed funds, and all Jewish men over the age of twenty had to pay an annual temple tax. Foreign kings, from Artaxerxes to Emperor Augustus, sent large caches of gold goblets and other valuables that were kept in special underground vaults. Rich families of Jerusalem donated large parts of their fortune. Herod himself was the largest donor, having paid for the construction from his own private fortune. Herod was a generous contributor to other causes as well. Thirteen years after he'd conquered Jerusalem, the city was plagued by drought and famine. Herod immediately spent the major part of his wealth to import grain from Egypt, just as Jacob's sons had done 1,500 years earlier.

But Herod's life was anything but idyllic. He was embroiled in numerous conflicts, often with religious Jews. He constantly feuded with the high priest, which is why he arbitrarily increased the power of the pharisee attendant high priest and thereby the influence of the pharisees. One of the most serious conflicts occurred when Herod was already ailing in his imposing palace near Jericho. He had a golden eagle, the Roman symbol of power, affixed above the main entrance to the temple. A group of religious students climbed up and destroyed it. Herod fired the head priest and imprisoned the students. After a summary trial on Roman premises they were all burned alive.

Perhaps it's not difficult to understand why modern Jews tend to shun the subject of Herod's Jewishness. They quickly change the subject, preferring instead to discuss his architectural accomplishments.

Herod died fairly soon after the burning of the students, in the year 4 according to our calendar. His death meant the end of a stable Jewish government in Palestine. After various conflicts and much confusion, when Herod's plans for his succession collapsed, the land called Judea was run by a Roman procurator who was stationed in Caesarea. It took 1,944 years until Israel was resurrected within the region.

It was now broad daylight. Was I in the wrong millennium? No, I was in my own time, about to meet a man named Ali and not . . .

Not what?

Well, who cares about people's names. I'm hungry, here and now.

LONG DAY'S JOURNEY INTO NIGHT

We ate our late breakfast a bit drowsily, assisted by far too many waiters and waitresses. They performed their chores with frozen smiles and absent eyes, their impersonal courtesy accompanied by stereotypical phrases. There was plenty of food and too few guests.

Suddenly something happened. The staff came to life. Their faces brightened with authentic smiles as they kept looking toward the entrance. We turned around and saw a short, rotund, and almost bald gentleman engaged in intense conversation with one of the waiters. Their exchange seemed very personal, as if between friends.

It was Ali. He was heading for our table, but kept stopping to chat with each member of the staff. He knew their names, asked about their families or about their kibbutz. His curiosity seemed genuine. Everyone's eyes sparkled. Suddenly the atmosphere was transformed as if through a magic spell.

He sat down at our table. After just a few moments I felt as if we had always known each other. He then invited us to his room. The door said General Manager. Below that was another sign with the words: *Dear guest, welcome. My name is Albert Elovic. I would like to get to know you. Please come in and say hello.*

"Do you always have time for all your guests? How do you find the time to speak with each member of the staff, how do you remember everyone's name, and how do you know so much about their families?" I asked.

"It is not at all difficult," he answered. "I'm interested. I've always been interested in people."

"How will you get this failing hotel to function properly?"

"There are still many problems. But we're on our way. One pressing issue is to convince the 'Sabras,' the native Israeli staff, to be polite to the guests. Most of them come from a kibbutz. They've been brought up to be spontaneous and independent. Their generation regards the European courtesy of their parents with suspicion. They associate it with a kind of 'ghetto mentality.' They see a connection between courtesy and what they mistakenly regard as the older generation's compliance toward the Nazis. The resistance against the British during the mandate may also have played a part. The British are polite. Here they're regarded as oppressors, and thus politeness is viewed as something to be despised. All this has to change. A prerequisite in this business is that the staff display a courteous attitude toward the guests."

"How can you get them to change their behavior?"

"It's not that difficult. First I have to get to know them personally, understand how they live and how they think. I like doing this because I'm curious about them. Most react in a positive manner when they're approached in a natural way and given respect as a fellow human being. I can also understand why young members of the kibbutz react the way they do toward wealthy guests. This is what I tell them:

"The people who come here have lots of money and many of them are spoiled. They think that what they eat and drink and everything else related to their comfort is the most important thing in the world. Both you and I know that there are more important matters. Some of them are quite decent people, but others represent the scum of the earth. We don't know which category they belong to when they arrive as paying guests. But we know that Israel depends upon a successful tourist trade and the foreign currency it brings into the country. We must encourage this as much as we can, and we can succeed only if we're as concerned about the guests' comfort as they are. If we can make them believe that we care, they'll enjoy staying here. The hotel will thrive and you and your kibbutz will profit. Don't think that a bit of courtesy will infringe upon your human dignity or integrity. It's all just a game for a good cause. And I can promise you one thing: The guests will face the moment of truth when I present them with the bill. I'll bite them like a poisonous snake. Most will pay without blinking. Their vanity is so great that they prefer to pay than to show that the sum matters. In this way, and through our common efforts, we can add to the country's reserve of foreign exchange."

"But what do you say in other countries?"

"It depends. I have to understand people's attitudes and motives before I can say something. I try to establish good personal contact with everyone from the start. Human motivation and behavior doesn't really differ very much from country to country. What I say after I've formed my opinion may be an exaggeration, like a kind of caricature. But I never say anything that I don't truly believe."

The man impressed me. But Eva was more skeptical. Was it because of his many amorous affairs that we'd heard about? In any case Eva was convinced that since Ali knew so much about human nature, he also knew what to say to make me like him. What he said to me didn't necessarily have anything to do with what he said to the staff or to other guests. He liked to please everyone, and knew how to do it. He was as mutable as Proteus. We only saw the face that he chose to show us.

I didn't really agree with Eva. It's true that this man is protean and that he wants to please. He wants to succeed and he does succeed. But I sensed something genuine behind his facade. When he said that he liked all people I believed him. This is probably what everyone senses about him. It's reflected in the spontaneous, happy smiles on the faces of the elevator boys as soon as they see him. It's as different from the polished courtesy of most hotel directors as a Mozart symphony is from pompous schmaltz.

Later that afternoon Ali appeared again and asked if we wanted to join him for a walk on the beach. When we passed the stable, Ali introduced us to a tall, blond, and extremely attractive Israeli woman in her twenties who was his current girlfriend. She was busy with the horses when we approached the stable, but her face lit up when she saw Ali. He spoke with her in a joking but intimate tone. It sounded as if they'd known each other since childhood, and one easily forgot their age difference. Ali later told us that she was well aware of the rules of his game. One week, maybe two, then it's over. But we'll remain friends. "I'll never be chained to a woman like you or Feri and most of my friends," he added with a wink. Eva heard and laughed instead of being irritated. I could hardly believe my ears. Had I misunderstood women during all these years? Did Ali know some secret that I wasn't aware of?

We continued our walk through the orange grove. "She's a very beautiful girl," I told Ali. "Forgive me for asking an indiscreet question: Is she employed at the hotel, or is she one of the guests?"

I regretted my question the moment I asked it. Had I been too forward and offended Ali? But he only laughed. "You can ask me anything you want. I never have affairs with a member of the hotel staff or with a guest. That would be against my principles. This girl is from a kibbutz in another area. I can invite my friends to the hotel, just as I've invited you and Eva, but I never invite a woman for the sake of an affair."

"How can you be so strict in this matter and so liberal in others?"

"When it comes to work I must obey the same principles as everyone else. I never employ married couples at my hotels, and don't accept affairs between members of the staff. If I become aware of such a relationship, I call both parties and ask them who wants to volunteer to leave the hotel. The other one can stay. If I find out about a homosexual affair, both must leave."

"What! Why can't two members of your staff have an affair like anyone else? How does this fit in with your liberal ideas? And why do you discriminate against homosexuals?"

"It's not a question of not being liberal, nor of discrimination. I've agreed to do a job. My task is to teach a sinking company to swim. So far I've never failed at this. We treat everyone as valuable human beings and I want them to understand that we all have to obey the same basic regulations. But a hotel also needs a disciplinary structure that has to work, same as on a boat or an airplane. When two people have an affair, the entire structure changes. Once a ranking member of the staff has met a subordinate in the most intimate of human situations, they can no longer function as they used to. They cannot give or take orders without being aware of their relationship. The entire sociology has changed, often in a disruptive way. I've seen too much of this and am determined to prevent it. One of the two must go.

"Due to the social discrimination against homosexuals their situation is even more complicated. I have many friends who are homosexuals and I have absolutely nothing against them, but I'm aware of their problems. In most countries where I work they belong to a more or less oppressed minority. They must hide their sexual preference and are thus subject to blackmail. In the various crisis situations that I have to solve, I cannot afford the added risks posed by this complication."

"But how can you exhibit such generosity that your employees simply glow when they see you, and also be so uncompromising regarding their sexuality—something of central importance to everyone which you, if anyone, should understand?"

"It's not a matter of understanding. I understand all people. But my hotels must adhere to the same kind of discipline as Feri's surgical clinic. This doesn't prevent us from socializing and enjoying each other's company. Everyone understands and appreciates the need for a certain degree of discipline."

We stood on the beach near the Roman aqueduct, that masterpiece of engineering which was one of the most important factors in the city's development. "Were you aware that the citizens of Caesarea had running water in their homes nearly two thousand years ago?" Ali asked. "They had public and private baths and irrigated their gardens and orchards. The mains from the sources on the Carmel mountain were between seven and twelve kilometers long. I was recently visited by a group of experts who were full of admiration for the system's hydrodynamic precision."

The sun began to set over the Mediterranean. I thought of the coins Titus had minted when he had conquered Jerusalem and leveled Herod's temple. *Hierosolyma est perdita*—Jerusalem is lost—said the inscription. But the city is still standing two thousand years later. Who today remembers that it was supposed to be known as Aelia Capitolina forever after? Gone too is the magnificent Roman Empire. Jerusalem continues to bear its Hebrew name, "city of peace"—an irony, a hope, a promise, an eternal disappointment.

The previous night's many hours in Feri's company ran through my head. Is this jovial, genial man who is explaining his success-oriented work ethic on a pleasant Mediterranean beach the one that Feri was telling me about? Is this driven professional also a rake full of zest for life? Is this the deeply serious clown who's survived the two greatest paranoiacs of the century, although both Hitler and Stalin did their best to annihilate him? Is he thinking about them now as he is standing just outside the most sophisticated port from antiquity built by the greatest paranoiac of its time? No, he doesn't appear to be. He's here with me, fully absorbed in our feather-light yet serious conversation. We could be conversing anywhere: on an airplane, in a hotel, or in the battlefield trenches. He doesn't even seem to notice that the sun is dipping toward the horizon while he is preaching.

Preaching what? His philosophy of life? Does he have any—other than that we must survive, in order to show them, to defy them?

Show who? Defy who?

Those who wish to destroy us.

Why?

To show our contempt.

Contempt for what?

Contempt for their hatred.

Is it worth paying such a high price for?

Of course it is. And we are richly rewarded.

If you're doubtful, just listen to Ali's song to life, to women, to his friends.

But where is he? Who is he? How can I grasp him? Why does he slip through my hands?

"Look!" Ali suddenly exclaimed, pointing to the small sand crabs scurrying quickly sideways before disappearing into their almost invisible miniature burrows. In vain we tried to figure out how they moved. "Actually, I wanted to become a scientist," said Ali, "but the war got in the way."

"Your curiosity would have suited the profession," I answered, "but you'd never have been able to endure the unavoidable monotony, the long periods of hard work when nothing exciting happens. You have just told me that you want to be as free as the wind! You don't want to be tied down by a wife or family and, least of all, by routine work. You don't have a homeland—not even a permanent residence. How could you have stood doing the same thing year after year in order to experience one single minute of the euphoria that you constantly seek? But now I'll change the subject and ask you an indiscreet question: How did you get all your medals during the war? Feri has told me about some of your exploits, but I want to hear what you have to say."

"It was nothing special. I've forgotten most of it. Feri has heard many of his stories from others. I only know that I was scared out of my wits and that I kept firing my gun. And that I drank constantly in order to endure my fear and my shooting. As soon as I spotted Germans I fired like a madman. I knew that they had killed my parents and the rest of my family. I received one of my medals after holding an important position against a German force, all alone with only a machine gun. But I didn't know what I was doing. I only knew I was scared for my life, dead drunk and mad as hell. I fired at anything German that moved."

"How could you become such good friends with the Russian officers?"

"They're the same as all other soldiers. We drank together and I told them raunchy stories."

"When did you first come in contact with Israel? Have you ever thought of settling here?"

"Settle down? No, never. But if I did settle anywhere, it would be here. I feel at home here. Ben Gurion himself asked me to stay, but I declined."

"How does Ben Gurion know you?"

"I played a certain part in shipping weapons to Israel during the war of liberation in 1948." Ali said it as airily as if he was talking about a shipment of Coca Cola to the hotel the previous day. I knew that the Czech weapons were of decisive importance to the ability of the small Israeli army to withstand the onslaught of the armies of the surrounding countries. That was the only time that weapons were shipped from Czechoslovakia to Israel.

We returned to the hotel and I returned to my work. But it was difficult not to think about Ali.

A few days later he disappeared as suddenly as he had appeared. But I ran into him several times during the following years. We met occasionally as he traveled from land to land, from hotel to hotel, from flower to flower. Half a year after our first meeting he appeared in Stockholm with a new Israeli girlfriend. She was young, dark, and beautiful. She looked at him with the same devotion in her eyes as her predecessor. Ali had come to Sweden to promote Swedish tourism to Caesarea. He wanted to "broaden" the quite intense but mainly American flow of tourists by offering special cut-rate deals to prominent Swedes, whose example would hopefully inspire their countrymen.

I asked if he knew much about the Swedes. No, nothing at all, but he was sure that he would find out the essentials in a few days.

We wandered around the Tumorbiology Department, a new and exotic place to him. In the corridor we came across one of my most attractive female co-workers with her young son in hand. "What a Nordic beauty, right out of a Bergman film," exclaimed Ali. I introduced them to each other. The eyes of the Swedish girl began to sparkle after just a few minutes. They could not have exchanged more than five sentences before Ali asked her who had fathered her child—was it really her husband? Instead of a well-deserved slap in the face, Ali was rewarded with a hearty laugh and their contact was firmly established.

Two days later Ali returned to report that he now knew everything essential about the Swedes. Tell us what you know, we said. Ali gave us a perfect show of mimicry. The famed "skål" ceremony, the body language, the expressions, and the tone of voice were right on target. He could have performed at a cabaret that very evening. Now I understood what Feri was referring to when he mentioned Ali's clowning as a teenager.

The night before his departure Ali was in a great mood. He suddenly began singing to us in Hungarian, Czech, Russian, Rumanian, and Yiddish. I knew that the goal of his trip had been accomplished beyond expectations. His girlfriend looked at him in a way that would have made most men green with envy. I joined in the general laughter. But at the same time I felt a lump in my throat. I pitied him, although I didn't know why. I couldn't explain it to myself and didn't want anyone else to notice.

I met Ali one last time in Hamburg, fifteen years after our first meeting. Caesarea was just a memory to him then. During his time the hotel became a great success, just like a series of successive hotels that

he ran for a while in Canada, Spain, Latin America, Germany, and the
Far East. When he called to invite me for a visit he was president of the
grand new Hotel Plaza in Hamburg. He mentioned that the city of Hamburg had made him an honorary citizen, and the mayor gave a dinner
gala in his honor. He eagerly accepted the invitation because it provided
him with a welcome opportunity to emphasize in his festive speech that
he was a Jew and that his family had been murdered by the Nazis.

At the airport in Hamburg I was met by Herr Schmidt, the hotel's
chauffeur, who looked like a German university professor of the old
school. I asked him how the hotel was doing.

He answered that ever since Herr Elovic took over they'd been
booked full every night. It is incredible! Unfortunately he'll leave us
when his contract is up. Then things will decline. His skills cannot be
taught; they are a gift one is born with.

Soon Eva and two of our children arrived and we dined with Ali in
the hotel restaurant. He had hired a prominent Gypsy ensemble from
our common home region which was now a part of the Soviet Union. But
the Gypsies still spoke the same colorful Hungarian as in our childhood.
Ali immediately put them in the right mood with some well-chosen pro-
fanities that were so obscene that I didn't even want to hint at their
meaning to my Swedish children. The Gypsies played Ali's favorite
music and he began to sing and dance. Smack in the middle of the
crowded luxury hotel's dining room and singing in Dionysian joy without
having drunk a single drop of alcohol stood this honorary citizen of
Hamburg, the hotel's respected and internationally renowned manager,
whose father, mother, and siblings had been gassed to death as vermin
by his host nation a mere generation ago. But it was obvious to me that
this remarkably skillful dancer was neither the hotel manager nor the
Hero of the Great Patriotic War. He was once again the impish ten-year-
old who refused to leave amorous couples alone until they'd bribed him
with a coin; he was the fifteen-year-old revolutionary who marched with
red banners and organized a workers' strike to the dismay of his family,
his friends, and the entire bourgeoisie; he was the tireless Casanova who
saw an entire continent of new horizons in every woman. But he was also

something else, something evident only to his closest friends. He was the disillusioned Socialist who knew that his most honest and altruistic ambitions had been built upon a mirage of wishful thinking. He no longer cared about anything that he'd held so dear in his youth. It no longer mattered whether he built hotels only for the very rich, the most indifferent, or the scum of the earth. He was the secret mourner who no longer revealed himself, since it would make no difference. He was the magician who could transform an incurable pain of loss into such a triumphant zest for life that this skillful juggler's act was evident only to the most perceptive and to his closest friends.

The Germans were exuberant. They laughed, applauded, and understood nothing. Quite unlike myself, I was carried along and shouted "encore!" along with everyone else while the Gypsies played on, but it pained me deeply. I saw everyone's and no one's brother, friend, and lover; everyone's host and no one's guest in his last great circus act. I knew that he was alone, beyond all companionship, poor as a churchmouse, and close to death.

Ali died a few months later, alone in a small hospital in Germany where he'd been taken after suffering a sudden heart attack while on a business trip. No lover, no companion, not even an acquaintance was present.

EPILOGUE

Tel Aviv, 1990. I am sitting opposite Feri's sister Agi. Feri has been dead for more than ten years. Agi is a well-known artist who had known Ali since they were young children.

Show me a photo from when all of you were still in school!

Agi finds a group graduation photo. The students could be sixteen or seventeen years old. Ali is easy to spot. He's at the back, somewhat separate from the others. Did he want to emphasize that he wasn't quite part of the group? His posture and gaze radiate intensity. He doesn't seem to distance himself in a demonstrative way, yet he's still on his own. He's self-contained.

"Did Ali isolate himself from his school friends?"

"He didn't isolate himself, he was a world unto himself. He could socialize with anyone. Throughout our high school years he was one of my closest friends. We gathered at the home of my parents for "serious" discussions several times a week and Ali was always at the center of the discussion."

"Did you discuss politics?"

"Oh no! Mostly literature, poetry, music, and art. These discussions led me to view myself as an artist long before I became one, when I was still a young teenager."

"Why has Ali always been so popular with women? Can you explain his power of attraction?"

"Are you thinking of what Leporello says to Donna Elvira in Mozart's *Don Giovanni*: 'But you know yourself how he does it'? If this is what you mean, I cannot answer. I've always liked Ali; he was perhaps my best friend during all these years, both when we were young and toward the end of his life. But I never had an affair with him. During my teens I was closely guarded by my two brothers. They were among Ali's best friends and knew him very well. They watched every step I took with him. Ali respected them and appreciated their friendship. Even in high school he had sexual relations with innumerable girls. But I cannot tell you 'how he did it.' I have myself never experienced it. I'm sure this was one of the reasons why our friendship lasted as long as it did."

"But I understand that he proposed to marry you?"

"Yes, more than once, both before and after the war. One day in 1946 or 1947, when I was a student at the Academy of Art in Prague and lived in a rented room, Ali woke up my landlady at two in the morning. His uniform was gaudy with all his medals, and he was quite drunk. He came from Constanza and had decided to wake me up to tell me that he wanted to marry me. When Ali wanted to do something, nothing could deter him from his goal. But he couldn't lie, at least not to me. I asked him why he suddenly decided to wake me with this message that I wouldn't accept. It turned out that he had gone for a long walk with my older brother, Feri. Ali, my younger brother, and I always turned to Feri for advice. It was as if we sought our murdered father in him.

" 'I have told Feri that I want to marry you,' Ali had said.

"What did Feri answer?

"Ali looked down at the floor. There was a long silence. His mouth trembled; he almost wept. But I knew that he wouldn't lie.

" 'He said that his sister would not be allowed to marry an alcoholic.'

"Is this what you came to tell me, in the middle of the night?

"The issue was never mentioned again."

While Agi made coffee, I wondered if Ali could be compared to Don Giovanni as we know him from Mozart's opera. No, not at all. Don Giovanni was an aristocrat, a deceiver, and, if need be, a murderer for his own amusement. Ali was never like that. But women have apparently fallen for him in a similar way.

Agi returned with the coffee.

"But you must understand something about his power of attraction upon women," I said. "He wasn't exactly handsome."

"I can only describe it with the word 'presence.' Ali was immediately the center of attention when he entered a room. Everyone wanted to see and hear him. It wasn't because of his reputation; I've seen it happen after only a few minutes with new people who knew nothing about him and met him for the first time. Everyone listened, men too. He was somehow—how shall I put it?—autonomous. Perhaps it was the force of his personality which gave him such charisma. It's the way he was, even without trying. It was spontaneous and unforced and everyone could feel it. At the same time he was down to earth, jocular, 'nice' in the trivial, everyday meaning of the word, and very entertaining. Yet this was still not the essence of his attraction."

Yes, that's how I also perceived him. "But where did his forceful personality originate; what was his inner source? Could it be that he experienced life as an open field with exciting and often unknown possibilities that were free for him to explore, to play with, to influence and be influenced by, or, simply, to master? Did he want to probe his ability to change his surroundings to the better, according to what he regarded as good in his own unconscious value system? Or did he just want to experience repeatedly how he could make everyone laugh and be happy, if only for a moment?"

I could have asked Agi if Ali was constantly "in flow," but this would have required a long explanation of the concept.*

"It's probably partly as you say," she replied, "but there are two things you mustn't forget: He was absolutely brilliant intellectually. He had a quicker mind than most and could readily verbalize essential matters; he only needed to listen for a moment to have a good grasp of the situation and its logical consequences. A second later it would all flow from his mouth as if he'd captured the message in flight. And he could do this in at least seven different languages. In addition, he was totally unafraid. He simply didn't know what fear was. He was the only person I have known who wasn't afraid of anything."

This didn't agree with my own talks with Ali. I guess this was the face he showed Agi or what she wanted to see in him. I remembered Ali's own words about his fear during the war, how he became a hero against his will and how he fired blindly at the enemy, often numbed by alcohol.

Was he constantly searching for flow in order to escape fear? Perhaps. How many times have I grasped for something that could put me into flow in order to escape my demons? Upon closer examination I regard it as my universal instrument. How often has my "inner watchman" observed my own metamorphosis, always with the same, somewhat aloof sense of surprise?—my transformation from a trembling bunch of nerves afraid of my own shadow into a "hero" proceeding like a steamroller toward a goal which I correctly or incorrectly believe is true; how I'm admired by all for my "selfless commitment" and "courage" while I'm at the same time fully aware that I'm fleeing an inner enemy who seems more frightening than all the terrors of the outer world.

Is this a form of deceit? Hardly. It's neither directed toward a goal nor a strategic calculation. Escape itself is the true goal.

I saw how Ali could suddenly enter a state of flow while studying the

---

*This concept is discussed in detail in the final chapter, "When Time Stops."

sand crabs and trying to understand how they moved. I myself can enter a state of flow as soon as I concentrate on some problem which I have a reasonable chance of comprehending. It can be a research problem, or something insignificant which has captured my interest, or an attempt to understand a foreign language. As long as the outer world doesn't interfere! After having experienced this countless times, I have, like many other flow-addicts, developed my own methods for protecting the process. You try to avoid everything that can prevent concentration and close the escape route from the inner threat. My earplugs and dictaphone are two practical, almost symbolic aids. The earplugs filter out many unwanted noises while allowing welcome, stimulating sounds (such as music) to enter. The dictaphone is that superb instrument which immediately jots down my thoughts, preserving them as a springboard for the continuous search for more flow. It also provides me the means of communicating with others without interference.

Was Ali searching for flow? Yes, that's exactly what he was doing most of the time. But it was probably more of an addiction than a search. Aided by his unusual ability to love almost anyone and be loved in return, he could enter a state of flow anywhere, under seemingly impossible conditions and with almost all kinds of people. He could do it in a variety of roles: the clown who made everyone laugh, the lover who put a sparkle in women's eyes, the entrepreneur who could resurrect moribund companies, the managing director who could inspire people to accomplish more and better than they ever thought themselves capable of. All of these roles had one thing in common: they inspired *joie de vivre*. Ali experienced flow by repeatedly perceiving his own ability to accomplish it in himself and in others.

An inquisitive journalist asked Mihály Csikszentmihályi, the originator of the concept of flow, how he achieved his own state of flow. By researching, recording, and describing how other people enter flow, he answered. Ali has given a similar reply, but without the psychological terminology. It wasn't hard to see how he beamed each time he was certain that he could transform inefficiency and stagnation into a positive, hopeful dynamic; how he could get the melancholy and the emotionally bereft to laugh at his clown's tricks.

Ali's flow addiction was also evident in his "abstinence symptoms." As soon as he'd successfully accomplished a task, the challenge disappeared and he immediately wanted to go forward, test his skills on a new person, a new group, a new woman. The territory that was already conquered lost its attraction; those vanquished and won over were—with the exception of a few lifelong friends—kindly but firmly set aside. The art students described by Csikszentmihályi in his doctoral thesis displayed a similar relationship to their artwork: while they were in creative production the painting was the most important thing in the world to them, but once finished it was discarded never to be touched again.

Ali's constant search for new flow experiences is most evident in his relationship to women. This tendency is also evident in his professional work. To reverse a failing trend, to transform disquietude and stagnation into activity and life, to jolt listless people into opening their eyes and smile out of the sheer joy of seeing him, this was Ali's art, his mountain to climb, his surgery, his bold coup, his pirouette in the air—in short: his flow.

Did Ali start to drink when he was prevented from using the methods of achieving flow that he had developed during his youth? Was the most stressful aspect of the war that he was denied the possibility of shutting out the external world, focusing his brain, and determining his own path? Or did he use alcohol to anesthetize sorrows and anxieties born from the unbearable loss of his family, from his disillusionment at being unable to become what he could have become, from the insight that genuine sharing was beyond reach? Did he use sex to gain temporary communion? Or did he instead want to constantly relive his own ability to triumph; did he want to open the floodgates of lust to be able to use his entire emotional register freely, to become poetic or spiritual or happy as a child, be the clown or the philosopher according to the needs of his mistress, to constantly experience anew how the hidden and archetypal gateway of the female body opens for the conqueror?

Ali, without great difficulty, was able to rid himself of his alcoholic addiction after his escape from Stalin's empire. This supports my theory that alcohol played only a surrogate role. He retained his sexuality and his search for flow until the end; these were essential to him.

On one point only was Ali mistaken. It concerned his grave monument, his last protean message. A few years before his death he assigned
Frank Meisler, an artist in Yafo, to construct an animated statue of him according to his exact instructions. The statue was equipped with electric
switches in order to emulate the natural functions of the body. It was conceived as a funny, serious, and somewhat obscene toy to amuse the cemetery visitors. In its right hand it holds an urn which, according to Ali's instructions, contains his ashes. The monument's epitaph has been written
by Ali in the form of a letter. It is addressed "Dear friend" and begins with
the same sentence as on the door to all his hotel offices: "My name is Albert Elovic." He then writes that he would have preferred that someone
else's ashes were in the urn and that he was now reading the inscription,
but unfortunately the opposite is true. Therefore he wants to convey
through the statue his thoughts about life. He hopes that the visitor won't
be shocked. Creative people are seldom respectable and he counts himself among their number. The statue resembles a small dwarf, but its
anatomical parts are unnaturally proportioned according to how significant they were to Ali in life. The large, smiling head stresses the importance of a positive attitude to one's fellow human beings. The battery-run
and clearly audible thumping heart represents generosity and uncondi-
tional love. The stomach, penis, and bowels can be activated with the help
of switches to emphasize the importance of good food, the glory of love-
making, and the ability to eliminate all waste. Ali wills his intestinal contents to the politicians whose actions lead to hate, suffering, and war. He
finally implores the visitor to love passionately every moment of life as
long as he or she lives, despite all suffering and sorrow. He also asks the
visitor to forgive his language and means of expression. He hopes that the
reader fully understands that he was anything but a British gentleman.

The statue remains in the artist's studio window in Yafo almost a
decade after Ali's death. No one wanted it—not even a kibbutz where
Ali was revered and which was initially intended as the site of the monument. Ali had obviously miscalculated. His message, which can be
summed up by the Roman adage "*carpe diem*," is not new. This wouldn't
really matter if the statue's form and language would move the passing

visitor, but it doesn't. Compare it with the short, pregnant motto, also from Roman times: *"Sum quod eris, quod es, ante fui, pro me, pregor, ora!"*—I am what you will become, what you are I have already been, please pray for my soul.

Ali knew that he could make his fellow human beings happy when he inspired them with his lust for life. As long as he was in constant flow he could create flow in others. How could he believe that he could replace his own living, exuberant *joie de vivre* with a poor and lifeless communiqué?

The statue will remain in the studio window in Yafo for a long time yet. It is as poor a reflection of Ali's real message as the ashes in his urn resemble the once vital individual.

PROTEUS II— CARLETON

When I first met Carleton Gajdusek at the home of a colleague in Stockholm in October 1960, more than a decade before he received the Nobel Prize for his discovery of a new type of infectious agent, I knew nothing about him. He arrived on short notice and my host hadn't had the time to inform me. I only knew that I would meet "a very unusual virologist."

I began with the routine questions: What do you do? Where do you work? His answer was anything but trivial:

"I'm a departmental head at the National Institutes of Health (NIH) in the United States. The federal government provides me with a salary and substantial grants even though I'm rarely there. Most of the time I'm in New Guinea or in Micronesia, and sometimes in South America, Iran, or Afghanistan. I chart new diseases that no one has yet identified, but these things don't interest me. Sometimes I've managed to reveal their causes and analyzed their origins, but this doesn't really merit any attention. I isolate viruses one after the other—boring stuff. I've discovered many previously unknown genetic defects, but I can't imagine that you'd enjoy hearing about them."

"What, then, are your interests?"

"I'm interested in one particular problem which I'll never write about nor receive any grants to explore. I'm trying to understand the thinking process of people who've never come in contact with the Judeo-Christian, Chinese, Japanese, Indian, or Mongolian cultures or any other major culture."

"How do you approach this question?"

"I've penetrated many areas in New Guinea that have never been visited by any white man before me. I've come in close contact with the natives, and have lived with them during long periods and learned several of their more than seven hundred different languages.

"I've also adopted children from Stone Age cultures in New Guinea, and they have lived in my home for years."

I didn't believe a single word of what the man was saying. I was convinced that I was listening to the ramblings of a mythomaniac. Later I found out that every word he spoke was true, with one exception: Carleton is passionately interested in his work. But at our first meeting he apparently wanted to play the role of the uninterested, aloof professional, perhaps in order to offset my presumed one-sided focus on strictly scientific matters.

"How do people who've never had any contact with our civilization think? Is their thought process in any way similar to ours? Can they, with their primitive languages and without access to writing, articulate intricate ideas?"

Gajdusek became angry.

"Your question reveals your prejudice. It's true that they have no written language. They've nothing to write on, not even sand or clay. The rapid mountain streams and high tropical rainfall would immediately obliterate any sign they would trace, so it would be meaningless for them to even try. But why do you think that their languages are primitive? Their syntax and grammar are more inflected than yours and mine. They have only rudimentary numerical systems, and count rarely beyond ten, but they can express precisely how two people are related who have a common forefather seven generations back. The terms resemble your

Swedish system with *morfar* (mother's father) and *farfar* (father's father) for maternal and paternal grandfather, *moster* and *faster* for maternal and paternal aunt, or *barnbarnsbarn* (children's children's children) for great grandchildren, but is much more complicated. They have no general word for 'yellow' but rather a dozen words for different shades of yellow that you and I have no words for. Languages that have no written expression can be more nuanced and grammatically precise than languages that for many centuries have been used by people who read and write. Latin grammar is more complicated than Italian grammar, and the Icelandic language features a richly inflected structure which your truncated Swedish overall has lost. The only more or less unchanged surviving language from antiquity, Hebrew, is more compact and subtle than many modern languages. A high degree of accuracy is required in a language which is spoken rather than written, and especially when verbal misunderstandings can lead to dangerous situations. In our modern cultures, where mass media dominate communication and most people are protected from violence by general laws, language inevitably degenerates. Grammar disappears and sentence structures become simplified, resulting in a language resembling that of a simple-minded comic book. You'll have to consider this subject a bit more thoroughly. I'm fed up with hearing Stone Age people described as primitive. It's only evidence of our unwillingness to relate to their way of thinking. Stone Age people rapidly grasp our concepts and see through our behavior once they've established contact with us."

"How did you contact the natives in what were then completely isolated areas?"

"When I lead an expedition in New Guinea I recruit my assistants from the villages we pass. Native boys from ten to fifteen move swiftly through the jungle and are familiar with all the paths. During the months when they're traveling with me I usually learn as much of their language as I can, but they often learn our language as quickly or even quicker. Sometimes they learn so effectively that we're forced to converse in French, German, or Russian in order to maintain privacy. One time they picked up much of our 'secret' languages, even French and Russian.

There's nothing wrong with their intelligence, but there are some things that they're unable to learn. I'll give you an example: We keep our biological reagents in a mobile kerosene refrigerator which is opened and closed by turning a knob. The boys have trouble managing to do this since they've never learned as children how to rotate their wrist in a plane. In Stone Age culture there are no knobs or screws to turn. We learn this seemingly simple hand movement as young children and regard it as very easy, but it is difficult to learn beyond early childhood. The teenage boys were too old to learn the correct movement and would repeatedly break the knob. It was difficult to repair, so when it happened a fifth time I became quite angry. I yelled and berated them, but the boys just laughed and drummed with their left hand in an odd manner. It turned out that they were simultaneously keeping triple time with their thumb and double time with their little finger. No Westerners can manage this, not even Arthur Rubenstein, but these boys learn it very early as a part of their drumming ritual. Their logic was obvious: They had given me a perfect retort to my scolding!

"If you want to find out how Stone Age people think, you must study their thought processes before your presence, or the presence of any other Westerner, has changed their patterns of reaction. Otherwise it's like studying the behavior of wild animals in the dark by pointing a searchlight at them. As soon as one year after the appearance of the first white man, everything has changed irrevocably. Each change brings on the next and thereby accelerates the dissolution of their original way of life and ways of thinking. As soon as the whites have explained to them what a road is, the natives want to begin building one. They work with great enthusiasm, but stop immediately as soon as they grasp the meaning of an airplane. Then all they want to do is build a landing strip, but eventually stop as soon as they see a helicopter. They're even willing to drag a cable through the jungle if you explain how the telephone works, but they'll quit as soon as they discover the radio. It doesn't help when we tell them how many centuries it's taken us to get from the horse and carriage to the train and the car—or, to put it in their terms, 'how many men's ages' that have passed during the development of these means of transportation. They'll shake their heads and laugh and ask: how many men's ages have *you* lived? Then they'll refuse to continue with what they regard as unnecessary work."

Gajdusek continues speaking for many hours. His subjects cover many fields: his research on previously unknown diseases in New Guinea, fiction that he's read in his youth, the American federal bureaucracy which he wants to avoid or battle at all costs. We listen spellbound. No one wants to leave, and no one moves. Gajdusek has an amazing ability to captivate his listeners and instinctively knows how to grab our attention. His "conversational partner" rarely gets a chance to ask questions or to express an opinion. Surprisingly, one doesn't feel any of the usual irritation toward people who dominate a discussion. One's ambition to actively influence the course of the conversation disappears, and one is content with listening. No one tries to break into Carleton's monologue, nor are other dialogues started on the side. A few peripheral questions are asked, but by and large the listeners settle for expressing their interest or astonishment with facial expressions. It's as if everyone has one wish in common: to help the evocative flow of his account reach as many listeners as possible. Is this the way old bards would sing? Are we experiencing a kind of Homeric fascination? But this bard isn't blind. His eye is sharper than the eyes of most men, and he speaks not about wars, heroes, or gods. Or is there a deeper and more archetypal connection between Carleton and the inventive Odysseus or the wise old Väinämöinen, the ancient Finnish seer?

It was only after several hours that I could summon the wherewithal to break the spell and leave. With surprise I noticed my skepticism give way to a sense of wonder which I tried to prevent from turning into admiration.

During the next several years I regularly experienced the same spell when I met Carleton at scientific conferences or at the homes of friends. He had an opportunity to exercise his ability to seize the attention of a large group of listeners when he received the Nobel Prize in 1976. Carleton exceeded the sacred forty-five-minute limit of the Nobel lecture without the slightest embarrassment, speaking as he did for two hours and ruining the schedule for the entire afternoon. Strangely enough, no worried organizer tried to intervene. The lecture hall was packed. Eager listeners sat in the aisles and on the floor, many were jostling in the back and still more tried to enter the hall in vain. Gajdusek obviously enjoyed the situation. "I know that most of you have come to see my exotic films from New Guinea," he kept repeating. "We'll get to them toward the end of my presentation, but first we must talk about science."

Whatever had enticed you to attend the lecture, you had no reason to regret coming.

THE KURU DISEASE

In 1951 Carleton Gajdusek, a twenty-eight-year-old Harvard research assistant in virology, infectious diseases, and pediatrics, was drafted into military service at the Walter Reed Medical College in Washington, D.C. The virologist Joseph Smadel, who was a decisive influence on Carleton's development, became his immediate supervisor. Smadel was supportive, but received the young man's often overambitious projects with constructive criticism and was the first to discover Gajdusek's remarkable talents as a field virologist. When less developed countries sought American expert help in connection with local epidemics, Carleton often got the assignment. During 1952 and 1953 he was, among other places, sent to Iran, Afghanistan, and Turkey, where his task was to trace the sources of rabies and identify pockets of bubonic plague, encephalitis, and various vitamin deficiency diseases. The search for known or unknown viruses and other pathogens provided Carleton with welcome opportunities to contact isolated and often very exotic ethnic groups. Carleton's assignments became increasingly challenging as he organized and led expeditions to the valleys of the Himalayas, and through the jungles of South America, Malaysia, and New Britain.

But the most decisive event for his ongoing work occurred during a period as guest researcher in Melbourne, Australia. Through his host department he was introduced to the large island which for several decades would become his most important medical and nonmedical area of research. The dense jungles, remote mountain ranges, hidden valleys, and treacherous swamps, and above all the indigenous populations of New Guinea have irrevocably held his interest ever since. In New Guinea he could search out isolated tribes which had never before encountered a white man. He could indulge his interest in human development and communication among primitive cultures completely alien to our way of life while simultaneously enriching medical knowledge in a groundbreaking way. It's impossible to say what meant the most to him since each activity was a means of reaching the other. Each can be regarded as a goal or as a means, depending upon the situation.

Carleton's answer to my query about the Swedish explorer Sten Bergman reveals a great deal about his approach. Yes, he'd met him on one of Bergman's expeditions and had received a positive impression. Then Carleton pointed out that Bergman was an ornithologist and explained that when visiting an isolated tribe for the first time one should preferably be interested in birds, butterflies, or flowers. The amused natives will regard the visitor as a complete lunatic, but they'll be willing to run great distances to find the rare butterfly or flower which he seeks and in this way he'll get rich opportunities to familiarize himself with their customs and habits. But the visitor who arrives with the declared goal of studying the natives will find all doors slammed shut.

Was Gajdusek mainly interested in the diseases of the population or did this fulfill the same function as the birds and the butterflies did for other explorers? We'll return to this question.

After a few years of working together, Smadel was convinced of Gajdusek's genius. As early as 1958 Smadel managed to create a unique position for Gajdusek as head of his own research laboratory at the large federal National Institutes of Health (NIH) in Bethesda, Maryland, a position Gajdusek retained for many years. It provided him with the freedom and the necessary resources for his work in New Guinea and other exotic regions. The venture was successful beyond all expectations and resulted in a new scientific speciality which is commonly—but, as we shall see, mistakenly—described as "slow viruses." The kuru disease was the first case found in humans. (The "mad cow disease" that has drawn so much attention in recent years belongs to the same group.)

Carleton came upon the first cases of kuru in the 1950s when he visited New Guinea while based in Melbourne. The disease was described by Gajdusek and Vincent Zigas in 1957 after three years of joint research in a few distant villages in eastern New Guinea.* Kuru is a rapidly progressing, degenerative disease of the central nervous system which primarily attacks the cerebellum. It probably first emerged at the beginning of the twentieth century in two small villages. The affliction manifests itself in increasingly severe tremblings which lead to a loss of balance. The word "kuru" means trembling in the local language, and all who were stricken with kuru died within a year after their first symptoms were visible. Most victims were older children and adult women, but rarely adult men. Oddly enough, only a small number of villages were stricken with kuru. By meticulously mapping languages, customs, and family relations Gajdusek and Zigas could demonstrate that the disease only appeared among the Fore people, who speak their own language and display a distinct culture which differs sharply from that of neighboring villages.

In his book† Zigas writes that he first believed that the kuru disease, which according to the firm opinion of the Fore themselves was caused by witchcraft, was a form of hysteria. Later Gajdusek and Zigas postulated that it was an inherited disease, since the Fore people only married within the tribe. The absence of fever and other common reactions against viruses indicated that it wasn't an infectious disease. Combinations of hereditary, hormonal, and endocrinological factors were also considered, as was the possibility of a connection with some form of poisoning. But only when Gajdusek had gained close contact with the tribe and become familiar with its rituals and way of life could he formulate a theory of infection which would later prove to be correct. It was a remarkable achievement made possible only by Carleton's unique combination of skills as a field virologist and expedition leader, his ability to quickly learn new languages, his determination and stamina. Already

---

*C. Gajdusek and V. Zigas, "Degenerative Disease of the Central Nervous System in New Guinea: The Endemic Occurrence of 'Kuru' in the Native Population," *New England Journal of Medicine* 257 (1957): 974.

†Vincent Zigas, *The Laughing Death* (Clifton, N.J.: Humana Press, 1990).

his detailed epidemiological mapping of the presence of the disease in a previously unreachable region was astonishing. His ability to set up a field hospital in the most primitive conditions imaginable was only one reason for his success. His warm and personal contact with the kuru patients and their families was perhaps his most important and unique asset. Without this contact he would never have been able to conduct the autopsies which made the kuru brains available for pathological and microbiological analysis, and for the decisive animal experiments.

Vincent Zigas, an Australian of Baltic extraction and a native speaker of German, vividly describes the first kuru expeditions. He had worked as a physician in New Guinea for about ten years before he first heard about the disease from the natives. Shortly thereafter he encountered a few cases. The afflicted were well aware that they had kuru and what this meant, but they took their inevitably deteriorating condition and approaching death in stride, laughing together with their families at the comical, clumsy movements caused by their worsening physical shape. They lived and died in an environment dominated by dirt, rot, rats, insects, and other parasites. Everyone was certain that kuru was the result of a spell and therefore saw no reason to turn to the Australian hospital for help. Only after many determined attempts at persuasion did Zigas manage to bring a few kuru victims there. The natives regarded his examinations with great skepticism. They said that since you cannot cure the stricken, it only proves that they're bewitched. When other diseases were cured at the hospital, the natives interpreted it as cases where the spell had been broken.

In the mid-1950s Zigas received a prominent visitor in Sir Macfarlane Burnet* (who won the Nobel Prize for Medicine in 1960 for his research on the body's reactions to skin grafting and organ transplants), one of the world's leading virologists and Australia's most famous scientist, who came to hear about kuru. Burnet became interested and promised to contact competent Australian scientists. Zigas sent kuru-stricken brains for examination, but the Australians failed to isolate any virus and developed no concrete ideas about the origins of the disease.

*See more about Burnet in my essay "When Time Stops."

On May 14, 1957, while still waiting for the Australian research group promised by Burnet that would begin field research in the kuru region, Zigas received a visit from an unexpected and unusual guest, whom he first believed to be a bohemian drop-out. The visitor didn't have a beard or long hair, but his tattered shorts and open brown shirt over a grubby T-shirt signaled that the man was a "refugee" from Western culture, perhaps on a personal quest for some paradisiacal island. He was tall, lean, and boyish with scruffy, badly cut hair. Despite the shabby exterior, Zigas was immediately struck by the stranger's gaze, which was unusually focused, as if his eyes strived to penetrate everybody and everything. The furrows above his eyes gave evidence of his concentration, while his protruding ears seemed ever alert for signals to process while simultaneously screening out all unnecessary noise. The man's torso leaned slightly forward, as if he were moving even when still. His entire being gave the impression of a search, as if he was in constant motion toward some distant goal.

When Zigas heard about Carleton's background (because, of course, that's who this bohemian drop-out was), he first thought that he had before him a "standard" ambitious scientist whose sole interest was to gather academic merits. He was surprised to learn that Carleton was interested in everything related to the natives' way of life and was eager to learn not just about obviously important things but also about relatively trivial details. Most remarkable was his ability to gain immediate contact with the natives. He spent a lot of time with the children, whom he obviously loved, and who quickly learned to call him "Kartun." Large groups of children always surrounded him whatever he was doing—even during the many hours when he wrote his reports on a typewriter in his lap. And what reports he wrote! According to Zigas they were sufficiently detailed and precise to be immediately publishable in any scientific journal.

Zigas was also surprised to find out that Carleton was never afraid of conducting medical examinations on seriously ill or dying patients even when the primitive conditions were beyond compare. He would conduct an autopsy anywhere, even on a makeshift dinner table. Both he and Zigas handled kuru brains without the slightest fear of infection.

After the first intensive days of work, Gajdusek wrote a lengthy report to "Sir Mac" (Burnet) in Australia. When perusing the report for comments Zigas was struck by Carleton's modesty. Everything he had done on his own he described as a cooperative effort. The text was rich in detail and crystal clear, and the reader was effortlessly drawn in, whether faced with objective descriptions of facts, temporary experiences or subjective impressions. Today, when I read Carleton's diary from this and later periods, I can only agree with Zigas's assessment.

After having finished a first series of autopsies and other examinations at the last medical station, Zigas and Gajdusek ventured directly to the remote southern part of the Fore region. Carleton wanted to determine the exact geographical boundaries of the kuru affliction. Zigas describes the expedition into the practically uncharted region as the most exhausting of all during his years in New Guinea. The Australian governmental patrols had earlier reported that the area was not under their control and could not be entered due to constant tribal warfare, the risk of sudden attacks, poisoned arrows, and rampant cannibalism.

Zigas and Gajdusek encountered no such dangers. What proved vastly difficult was traversing the dense, mountainous jungle. They were literally forced to climb up to an elevation of over 9,000 feet. After reaching the top they had to descend to the valley at an elevation of 3,000 feet before climbing another peak at over 6,000 feet. It was like playing yo-yo: straight up, then straight down, and then up again during many difficult hours. When they had finally reached the mountain crest they found themselves in a swampy area where they were assailed by countless leeches. They were also attacked by wild bees, mosquitoes, and other types of blood-sucking insects that took turns tormenting the expedition according to the particular twenty-four-hour cycle of each species. They attacked in large swarms while the members of the expedition slashed and cut their way through the rough terrain. The high elephant grass with its razor-sharp edges and the thorny bushes contributed to their misery. The thorns, which resembled hooks and were often attached to the underside of vine-like plants, cruelly and inevitably stuck to the socks and trousers of each expedition member, literally grasping to puncture the bearer's skin. It was a "to this point but no further" shrubbery that seemed determined to open the intruders' skin to an invasion of assorted parasites and larvae. Foot wounds were especially dangerous since they could provide entry to insect-borne spirochetes which caused the severe tropical disease Yaws or Framboese. The expedition continued, step by step, on their tortuous but unstoppable journey. They defied all obstacles in order to establish just how far a mysterious, incomprehensible disease had spread within a small, primitive, and isolated ethnic group that held no importance to the world or the region. At the time, no one could surmise the future global importance of this and Carleton's later, seemingly harebrained expeditions.

Already at the start of the first expedition Zigas greatly admired his new colleague and friend, and this crew-cut maverick's manner of coping with all hardships. Each time they arrived in a village, soaking wet, exhausted, and out of breath, most of the members of the expedition would want to collapse and just sleep—except Carleton, who would immediately befriend the inhabitants in order to get them to donate blood samples. His practical skills were phenomenal. Full of admiration, the physician Zigas describes Carleton's quick and faultless method of taking blood from the thigh veins of very small children. He was just as quick with his camera, documenting everything for future study. The natives were remarkably positive toward Carleton's taking of photographs, the purpose of which they couldn't understand—although they concluded that the camera's lens was a magical eye which could see deep into people and objects and discover hidden connections. An old man whose pig had been stolen asked Carleton to identify the thief with his camera eye.

Carleton seemed totally possessed by the kuru problem and would scarcely speak of anything else. He wanted to construct a complete scenario from the many details, and his total devotion to the task was combined with complete disregard for other matters. The large postal sacks from the lab in the United States were left unopened for weeks and months, and he resisted all temptation to involve himself in other tasks.

During the course of this feverish work in New Guinea the scientific establishment in and around Melbourne arrived at the conclusion that Gajdusek had no rights to conduct kuru research on Australian territory. They wanted the investigation of the exotic disease to be an exclusively Australian affair and sent emissaries to New Guinea to convince Carleton to abandon his project. One after the other returned without having achieved his objective, and a few of them were actually converted during their visit, arriving at the conclusion that only Carleton had any chance of solving the mystery.

But solving the kuru mystery wasn't easy. Carleton explored every possible avenue. Since he first suspected the local diet and possible poisons, he collected samples of food, plants, and minerals. These were analyzed in both Australia and the U.S. but yielded nothing of interest. While in New Guinea Gajdusek and Zigas tried various forms of therapy on the patients in order to draw possible conclusions *ex juvantibus* (from whatever helped). But neither antibiotics, vitamins, antihistamines, cortisone, hormones, nor antidotes to various poisons had any effect. When they were still without a clue after seven months of hard work, Zigas was at the end of his patience, wondering if there weren't more important and fruitful problems to investigate. In addition, the Fore people began to grow tired of the intrusive research and especially the constant tests. They realized that the white doctors could help them with simpler ailments but were convinced that the "kuru bewitchment" lay beyond the doctors' powers and understanding. But although the Fore considered the quest for the "solution to the kuru problem" as pretty ridiculous, they didn't oppose the effort.

Carleton remained convinced of his course, however, and regarded the first six months as just a start. He viewed kuru as a gateway to understanding other chronic degenerative diseases of the central nervous system. Carleton's patience seemed endless and boosted the failing motivation among the others.

After ten months of intensive work, Carleton made his first visit back in the United States. Zigas, who didn't yet know that Carleton would keep returning in order to continue his stubborn research, regarded the past period as a bizarre mixture of hope, despair, frustration, and illusory victories. But he knew that he had learned more from Carleton during those ten months than during his previous thirteen years of medical studies and practice.

But Carleton had begun to formulate his theory and was full of confidence. He received a letter from the British pathologist Bill Hadlow, who noted the similarity between kuru and scrapie, an infectious disease among sheep which caused great financial loss in Scotland and Iceland. The course of the diseases and the pathological changes in the nervous system were so similar that Carleton began to suspect that kuru could also be caused by some form of infection. But his attempts to infect laboratory animals failed. Neither was he able to cultivate the suspected infectious agent in cell cultures.

During his stay at home he lobbied intensely to be able to inoculate chimpanzees and other apes with kuru brain matter. This demanded a large investment but he finally managed to convince the National Institutes of Health. The attempts at inoculation demanded more patience than the optimists had expected, but gave positive results.* The chimpanzees became ill eighteen to thirty months after the inoculation, demonstrating symptoms that fully corresponded to the kuru disease in humans. Their brain tissue showed the same type of pathological change and was highly infectious. After one chimpanzee passage the incubation period was shortened to one year.

These experiments definitely proved that kuru could be transferred by an infectious agent. But how did the contagion spread among people and why was the disease limited to the Fore tribe?

We might never had an answer to this question without Carleton's close contact with the natives and their culture. Zigas notes with sarcasm the contrast between Gajdusek's close daily contact with the entire tribe and the run-of-the-mill white doctor who lives totally isolated among the natives, cut off from his own culture and often taking solace in the colonialistic myth of Western superiority while succumbing to alcohol and drugs.

---

*D. C. Gajdusek, C. J. Gibbs, and M. Alpers, "Experimental Transmission of a Kuru-Like Syndrome to Chimpanzees," *Nature* 209 (1966): 794; D. C. Gajdusek, C. J. Gibbs, and M. Alpers, "Transmission and Passage of Experimental 'Kuru' to Chimpanzees," *Science* 155 (1967): 212.

Carleton's dissimilarity to this stereotype early on made him aware of the Fore tribe's ritual cannibalism in connection with their burial ceremonies. Tradition demanded that families eat the bodies of their relatives after they had died. It was a sign of respect, since the relatives would then be able continue to live through the bodies of their surviving family members. The kuru-afflicted Fore tribe and their neighbors in the Eastern Highlands employed this ritual. It was this cannibalism that was spreading the disease as well as limiting it to the Fore people.

The Australian government prohibited ritual cannibalism during the 1950s. Missionaries, the Salvation Army, and small groups of fundamentalists who arrived in the region around 1957 did what they could to convince the natives to discontinue their ceremonial habit, and were helped by the fact that the natives wanted to "resemble Europeans." When the practice of cannibalism was abandoned the kuru disease eventually disappeared among the children (about five years later) and among adolescents (ten years later). In the early 1980s the disease was practically gone. No one born after 1956 has been infected, although the disease still appears among old people more than thirty-five years after the assumed moment of contagion in their infancy, which can be determined precisely in certain cases.

The age and sexual distribution of those afflicted with kuru also reflected the traditional mortuary rite. The brains of the deceased, which animal tests had proven to be more infectious than other tissues, were mainly handled by children and women, who were also at greatest risk of catching kuru. They were probably infected through skin wounds and the mucous membranes of the eye and nose.

One may wonder if the discovery of an unknown and already eradicated disease which affected a small, primitive tribe really was important enough to warrant a Nobel Prize. It certainly did. It turned out that the infectious agent of kuru did not belong to any previously known viral category. It differs in principle from all earlier known infectious agents, including all viruses, with scrapie the only important exception. The kuru and scrapie agents cannot be called viruses for the following reasons:

A virus carries its genetic information in nucleic acid, as do all other living creatures. All cells contain two types of nucleic acid, RNA and DNA, while a virus contains only one, either RNA or DNA.* The RNA- and DNA-borne information is written in the same code, or rather in very similar "dialects" of the same code. The viral nucleic acid contains all instructions needed for the construction of new viral particles within the infected cell. If the viral nucleic acid is damaged by radiation or chemicals, the virus is inactivated. Therefore it was a great surprise when it turned out that neither the kuru contagion nor its "sheep cousin" scrapie followed this rule common to all viruses. They were highly resistant to both ultraviolet and X-rays, and to many chemical disinfectants. At an early stage Carleton began doubting that their genetic information was written in the code of nucleic acid. He was well aware that the absence of nucleic acid in an infectious agent would be a revolutionary conclusion, since all genetic information throughout the biological world was known to be written in RNA- or DNA-code.

During his Nobel lecture Gajdusek produced a blackened plastic tube. It had been subjected to radiation for so long that the plastic had become black, yet it still contained an active infectious agent—the radiation had had no effect. The agent also couldn't be damaged by chemical disinfectants like formalin or propiolacton. It remained active at 80⁰C and was only somewhat weakened when boiled. The presence of infectious material could also be proved in pathological specimens embedded in paraffin, even though these had been subjected to formalin, alcohol, and organic dehydrating agents. The kuru and scrapie agents have, however, been partially destroyed through oxidation, autoclaving (i.e., high-pressure sterilization using steam) at a temperature of 121⁰C and by phenol. But the formalin-treated agent resists autoclaving.

The kuru and scrapie agents differ from conventional viruses in another important respect. They don't contain any detectable foreign protein. Electron microscopes reveal no viral particles in the diseased tissue and there are no signs of immunological reactions. The 100 per-

---

*For a more detailed discussion about RNA- and DNA-viruses see George Klein, "Coexistence between Virus and Man" in his *The Atheist and the Holy City*, translated by Theodore and Ingrid Friedmann (Cambridge, Mass.: MIT Press, 1990).

cent fatality rate also indicates the absence of any immunological response in the host.

After continued research, kuru and scrapie have been joined by other diseases afflicting the central nervous system among humans or animals that are caused by the same spongelike ("spongiform" in medical parlance) degeneration of the nerve cells. The rare Creutzfeld-Jakob Disease (CJD) in humans is of special interest. Like kuru, CJD is characterized by a rapid and fatal degeneration of the brain. The disease occurs globally with a frequency of about one annual case per one million people, but its exact frequency varies between different ethnic groups. It often manifests itself in patients around sixty years of age and strikes both men and women in equal proportion. Like kuru, it primarily afflicts the cerebellum, resulting in loss of balance and decreased muscle function. C. J. Gibbs and Gajdusek have inoculated brain suspensions from cases of CJD into chimpanzees and other apes, and the animals developed the same disease as they did after similar tests with kuru.* Gajdusek concluded that kuru is a variant of CJD that has spread within the Fore and neighboring peoples through ritual cannibalism. Further support for this theory was provided by the discovery that the CJD agent was as resistant to radiation and chemical treatment as is kuru. The route of transmission could only be hypothesized. For instance, CJD appears more often among Libyan Jews (thirty-one cases per million) than among Jews from Europe (0.4 to 1.9 cases per million). Gajdusek suspects lamb eyes as a possible source of infection, since that is a popular delicacy among Libyan Jews. P. Duffy mentions a case of a cornea transplant from a donor suffering from CJD as a clear confirmation of infectious transmission.† The recipient fell ill with a typical case of CJD eighteen months after the operation. Three cases of CJD have occurred fifteen to seventeen months after cases of brain surgery. Neurosurgeons are at greater risk of contracting CJD than other medical doctors. Brain matter from a neurosurgeon who had died after a complicated brain disease was

---

*D. C. Gajdusek and C. J. Gibbs, *Perspectives in Virology* 8 (1973): 279.

†P. Duffy et al., "Letter: Person-to-Person Transmission of Creutzfeldt-Jakob Disease," *New England Journal of Medicine* 290 (1974): 692.

shown to cause a characteristic case of CJD in apes. Approximately 10 percent of CJD occurs among relatives, but even this seemingly hereditary form may be transmitted to apes through inoculation.

The term "slow viruses," which includes scrapie, kuru, and CJD, was coined by the Icelander Björn Sigurdson. Certain infectious diseases among minks and cattle also belong to this category. "Mad cow disease" or BSE (Bovine Spongiform Encephalitis), falls into this category and has caused a special sense of alarm. BSE has been rampant in Great Britain since 1986, and at least 15,000 head of cattle have been slaughtered in emergency measures to prevent further spread of the disease. Felines and antelopes at British zoos have also been infected. The fear of human infection has caused meat prices to plummet and caused serious crisis in Britain and elsewhere. *Deadly Feasts,** a recently published book by Richard Rhodes, gives an excellent account of the scientific findings and political consequences of the disease.

How do the slow viruses transmit the infection, and what type of molecule carries the relevant information? Could it be nucleic acid, after all—the only known molecule which speaks the language of the genes? The possibility that a very small RNA molecule could resist all the drastic treatment that the kuru and scrapie agents have been subjected to cannot be excluded with absolute certainty, but it's highly unlikely. Carleton has proposed a different explanation.

CHEESE-MAKING, TIRES, AND OLD WALLETS

Gajdusek's Stockholm lecture in 1986 astounded the audience. Suddenly he began talking about women who manufacture cheese. When the milk curdles, strings are produced which spread over the entire batch and eventually solidify. This is because the round, globular pro-

---

*Richard Rhodes, *Deadly Feasts: Tracking the Secrets of a Terrifying New Plague* (New York: Simon & Schuster, 1997).

tein molecules are transformed into long fibers—even though their chemical composition is unchanged. Gajdusek proceeded to display two wallets, one old and one new, which had both been made from the same kind of leather. When he bent or squeezed them, the old one emitted a creaking sound while the new one remained "quiet." This is due to the fact that the proteins in the old one had "aged" and changed their structure. Another example is the contrast between old and new tires, where old ones can be damaged merely by kicking since their proteins have been pulverized. In both examples the "aging," which resembles a process of crystallization, had begun in one or a few "cores" and then spread through the wallet and the tire. According to Gajdusek, degenerative changes in the nervous system develop in a similar way. Kuru, CJD, and scrapie begin from one or a small number of initial sources— perhaps when an indigenous protein of the organism happens to change its normal structure. The change would then be transmitted to other similar molecules. The "spread of the contagion" between the cells would be conveyed by the millions of interlinked nerve fibers, in a similar way as when milk is converted into cheese. In contrast to viral encephalitis, such a process does not need to provoke any immunological reactions. Normally, the organism doesn't react against its own proteins.

PRION—FROM CONCEPT TO MOLECULE

In order to distinguish the unconventional scrapie, kuru, and related agents from regular RNA- and DNA-viruses, Stanley Prusiner* has introduced the term "prion." Gajdusek, who many years before Prusiner had begun his research had postulated that the scrapie and kuru agents don't contain a nucleic acid, was reluctant to use this designation. He still prefers to talk about infectious protein. The term "prion," however, has taken root and is now commonly used, regardless of priority.

---

*S. B. Prusiner, "Novel Proteinaceous Infectious Particles Cause Scrapie," *Science* 216 (1982): 136.

The biological research which led to the prion theory picked up speed when scientists succeeded in infecting mice and hamsters with scrapie. This was a precondition for the purification and closer characterization of the agent. As far as we know, the experimental findings that have been made on small laboratory animals are valid for the naturally occurring scrapie disease in sheep as well as for kuru, CJD, and related diseases in humans.

The purification of scrapie prions taken from infected hamster brains have led to the identification of the infectious prion protein PrP. The purified proteins have been "sequenced," i.e., analyzed, for their building blocks. The amino acids that make up the protein were identified and their exact order in the protein was determined. With computer help, this information was translated into the language of nucleic acid, and the exact genetic code that carries the inherited information for the protein could be determined. Using synthetic pieces of this text called oligonucleotides, the corresponding gene could be retrieved from gene libraries, derived from normal cells. This whole process has been successfully carried out for PrP.

The infectious protein identified in the scrapie brains has been termed PrP^{SC}. The same protein is prevalent in a somewhat different form in the normal tissue of uninfected animals. Thus, as has been suspected all along, it's a cellular and not a viral protein. The PrP proteins exist in two different forms. The normal form is called PrP^{C} and is not infectious. Both PrP^{SC} and PrP^{C} are encoded by the same gene. This means that they're defined by same genetic code letters and mutually corresponding protein building blocks (amino acids) (with the exception of a common form of CJD, GSS, as discussed below). The only difference is the protein's form and higher structure, just as Carleton suggested with his metaphors about cheese production and crystallization. In other words, the difference between PrP^{SC} and PrP^{C} must develop after the protein has been formed.

Molecular biologist Charles Weissmann has summarized "the advancement of the prion" in the magazine *Nature*, suggesting that the prion has "climbed from the Ditch of Doubt to the Mountain of Respectability. So far, it hasn't yet reached the Peak of Universal Acceptance, but it's on its way."*

All prion-transmitted diseases are sorted under the umbrella term "spongiform encephalopathies," meaning spongelike brain degeneration. Besides scrapie, kuru, and CJD there is yet another unusual human brain disease called Gerstmann-Sträussler-Scheinker syndrome (GSS). This is a very rare variation of CJD with an earlier onset, slower progress, and a more extensive process of degeneration. Besides the cerebellum, it afflicts part of the spine. Gajdusek has identified GSS among at least twelve families.†

PrP^C is a normal component of the outer membranes of the nerve cells. PrP^{SC} differs from PrP^C in certain physical properties, for example solubility and sensitivity to certain degradable enzymes. PrP^C is the biochemical precursor of PrP^{SC}, but the exact details of the transformation are not yet understood.

The transfer of the scrapie prion between different species has provided important new information. Inoculation of scrapie-infected hamster brain to mice transmits the disease to the recipients, but it appears only after a long delay, starting 500 days after the implantation. But on the next passage from mouse to mouse the incubation period decreases to 140 days. The same is true in the opposite direction. Mouse scrapie prions induced the disease in hamsters after 400 days, but already by the next passage from hamster to hamster the period of latency is shortened to 75 days. Transformation of the host's PrP^C derived from a foreign species is therefore a relatively rare event. But once it has occurred, the new host's PrP^{SC} can effectively transform PrP^C to PrP^{SC} in the same organism, and, after passage, in other organisms of the same species.

The Gajdusek team and others have recently shown that the usual form of the GSS-syndrome depends on a mutation in the normal PrP^C

---

*Charles Weissmann, "The Prion's Progress," *Nature* 349 (1991): 569.

†C. L. Masters, D. C. Gajdusek, and C. J. Gibbs, "Creutzfeldt-Jacob Disease Virus Isolations from the Gerstmann-Straussler-Scheinker Syndrome with an Analysis of the Various Forms of Amyloid Plaque Deposition in the Virus-Induced Spongiform Encephalopathies," *Brain* (1981): 104–559.

gene.* This mutation always occurs at the same place within the gene. It is believed that the mutation facilitates the spontaneous transformation of PrP^C to PrP^{SC}. This has been confirmed through the transfer of the GSS-mutation to mice. The mutated human gene was inserted into fertilized mouse eggs. The baby mice that carried the mutated gene died between seven and thirty-nine weeks after birth, and their brains displayed the same type of spongelike degeneration as the natural diseases.

This is where one begins to suspect a connection between the hereditary and the infectious forms. The mutation increases the probability that PrP^C can change to PrP^{SC} among GSS-stricken families. The infectious disease appears when the protein, which for unknown reasons—but not necessarily or solely through mutation—has been changed from PrP^C to PrP^{SC}, is transferred horizontally through either natural or experimental means, i.e., when the agent is passed from one person to another.

CARLETON'S EXTENDED FAMILY

Washington, D.C., 1975. We are in Carleton's large house located on the city limits between Washington and Chevy Chase. The outside of the house comes across as any ordinary American family home. Four or five black teenagers are playing basketball in the back yard. They're Carleton's youngest adoptive sons and are still living "at home." The earlier "litters" have already left home. One of the oldest has returned to Papua-New Guinea and is now the new nation's Nature Museum Director. Several are teachers or doctors. A few of them have found a place in American society. The very polite young man who has driven us here is a college student with good grades in math who has just been elected class president.

I ask the boys if they have any contact with their biological parents. Their answer is somewhat tentative, but Carleton helps to explain. Boys from Melanesian and Micronesian islands who've been in contact with our world often keep in touch with their families and a few of them

*G. Goldgaber et al., "Mutations in Familial Creutzfeldt-Jakob Disease and Gerstmann-Straussler-Scheinker's Syndrome," *Experimental Neurology* 106 (1989): 204.

sometimes visit their home villages. Others are content with writing a letter now and then. Most remember their childhood and sometimes talk about their memories. The boys from the previously completely isolated Stone Age villages of New Guinea, on the other hand, seldom or never talk about their families, as if they've suppressed the memories of their childhoods. The cultural gap appears to be too wide. When Carleton first arrived at the most primitive villages in the region, the natives had never seen a person wearing pants or shoes. Neither did they have any conception of what an airplane is. One of the boys whom Carleton brought to the airport thought that the entire terminal would fly away.

Carleton leaps to one of his favorite topics, shooting off like an unstoppable rocket:

One must realize that Stone Age cultures change beyond recognition already a year or so after having received their first white visitors. Today there are no remaining villages in New Guinea that are unaware of "the civilized world." Neither are there still any outright hunters and gatherers or isolated primitive farmers. Airplane traffic and at least a few industrial products have by now made their way even to our planet's most isolated forests and mountains. Shortly after the process had begun, the tribal groups began losing their earlier profound and undisturbed contact with their own past. The youths were the first to realize that there was a world beyond their territory and that people there were capable of many things that their own (until recently) respected elders knew nothing about. Thus their traditional reliance on the wisdom of their elders was irrevocably disturbed. Only a few years later their ancient culture, which had remained more or less unchanged throughout the millennia, had eroded.

The first Western visitors often change the social structure without realizing what they have brought about. Before Carleton understood this he could, for example, reward a helpful youngster by giving him an ax— something comparable in our culture to instantly turning a poor worker into a millionaire. The youth would inevitably obtain greater authority than his father or the village elder, and may not have been able to handle it.

I try to bring the conversation back to the boys. How is it possible for some of them to have become elite students in the United States?

Carleton's monologue immediately changes direction. "I've chosen them carefully," he says. "They've first worked as assistants during my expeditions and I've gotten to know them well. Local teenage boys are our most important assistants, and we wouldn't be able to move between different tribal groups without them. The youths are the most valuable sources of information and also the best company. I usually establish good contact from the beginning by learning their names for everything I see. This always breaks the ice. I'll point at an object, listen to the sound, and then try to repeat the word while asking the youths to correct my pronunciation. This always elicits great bursts of laughter since it's difficult to imitate their sounds exactly; they are often very alien to us. Usually large groups of people immediately gather around me. Everyone speaks at the same time and wants to educate me as if I were their playmate. By the end of the day we really enjoy each other's company and have become friends. Massive barriers of suspicion and prejudice have evaporated. Since the natives are very fond of their children, getting to know them and the youngsters is like an admission ticket to the entire village."

"How are you able to pass between hostile villages and tribes? In your charting of the kuru disease you must have crossed such borders repeatedly."

It's not like moving between two cities in Sweden or the United States. Villages in two bordering valleys a few kilometers apart may be culturally and linguistically more dissimilar than Sweden and China. The borders that have been established by the feuds and wars of many generations may appear unsurmountable. But you can always assume that there are old paths between nearby villages even if they haven't been used in many generations. If the neighborly relations are hostile, no one wants to volunteer or admit that there are people on the other side. When I asked the adults what was in a certain direction where no one ever went, they would answer 'nothing' or 'hell' or 'evil spirits.' But I have learned to find the paths eventually with the help of the children."

"How?"

"When I've reached the last available village and understood that I've come upon a line of demarcation, I've stopped and pitched camp there. Sometimes I've stayed for weeks or months and learned a good portion of the local language. Don't be surprised! Anyone with a normal intellect can learn a wide vocabulary and some verb structure in a totally unknown language in a few months if you socialize intensely with people who don't speak any other language."

"Wasn't it ever difficult to achieve the close contact that you seek? How often have you failed?"

"Almost never. Remember that I take an interest in the villagers' illnesses and begin treating every ailment that I'm able to treat as soon as possible."

"Didn't you ever meet with sustained suspicion?"

"Yes, sometimes. If they're suspicious or fearful to begin with because something has gone wrong or for some other unknown reason, they can doubt the sincerity of every word that you say. In that case they'll accept no smiles or pleasantries but instead behave as if they'd want to pick everything apart. Oddly enough even the severest attitude can be overcome if you manage to redirect your contact toward the prevalent hospitality ritual. For instance, a visit to the 'men's dwelling' can do wonders. There you'll meet hardened warriors, but tradition demands that even the cruelest among them—who are at any time prepared to fight until death for their own garden or their friend's garden, their pigs, or their women—will be polite toward the visitor. It's striking how these men, who are armed to their teeth and always ready to avenge any sign of disrespect, will in the course of a few minutes be transformed into their own opposites. They'll beam with cordiality, a soft and sensitive dignity, and natural affection. But there's no guarantee that the effect will last once you leave the men's dwelling. Sometimes the ice is definitely broken, but at other times the fear and suspicion may return. This is perhaps not surprising in a society where a man's ability to survive is directly dependent upon his physical and mental strength and resistance. There are only a few situations when men are allowed to express friendliness and affection. The guest in the men's dwelling is regarded as an ideal friend and thus fulfills a ritualized need: the dream of a perfect friend, which, for example, was every male's dominant fantasy in the

Fore tribe. They would always imagine such a friend as a stranger, since all men from their own tribe or from linguistically related neighboring tribes were regarded as potential rivals and enemies. This is easy to grasp when you know how vigorously they have to compete for all available resources. Consequently, friendship, trust, and understanding are rare among these men. Yet—or perhaps for this very reason—they cultivate the dream and act it out ritually as soon as the opportunity arises. Communication with the children is much more natural and full of trust.

"The children are very fond of group games. Once, when I was really stuck in a village where I knew the children well, I began with a ring game. We clapped our hands and sang. Suddenly I pointed to a nearby mountain and sang the mountain's name. Everyone joined in. We then sang all the mountain names I knew and pointed in their corresponding directions. Suddenly I pointed in a direction that was alien and obviously taboo, and the children sang the taboo name without balking. By using the same method I could find out where the secret path was located. And as soon as we found it, we could move on."

Carleton continued talking with Eva, while I looked around the renowned house. This was not the way I had imagined it. I had expected a kind of "intense chaos" of excitement and complications, but instead I encountered a relaxed family atmosphere. The boys kidded with each other and playfully tried to tease Carleton. They talked to him the way you talk to an eccentric and somewhat untrustworthy older brother, not to a respected father figure. The older boys each had their own room while the younger ones were two to a room. There were plenty of bookshelves in all rooms, and the books had obviously been chosen with care and included some of the best European and American fiction. Besides books in English there were books in German, French, and even a few in Russian. A few of the older boys were busy sorting and registering native art from New Guinea. I was told that Carleton had collected works of art during all his expeditions and intended to donate them to the Peabody Museum of Salem as soon as they'd been systematized.

Someone called for the boys who were playing basketball in the yard to come and set the table. Only then did I notice Joe, a somewhat corpulent older gentleman with a cigar firmly rooted in the corner of his mouth. He didn't talk to us and was obviously very busy. He saw to it that the housework was taken care of, that the boys polished their shoes, did their homework, and tidied up in their rooms. In addition he had apparently prepared our dinner.

I took no particular interest in Joe. I assumed that he was employed as a housekeeper, and that he just as well might have worked somewhere else. Only long after our visit with Carleton did I learn that Joe Wegstein was one of the most important pioneers in the field of computer language.* During the workday he held a high position at the National Bureau of Standards. Carleton and the boys were his family. Carleton's house was his home, and the household work his leisure activity. Joe invented the computer language "Cobol" and was one of the three people who assembled "Algol-60." He was best known as the inventor of the Wegstein method for the computerized processing of fingerprints, the first method for this form of computer analysis which has been used in other criminological contexts as well by the FBI, Interpol, Scotland Yard, and others. According to what Carleton later told me, his adoptive children really dislike what they perceive as "computer-controlled people" and often affectionately ribbed Joe for his achievements, for instance by pretending to put arsenic in his food in order to "protect humanity from him and other controllers."

Spirits were high during dinner. The boys' constant ribbing of Carleton stayed within the borders of good taste as in any properly educated family. But unlike most stereotypical cases of "the discreet charm of the bourgeoisie," I couldn't detect any signs of forced or strained friendliness nor any polite excuses or evasions. The boys had obviously adopted aspects of Carleton's style but without abandoning their individuality. On the surface this could have been a typical slice of regular, everyday,

---

*See, for example, J. H. Wegstein, *Accelerating Convergence of Iterative Processes* (National Bureau of Standards, Washington, D.C.: ACM Communications, June 1958); and W. E. Grove, *Brief Numerical Methods* (Englewood Cliffs, N.J.: Prentice Hall Applied Mathematics Series, 1966).

American teenage culture, but it contained a different and mysterious aspect which I still hadn't been able to define.

Carleton's monologues, which were seldom and only intermittently interrupted, dominated the evening as usual. After dinner a third guest arrived; a Hungarian-Australian virologist whom Eva and I knew from our student days in Budapest. He was as famous for his analytic sharpness as for his sarcastic and often spiteful attitude toward most of his fellow human beings. I had never before heard him say an appreciative word about anyone and was therefore fairly surprised to hear him praise Carleton during our shared cab-ride home after dinner. If there was a living genius in the world today who really deserved to be praised as such, he said, it was Carleton. I agreed that Carleton was unique, but I also felt a certain disappointment over the last two hours of the evening's conversation. After the exciting tale about human contacts in New Guinea, Carleton had slipped into his least interesting favorite subject: vilifying the bureaucracy at the National Institutes of Health. He was surely on target in many respects, but the matter was trivial compared with his other "monologue topics." But I knew it was anything but empty talk. Carleton had for many years battled the bureaucracy's often quite unrealistic rules. He had had the courage and the strength to build his own system within the system and also became a master at circumventing meaningless directives. I could understand how he was allowed to get away with this now, when he was famous, but how had he managed to pull this off in the beginning, long before he won his fame? Why didn't the bureaucrats put an end to what they must have regarded as his irritating elitist eccentricities?

Our Australian colleague explained that Carleton has always been protected by his closest superiors. Even those who were unaware of his scientific talents soon discovered his remarkable skills as a practical field virologist. For example, during the 1950s an urgent request was sent from Bolivia to the United States. A Japanese settlement in a hard-to-reach rain forest near the Brazilian border had been struck by an unknown epidemic, and the settlers now asked for immediate help from experts. Almost half of the inhabitants (46 percent), who originally came from Okinawa, were taken ill with a severe "jungle fever," and many of them died within a few weeks.

The health authorities in Washington, D.C., sent Carleton to investigate. He took a flight to the last possible airport, continued by helicopter to the last possible landing pad, and then traveled by boat up a river for several days. Upon arriving at the isolated settlement he found that no one could speak anything but Japanese. According to his curriculum vitae, Carleton's knowledge of foreign languages includes "German, French, Spanish, Russian, Slovak, New Melanesian, Persian, Bahasa Indonesian, Dutch, and several languages from Papua-New Guinea, Melanesia, and Micronesia," yet this time he fell short. Nevertheless he managed his task.

He began by reconstructing the course of events. The Japanese were told to illustrate on a calendar everything that had happened during the weeks prior to the outbreak of the epidemic. It turned out that they had felled several large trees in order to extend their site. Using sign language Carleton asked if any wild animals had lived in these trees. The Japanese drew frightened monkeys running around the settlers, which led Carleton to suspect that a mosquito-borne encephalitis virus could have been transmitted to man from its natural host, the monkey. His hypothesis proved correct. After only a week he managed to isolate a previously unknown virus which could be linked to the disease that was named Uruma after the Japanese settlement.

Carleton's practical skills—mentioned by anyone who has joined his expeditions—contrast sharply with the increasing bewilderment of modern virologists and clinicians during field work. At one point he visited isolated islands in Micronesia with fewer than a thousand inhabitants on each. The islanders' only contact with the outer world was through one or a few visiting boats per year. All of the islanders were more or less related, and they displayed an intriguing range of diseases, including various rare anemias, endocrinological disturbances, and parasites. Carleton invited eight prominent professors from Boston to join a one-month expedition to study the diseases that belonged to their particular specialties. But only a few short days after the experts in hematology, nutrition, parasitology, childhood diseases, endocrinology, and internal medicine had stepped ashore, Carleton realized that this time he'd bet on the wrong horse. Instead of filming the natives, as he customarily did, he turned his camera on the impractical professors who couldn't manage without their well-stocked laboratories and skilled assistants.

In another context I heard Carleton speak about an unexpected observation he'd made alongside his usual work—and again he wove the information into a lecture which was actually about something else. During a visit to the central highlands of western New Guinea, two Indonesian doctors drew his attention to an "epidemic" of substantial and often life-threatening burns which afflicted older children and adults of the isolated Ekori tribe. The small regional hospital at the Paniai lake received forty to fifty patients with burns each year from the same circumscribed region. Many were burned so badly that entire limbs had to be amputated. Carleton immediately went to the region. The inhabitants, who lived at an altitude of 2,000 meters, used no textiles and were practically naked. The nights were very cold and everyone slept around the open fire. Carleton immediately realized that the severe burns must have been caused by rolling into the fire. But a normal sleeper would immediately wake up and recoil from the pain. Carleton came to the conclusion that those with burns must have rolled into the fire while in a state of temporary unconsciousness. As soon as he could construct an understandable sentence in the local language his first question was: How many dead bodies have you pulled out of the fire during the last month? Five, was the answer.

Carleton was convinced that the burns must be caused by epileptic fits. But why would such seizures be endemic? He noticed that the burns were limited to a small area were pigs were raised. The Indonesian doctors had noticed that several villagers had small knots on their skin, which seemed to indicate a parasite. Carleton guessed that it was the worm *Taenia solium*, which may cause the disease called cysticercosis. The worms encapsulate themselves in liquid cysts in the brain and under the skin in both humans and animals, and are easily spread through infected pork. The worm was previously not believed to be present in that particular region, but the inhabitants had seen cysts in their pigs recently. Carleton asked to perform autopsies on the deceased burn victims. Their brains looked like Swiss cheese and were riddled with parasite cysts. After much detective work he could not only confirm the diagnosis, but also traced the source of the contagion to an infected pig that had been brought in from another area.

As soon as the diagnosis was complete, Carleton embarked on a round of intensive preventive work.* As usual he undertook this entirely on his own initiative. It would have been futile to try to get the Ekori tribe to kill the infected pigs and refrain from eating their meat without first convincing them of the causal connection. Typically, and as an illustration of Carleton's respect for all people regardless of their background and level of education, he chose the same method to convince the natives he would have used to convince a class of medical students. First he showed them that the sick pigs and the stricken people had the same kind of cysts. Then he treated a couple of patients who displayed the knots under their skin with anti-parasitical medicine and pointed out the live worms in their excrement under the microscope to everyone who wanted to see them. After this demonstration it was easy to convince the villagers of the connection between the pigs and their own cysts. He could also explain how the worms that they had seen under the microscope encapsulated themselves in cysts that were not just under the skin but also in the brain, and how this could cause epilepsy and unconsciousness. As soon as they had realized the link between the brain cysts and the nightly risk of being burned they killed all the afflicted pigs on their own initiative and carefully buried the remains. They also understood that the larvae in the excrement could infect other people, and so they ordered their children not to defecate close to the village, which they'd been doing before. Nine- to fifteen-feet-deep latrines were quickly built for the adults.

Who and what is Carleton? A practical genius? An untiring, devoted scientist and physician? He certainly is, but also much more than that. Only after several years of knowing him did I realize this. His scientific and medical efforts are so important that one tends to forget his other di-

---

*D. C. Gajdusek, in *Health and Disease in Tribal Societies* (Amsterdam; New York: Elsevier/Excerpta Medica/North-Holland, 1977).

mensions. Perhaps this is what he prefers. Perhaps he wants to keep an unreachable inner self to himself and those closest to him. Sometimes there are indications of this, but at other times one may encounter the exact opposite: a streak of fleeting exhibitionism, a sudden opening to his innermost core that slams shut before you have the time to draw your breath, a moment of boyish coquetry behind his serious, seemingly reserved facade. Is it only a game when he lifts the curtain, or is it real shyness, a painful but necessary inner loneliness seeking contact?

I must see and hear more.

Frederick, Maryland, 1987. I am visiting Carleton in his "new" house. It's large and by American standards very old, a somewhat dilapidated wooden villa from the eighteenth century surrounded by a large, wildly grown tract of land. A somewhat rusty official sign reveals that the house is a historical landmark, since it once served as a general headquarters during the Civil War. Carleton moved here when he'd been given new workspace in the large federal laboratory complex at nearby Fort Detrick. The complex was originally built as a top secret military plant for, among other things, the production of biological weapons. This highly dubious research has now been discontinued and replaced by an open facility for cancer and virus research run by the NIH.

We're lounging on a large terrace while those of Carleton's adoptive children who are still at home are preparing dinner. Joe has been dead for a few years now. The kids belong to a new generation, and are playing like their predecessors but have more space. There are now also a couple of adopted girls. One of them is the daughter of one of the first adopted sons from New Guinea, and as such the household's first "grandchild."

Carleton is sitting opposite me talking about Witold Gombrowicz's novel *Ferdydurke*, in which he is engrossed in at the moment. Two of the boys approach, looking at him in silence. "Do you need money?" Carleton asks. They signal with their eyes in a barely noticeable way. They receive five dollars each and run off smiling.

"Who's in charge of the house now?"

"The responsibility rotates between the thirteen- and fourteen-year-olds according to an agreed-upon schedule."

"Why not the older ones?"

"They're less suited to the task. As soon as they start dating American teenagers they loose some of their loyalty toward the house. The younger ones are affectionate and more reliable. I'm leaving for Europe tonight, although no one here knows it. They're preparing a big party for their friends, and I'll disappear in the middle of the party. They're used to me coming and going without notifying them in advance. The house is in order every time I return."

"Are you content with your large and constantly renewed adopted family?"

"I'm used to living with young Melanesians and Micronesians. This is the fifth generation. My older adopted children have grown up and left the nest. Many of them are constantly traveling between different cultures like me. I'm used to working, thinking, and writing under fairly chaotic conditions. A certain turbulence in my immediate vicinity is necessary and alleviates the integration of my various psychological levels. Each attempt to structure my life more rigorously, to introduce one or several regular routines immediately produces boredom—ennui." Carleton emphasizes and repeats this word. "Ennui produces anxiety which quickly escalates to outright panic that forces me to flee. Ennui is what I can tolerate least of all."

"Can you tell me more about your five generations of adopted children?"

Carleton shows me a large chart. The upper part lists thirty children who've been educated or are in the process of being educated in the United States. The lower part contains another sixteen adopted sons whose education in New Guinea Carleton has paid for. Most of them were adopted when they were between the ages of eight and twelve, but his first contact with them was much earlier—in some cases immediately after they were born. Some carry the last name of Gajdusek, but most have other ethnically correct names. Their birth dates and home villages are carefully registered, along with their father's and/or mother's name(s). Listed are many well-known American colleges, for example the University of Rochester, Hamilton University, the University of New Mexico, Reed College, the University of Oregon, Washington and Jefferson College, the University of Hawaii, California State, the University of Vermont, various schools of art, aeronautics, and other specialties. There are also notes indicating where the boys have moved to after their schooling. Many of the older ones have moved back to their native countries. Among their current home addresses are Papua-New Guinea (PNG), Federal States of Micronesia (FSM), Republic of Palau (RP), and Republic of the Marshall Islands (RMI). One of the boys, Jesus Raglmar (born in 1952 and educated at Hamilton College and the Foreign Service Institution), has become ambassador and later Foreign Minister of FSM. One of the first, Ivan Mbaginthao, is the director of the National Museum in Goroka, PNG. Among them is a school principal, several hotel managers, a corporate executive, and a few teachers. One is the head of the school department in Guam. Some have chosen to stay in the United States.

We take our seats at the table. The dinner is characterized by the same happy atmosphere as my earlier visit, and the delicious meal has been made solely by the kids. There are many courses, among them scrambled eggs with large blueberries. Eva asks if this is a specialty. The boys laugh. Yes, this is the Specialty of the Day which has just been invented by the Chef of the Day.

Our grandchildren are tired and whiny. Two of the teenage boys begin talking to them without being asked to do so. They manage to capture our grandchildren's attention and console them in a natural and unaffected way. We feel as if we're part of the extended family.

Carleton is holding forth as usual but also observes what's happening around the table. His thoughts are on the problem of Alzheimer's, a disease where the degeneration of the brain resembles kuru. There's no reason to suspect an infection in the case of Alzheimer's, but it may be that the changes in the protein disseminate between the nerve cells in a similar manner.

After dinner we sit down with Carleton in a room full of books. Suddenly he shifts to another topic: poets who have meant much to him. Knowing that he understands some Hungarian without being able to speak the language, I ask him if he's familiar with any of the great Hungarian poets. I can't resist the temptation to recite long passages from some of my favorite poems. To my astonishment he becomes completely silent. It's the first time that I have seen Carleton listening intensely instead of talking—in fact, I've seldom seen anyone listen with such concentration. He wants to understand all the words, put them in their right context, or at least capture a bit of the atmosphere. I suddenly realize that I know only a small portion of the phenomenon that is Carleton. Is his constant monologue only one among several instruments, one he especially brings into play with scientists? Carleton knows that few scientists are fond of conversing about anything else but science, except for the general trivialities that Carleton detests. Is his constant torrent of words at least partly intended to block all roads that may lead to trivial everyday chit-chat? Can he completely immerse himself in listening when he wants to? Is this how he listens to ancient, entirely alien languages when he wants to understand hidden connections, capture atmospheres, or imagine the mindscape of Stone Age children? Is this how he tries to understand the thoughts of people who know nothing about our culture?

"Aren't you writing, yourself, Carleton? Poetry or prose?"

"You have my numerous, unorganized, pedantic, and rhapsodic diaries. Everything is in them. I have nothing else to add."

"Yes, I've often browsed through them, but I've only read a fraction of the vast material. Everything is there, except what's essential. It's an unwritten epic about your life; it rolls on just like life, from day to day, but remains as opaque as life itself, offering no explanations. Despite the detailed, often fairly intimate descriptions of your thoughts and feelings and your relationships to people or to scientific problems, I'm full of questions about you and your motivations. You seem to protect an inner region where no one may tread. I neither can nor will enter uninvited, but unless you help me I may run the risk that my imagination looses contact with your reality. Can you give me a key?"

Instead of answering Carleton opens a page of Gombrowicz's *Ferdy-durke*. "Here's my answer," he says:

How different would our attitudes be if we looked at the world with new eyes, instead of letting ourselves be influenced by millions of philosophers, shapers of ideas and aestheticians, and if we gave ourselves a chance to feel the tremendous influence of form on our lives. If one would still want to use one's pen after that, one wouldn't do it in order to become a great author and create art, but to better express one's personality by painting a clear picture of oneself for others to observe; or in order to create order within oneself and through one's confessions cure one's own complexes and lack of maturity—and perhaps also in order to deepen one's contacts with others, render them more intimate and more creative. One would draw them in sharper outline, so that they would further one's capacity for thinking and development; or one would try to fight against rigid customs, prejudices, and principles that run counter to one's nature. At other times one would write only to make a living. One wouldn't spare any effort to give one's work an artistically pleasing form, but the main object would remain the same whatever one did: to reach oneself and not art. One would cease to write pretentiously, to try to educate, to obey, to lead one's fellows, and to moralize. One would at all times remain conscious of the most important aim: to raise oneself and to develop further. The text would not rush forth from an inner maturity which had found its form of expression, but from an immaturity, from a humiliating effort to find one's form. One would make a fool of oneself many times while continuing to climb toward the peak, sweaty as a mountain-climber on one's way toward self-realization.

And if one then happened to write a stupid and worthless book, one would say to oneself: all right, I have written some rubbish, but I have never signed a contract with someone to write a wise or perfect book. I have expressed my stupidity and I am glad, since I have been shaped by the harsh judgments that I have myself provoked from others. Now I feel as if I am born anew. An artist who subscribes to this healthy philosophy is so strongly grounded within himself that neither stupidity nor lack of maturity can frighten or hurt him; he can look at himself from without and hold his head high, despite his insensitivity, while the rest of you never can express anything, since your fear robs you of your voice.

I lay aside Gombrowicz's book. "I understand what you want to say. But now I'll let you listen to some more Hungarian poetry. The poet Babits, whose name you've heard, has written something similar. Yes, I believe that he's given part of Gombrowicz's thought its perfect poetic form."

I recite one of my most treasured Babits poems for Carleton, who listens intensely. It's the introductory poem to the collection *Racing against the Years*, which was written between 1927 and 1932, but the poem itself has no title:

> Like a dog in its lowly corner,
> always last in the pecking order,
> battered and bruised. Mud on his shoulder,
> faithful, bold, defiant soldier,
> howling away, even louder, bolder
> cold, as the wind turns even colder:
> That's how I howl it, growing older
> in solitude, in dark disorder,
> kicked and muddied from flank to shoulder,
> trembling, faithfully, louder, bolder.
>
> I am left alone, all on my own,
> my voice is like the old dog's monotone
> or the echoes of a wheezy groan
> from a gaping prison catacomb
> deep below. (I am the catacomb.)
> When it leaves my lips, the tone
> is hushed by a hundred walls of stone,
> for life has washed me in the filthy foam
> whose dulling, dumbing mud and loam
> has silted up my windows. I'm alone.
>
> Sometimes in my cluttered cupboard
> I find ribbons, fancy, colored
> knick-knacks. Faded, quaintly puckered,

fashion fossils, re-discovered
bygone wealth: a sombre record.
And I say: "My children, voices,
pick some ribbons, pick your choices,
cherry-reds, yellows, turquoises!"
And they pick their fancy choices
my children, the faded voices.

Even so they remain unsightly,
more awkward, as they fidget shyly
—in hand-me-downs—stilted, untidy,
my beggarly begrudgers deride me:
but the voices just come and hassle
they come regardless, hatch and nestle,
stumbling but new, in virgin vessel,
struggle through stone and mud abyssal,
they drown and drill and work and wrestle
until their rags drop all in a frazzle.

I question them: "What are you trying
dimmed and drowning, shivering, shying?
Why show your shame to all the prying?
Why should you come here stammering, crying?"
They reply: "Though straying, stammering
we must come, a word we're ushering
a word will come forth after our stammering,
we are envoys, road builders, laboring:
Great word, a great word is our future king!
We stammer, but one day he comes conquering."

(Translation by Peter Zollman)

THE MASSIVE DIARY

Gombrowicz is a useful key. Wherever I dive into Carleton's thick volumes of diary—there are some forty of them—I see a combination of outer disorder, inner order, keen observations and continuous, sharply focused mental activity. I can imagine him night after night typing on his small portable typewriter, often by the light of a kerosene lamp or a candle, surrounded by inquisitive children and youths. His location may be a many-day, difficult hike from his next stop. The kids talk and cuddle with him. Some of them may be his new friends whom he has only known for a few hours. Each contact may give rise to a friendship spanning over many years. The closeness, energy, or mere presence of the boys would disturb most others. Carleton regards it as almost a precondition, he has to "start up his limbic system from a condition of chaos."

The never-ending supply of tales from his diaries register all the diseases he's diagnosed and treated, names all the people he's spoken to, among them countless teenage boys who've been angry at him or who he's made happy, who've become fond of him or only flirted with him. He's also recorded all the thoughts that have ever come to him, from the practical and simple to the serious and philosophical. He's also made notes about his Western colleagues and friends. In a laconic note in a journal from the end of the 1960s I suddenly find my own name: "Passing through Paris. A cocktail party at X (the name is indicated). Meet George Klein for the second time. How can an intelligent person like X invite so many guests that no one can hear what the other person is saying?"

Who are these diaries intended for? For a few close friends or an undefined surviving world? Or is Carleton writing to his own unreachable self? Is he himself the target of his search, night after night, year in and year out? Is he seeking to find the entire world within himself, and himself in the world, through the countless million eyes of the human species? Does he want to liberate himself from the artifacts of our commercial civilization in order to reach some inner core? Is his entire multifaceted life only an attempt to illuminate the human condition? Is his great interest in the psychological development of children the most important part of his search? One notices a certain pride when he says that his department at NIH was set up with the unusual—and at first fairly unrealistic—object of studying *child growth, development and behavior, and disease patterns in primitive and isolated cultures.* Carleton regards this as the basic theme of his activities ever since he was twenty years

old. In his discussions with neurologists or psychologists he rephrases
the question in the following manner: How large a part of our higher brain
functions and our emotional reactions are built into our genetic code?

You're forced to speed-read or skim through large parts of the diaries. Carleton has also kept a kind of logbook over all the activities
during his expeditions. In connection with his occasional but no less
careful medical treatment of patients he notes the personalia, tribal
identity, and symptoms of each patient. Even these routine notes seek
out what's essential in each single case, and thus they surpass the often
soulless journals of most modern clinics. On the few pages I've had time
to browse through, I find, among other entries, an inquiry about various
recent deaths, a diagnosis of "the large spleen syndrome," notes on neurological diseases, fungus infections, cataracts, and diabetes. Skin tests
are conducted on both sick and healthy patients in order to measure immunological responses. Carleton also jots down notes about trivial
everyday problems such as faulty tape recorders and film cameras or the
problems caused by his big toe which he happened to injure on a rock
during a swim. A recurring theme is his ambition to keep all the members of the expedition active with meaningful chores. Even the youngest
and least educated assistants are given challenging tasks, for example
conducting certain blood tests. He has also the time to note his gratitude
to various people who are willing to have their blood taken, their skin
tested, and be given the BCG vaccine, which protects against tuberculosis. There are detailed descriptions of children's games, with each
child's age carefully recorded. There's information about food, insecti-
cides, the landscape, the ebb and flow of the tide, and about water
sources and water usage. Dry, factual passages of information may suddenly be interrupted by an unexpected poetic description of the dawn,
and may then immediately give way to a list of words in the local tribal
language. On the next page I find detailed descriptions of settlements
and social customs including the studiously protected niches of private
life. I browse and skip through the pages. There are thoughts on Micronesian migratory patterns; activities in the local school; problems
with the expedition's laundry; the mending of clothes; the lunch menu;

a tour of an island with local boys during three days and nights; the rav-
ages of the recent storm; the mixture of local and imported languages;
problems with contacting the research ship by radio; social, anthropo-
logical, and genetic information for the expedition's scientists; marriage
habits; studies of the genetic flow; practical problems in connection with
storing specimens and their solutions; visits to a volcanic crater and the
concomitant careful charting of the blisters and other afflictions of the
expedition members; the lengths and weights of the natives; a checkup
of hearts, lungs, and abdomens in the school; quests for local art and
handcraft; the purchase of a pretty, transparent rock for two dollars;
flaming sunsets, black and white beaches, steep cliffs, narrow valleys,
small streams flowing toward the sea; a visit to an isolated village inhabited by fourteen people belonging to four families—a depressingly
decrepit place which, after a thriving period, has been gradually emp-
tied of people during the last 150 years. Carleton doesn't want to linger
here. "Since there are so few villagers I'm not sorry to leave the village
as early as tomorrow. These surviving remnants of a once large population cannot offer me the multitude of personalities and human contacts
that I love to enjoy in the larger villages."

What can these contacts lead to?

Stockholm, autumn, 1990. I receive a new "medium-sized" Gajdusek
package by mail. It arrives as unexpectedly as the many earlier packages. Small and medium-sized packages usually contain scientific articles which flow from Carleton's laboratory in a steady stream. Nowadays
they're mostly about various new kuru-like diseases. Sometimes there's
an article about children's development in primitive cultures or the
physical and psychological characteristics of Stone Age people. The
large packages usually contain new diaries.

But this is something else. At first glance it seems like a book about
primitive art with beautiful color photographs and essays. On the cover
is an extensively festooned black man with an enormous wooden shield

visible behind him. According to the caption the man is adorned with white cockatoo feathers, a headband of cuscus, and a necklace made of large, sharp dog's teeth. The shield is named after one of his forefathers. The man has made it himself and believes that it contains the powers of his forefather.

Why have I received this? It appears to be a guidebook to an exhibition called *Embodied Spirits: Carvings of the Asmat.* The subtitle reads: "*A traveling exhibition on the Gajdusek collection of the Peabody Museum of Salem and the Crosier Asmat Museum Collection of Hastings, Nebraska.*"

Contrary to his habit, Carleton, who despises conventional niceties, has written a dedication by hand, which reads:

> To George Klein, in the interest of sharing with you a bit more of what has captivated me in New Guinea and what draws me to Melanesian culture and societies and has yielded for me the most satisfying loves and friendships of my restless quest throughout the world. In friendship, Carleton.

The introduction is by Peter Fetchko, director of the museum. He emphasizes that the entire exhibition is the work of one man, the material having been collected by Carleton Gajdusek on various expeditions during the 1960s and 1970s. Gajdusek "excuses himself," writes Fetchko, for having done it "on the side," while conducting scientific research. The unprepared reader may therefore assume that the five thousand objects that Carleton has donated to the museum would have demanded a considerable amount of research and documentation from specialists. But this isn't so—quite the opposite. A better and more carefully documented collection from this region simply doesn't exist. Some of Carleton's notes are beyond compare. The tiniest village where an object has been made is listed with exact geographical and ethnic information. In many cases the name of the artist or owner is mentioned. For further documentation Fetchko refers to Gajdusek's extensive diaries and his enormous collection of films and photographs.

In his article Carleton writes that the Asmat are a people who are constantly busy carving objects. Their world is inhabited by spirits who determine everything, from the weather and the hunter's fortune to virility, fertility, childbirth, and good or bad fortune in war, disease, and death. The spirits of close relatives continue to haunt the living until their deaths have been avenged. Revenge may be directed against the perpetrator or someone from the perpetrator's tribe. It may also strike someone who is suspected of having inflicted a magic curse upon the deceased. The restless ghost is only satisfied when a member of his closest family has proved his masculinity by decapitating a carefully chosen object of hate.

According to Asmat faith the first wooden figures were carved by Fumeripitsi, the Creator. One day when Fumeripitsi was out fishing he happened to fall into the water and drown. His body was washed up on a small island. The birds saw the body but didn't know if it was dead or alive. They tried to revive him with medicines and balsam but without success. They flew to the great sea eagle War and asked him for advice. War sent the birds to get other medicines and then flew to the island himself. He smeared medicine on a stick and anointed the body's joints, chest, and forehead. It didn't help. The birds were sent for more medicines. After further treatment the body began to move. Suddenly Fumeripitsi cried out, and all the birds were frightened off. Only War stayed. Fumeripitsi got up and said: I am Fumeripitsi. The sea eagle answered: I am War.

Fumeripitsi went into the jungle and built himself a large house, but he felt lonely. He began to chop down trees and carve figures with a head, body, arms, and legs. Some were male, others female. He put them in his big house which he had built for feasts. But nothing happened and he still felt alone. He chopped down another tree, hollowed it out and stretched the skin of a large lizard over one end. He fastened it with a mixture of glue and his own blood and began beating on it. As soon as the wooden figures heard the drum they began to move. Their movements were clumsy to begin with, but after a while their joints loosened up and eventually they could dance quite naturally. Soon thereafter they began to sing. This is how the Asmat people were created.

A while later Fumeripitsi was attacked by a crocodile. He cut it to pieces which he then threw up toward the sky. When they fell down and touched the earth the pieces were transformed into people. This is how all other tribes and peoples were created.

The story of Fumeripitsi is the only creation myth of the Asmat tribe. Figures are carved for all religious rituals and feasts. Each figure that is given the name of a newly deceased relative is regarded as possessing the strength of the deceased and is given its own life in the minds of the family members and the tribe.

Carleton's article makes clear that his expeditions to the Asmat settlements had well-defined medical purposes, and that the collection of more than a thousand art objects was a byproduct of his regular work. A neighboring tribe to the Asmat was often stricken with the rare neurological disease Amyotrophic Lateral Sclerosis and also Parkinson's disease. When Carleton studied these diseases he collected thousands of blood samples. The distribution of blood group and serum proteins were of great genetic and ethnographic interest. It was possible to distinguish unknown kinships between certain ethnic groups, while others seemed wholly separate. There was a demonstrable connection between the gene flow and the cultural contacts, even in the artworks. But to Carleton this was only a parenthesis. He also took the opportunity to study the presence of antibodies against a large variety of viruses and other pathogenic organisms and thereby map the incidence in the area of several infectious diseases.

Like other Melanesian ethnic groups, the Asmat have been head hunters since time immemorial. They practiced cannibalism, but not in ritualized form as did the Fore tribe. Human flesh was eaten as naturally as other kinds of meat and was often mixed with animal meat and fish. Cannibalism is now prohibited, but the earlier traditions still typify the culture. Carleton discovered that the head hunters had used the same method of opening the skull and extracting the brain as prehistoric tribes. Neanderthal skulls exhibit the same damage to the base of the skull after the moment of death as the captured skulls of the Asmat in modern times. The method must have been practiced for at least a quarter of a million years.

As usual, Carleton doesn't content himself with a superficial description of customs and rituals. In contrast with the anecdotes of traveling researchers and the often dry factual reports of anthropologists, Carleton combines his exuberant curiosity and delightful story-telling abilities with a thorough factual analysis of headhunting and its cultural significance. Some of the incentives are revenge, aggression, insecurity, and fear, but also the craving for status and prestige common to all human cultures. Head hunting also carries a deeper symbolic significance. The father of a son in prepuberty would hunt heads to ensure that the boy would mature to be a man. If the father managed to conquer a skull, the boy would sleep with it between his thighs. Those who could "afford" it would hang the skull in their garden in order to ensure a better harvest. The most "affluent" would put skulls on poles around their dwelling as status symbols. Skulls have also been used in connection with initiation and fertility rites, at the instigation of sexual relations, and as an expression of the dignity of old age.

The skull would not have to be won in battle. Cunning and treachery were accepted methods. A not uncommon ruse was to offer allies or close friends lodgings for the night on the pretext of preparing a mutual attack against a third party. If the "friend" took the bait, he might loose his head. There was an interesting exception reminiscent of our tradition of diplomatic immunity. A young man who had grown up with the skull of a named person between his thighs and/or had inherited the name of a decapitated person would be treated as a kind of relative to the victim's kin who would then protect him from possible revenge. Even if he had been sent out with the stated purpose of scouting out his host's house and especially the location of the sleeping quarters as preparation for a new attack, he would be treated with the warm hospitality accorded any family member. If the visitor's mission was known, attempts would be made to "convert" him. Everything would be done to dislodge his loyalty to his own family and win him for the cause of his hosts by emphasizing his mystical identity with the murdered person whose skull he owned. In our parlance it would be an attempt to convince a spy with diplomatic immunity to defect.

The older men would train the younger men in the art of head hunting.

Individual contacts were established which at first would resemble the bond between a father and a son, but as a rule would turn into a homosexual relationship. A youth who didn't take part in this training or the following head hunt would be regarded as insufficiently virile and fertile.

Life and death, murder and fertility rites are thus closely linked in the tradition of head hunting, the mystical ambivalence of which is underlined by the fact that the victim was often picked from among the friends and neighbors of the perpetrator. Particularly interesting is the link between the growth of a person and the growth of crops. The presumed effect of the skull on the fertility of both man and crop exceeds that of a mere metaphor. The human body is often compared to a tree. The roots correspond to the feet, the body is the trunk, the arms are the branches, and the head is the fruit, for example a coconut. Thus the head hunters become the "brothers" of fruit-eating birds and squirrels. The seed of the fruit is likened to that of the maturing boy. The generating power of a decapitated head can affect women's wombs and boys' genitals as well as fruit orchards. Carleton points to the deeply human dimension of these seriously meant analogies. The symbolism has no parallel in the animal world and is consequently limited to our human frames of reference. It's flexible enough to be used according to need and is always open to new, enriching fantasies.

Increased enforcement of peaceful relations, missionary work, and governmental control has made head hunting much more difficult. Carved heads are increasingly used in the place of real heads. In this way the ritual has spread more easily. The Asmat have been transformed into respectable Indonesian citizens. But the nudity, the cannibalism, and the head hunting lives on in the wonderful wooden sculptures that have earned worldwide respect.

FIVE PARADOXES

Is Carleton satisfied with his scattered diary notes? Is there no summary, are there no conclusions, or an attempt at a synthesis?

Yes, there is. In the journal *Pediatric Research** Gajdusek has formulated "five paradoxes" that arise when isolated cultures confront our
world. He begins by saying that he should have called his essay "Escape
from Paradise" and then proceeds without further explanation, taking
hold of the reader's attention in a way reminiscent of his verbal monologues. He literally grabs us by the collar and forces us to open our eyes
and listen. He wants to wake us up and shock us. He knows that he can
elicit a mixture of skepticism, surprise, wonderment, and admiration,
and he welcomes it. The reader is first told that Carleton has organized
and led many lengthy expeditions to New Guinea, the Solomon Islands,
the New Hebrides, and some of the most remote and seldom-visited
Polynesian and Micronesian islands and atolls. He's neither modest nor
boastful when he continues to inform us that he's stayed in inaccessible
indian villages in South and Central America, among aborigines in Australia, and among remote peoples in Afghanistan, China, Siberia, and
Africa. He adds that he has, over the years, adopted forty-six children
from New Guinea and Micronesia, thirty of whom he's raised in the
United States.

I wouldn't be surprised if the inexperienced reader, who's never met
Carleton, begins to shake his head and take refuge behind a protective
curtain of doubt. No person can have lived in this way; it can't be true.
I reacted the same way at our first meeting when I regarded Carleton as
a mythomaniac. But now I prick up my ears, full of curiosity. How does
Carleton sum up his experiences in four fully concentrated pages?

He begins with some factual information about Melanesian village
life. The people, who lack writing and signs, live in settlements of between fifty and three hundred people. Each person comes in contact
with a thousand people at the most during his life. The social structure
is based on mathematically precise definitions of kinship stretching
back over many more generations than we can keep track of. The choice
of mate is limited by strict rules against inbreeding. There are usually
very few eligible candidates—sometimes only one in the entire area.

---

*D. C. Gajdusek, "Paradoxes of Aspiration for and of Children in Primitive and
Isolated Cultures," *Pediatric Research* 27, supp. 59 (1990).

Married couples must produce at least six live births so that two may survive and procreate—a number equal to those of other primitive societies. Before the region had come in contact with the world of high technology, more than half of the total population was below fifteen years of age, sometimes under twelve. The children's contribution to their parents' economy is therefore very significant. The obvious importance of their tasks and their intense, close contact with the extended family promote the development of their personalities.

The extended families can be regarded as a wide network of material and psychological dependence among many individuals whose last common parents lived six or seven generations back in time. The intrusion of Western culture often destroys this network. Carleton's five paradoxes are born from this confrontation.

The first paradox arises when an isolated society is invaded by portable TV, radio, film, Coca-Cola, cold beer, and rock music, and eager youths are overcome by a strong wish to "get out and see the world." Western anthropologists, sociologists, doctors, missionaries, and administrators often close their eyes to this phenomenon even if they've experienced it repeatedly. Some of them cultivate a romantic picture of the "noble savage" and probably wish to retain their nostalgic illusions about "paradisiacal islands." But their wishful dreams mean nothing to the native youngsters who want to move to the real or imagined centers "where the action is." The phenomenon isn't new. Underdeveloped societies have always exported their adolescents when possible. We who live more or less isolated from a broader, more extensive human communion and have become totally dependent upon a small group of people in our own immediate family with all of the attendant complications, often feel rootless in our electronic and automotive paradise. We therefore have a hard time understanding why the "inhabitants of paradise" want to escape to our mechanized hell. Yet they persist in coming. I have often wondered why so many Puerto Ricans flee their beautiful island to move to the worst slums in New York. Neither have I been able to understand the Indians from the south of the subcontinent who leave their lovely coasts, which are poor but where everyone can find warmth and nourishment, in order to sleep under a newspaper in the streets of Bombay and Calcutta. I also remember the rootless and often drunk youths in the cities of Africa who've left their ancient tribal homes with their warm family environments. I'm obviously suffering from the same limitation that Carleton mocks. I should know better. Isn't it the constant search for new flow experiences which propels the adolescents' longing for the "exciting dynamism" of the big cities, a search I can greatly sympathize with when it comes to groups that are closer to home?

Before Carleton leaves his first paradox he offers a panoramic sweep through world history, from the Greeks of antiquity who moved from their idyllic islands to the cultural and political centers of their day, to today's ten million illegal immigrants in the United States. He makes a detour to the many Polynesians, Melanesians, and Maoris who crowd the cities in New Zealand after having traded their family security, their tribe's traditions, and their own natural sense of identity for the loneliness, frustration, and anxiety of metropolitan life.

Gajdusek's second paradox starts with our ambivalence toward our own culture. We greatly value our family, our nation, and our traditions; we regard them as our "roots." We easily mobilize warm feelings toward our own ethnic group, however much we try to convince ourselves of the opposite in our universalist wishful thinking. Those who are ideologically repulsed by Carleton's claims need only look at today's Eastern Europe. As soon as the authoritarian oppression disappeared, the old ethnic enmities were inflamed anew, as if they'd never died down. In many areas these hatreds can quickly become deadly, even though it's been assumed for decades that they were finally extinguished. But the opposite of a deep and unshakable ethnic identity is also true. Man is a "cultural improvisor" says Carleton. Languages, myths, art, and social organizations are "inexpensive"; they can easily be changed. They can be reinvented when the circumstances so demand. Assemble a small group of culturally diverse people who lack a common language, then isolate them or bring them on an expedition to a remote area. Observe the behavior of people who previously didn't know each other, but who have been brought together by a natural disaster or an act of war and then have had to rely on each other. Such people can create a new language and invent a new culture. In just a few months' time they can build unconventional social structures, establish new rules of behavior, create a new form of art and even a new cuisine. Throughout history we find the same recurring phenomenon. Ethnic groups, who willingly or unwillingly have moved to new areas dominated by other groups, adapt and change in a remarkably short period of time. Carleton mentions the Trojan women who were brought to Greece by force; Greeks, Carthaginians, Gauls, Slavs, Germans, and Celts in Rome; Mongols in China; the Aino people in Japan; Jews and Muslims in Spain; the Portuguese in Japan; and exiled French-American colonists who "went native" and became indians.

People who've survived a large disaster and who've previously been prepared to defend their country and their religion with their life and blood can quickly adjust to completely new and alien social systems when there's no other recourse. Gajdusek regards this ability to adapt and improvise as one of man's most admirable traits, which must have enabled our species to survive countless calamities.

Carleton's third paradox is not as clearly defined as the previous two—perhaps intentionally. If you know him fairly well and have for many years more or less in vain searched for the key to his protean personality, which is as concealed as the ancient jungle paths in New Guinea, you suddenly sense that for just one second he wants to give us a small glimpse before he quickly closes up again.

In many primitive cultures—and the Melanesian in particular—even the youngest children learn to think before they speak, and to make a great effort to say what they instinctively feel that the adults want to hear. They don't want to hurt the feelings of their elders and wish to protect them from the risk of loosing face. "Dissimilation and discretion are the cardinal virtues inculcated in a young child already at toddler age," Carleton states. It's simply a given that the truth must be angled, adjusted, twisted, changed, or forgotten if you can thereby minimize the risk that someone loses his dignity. The cardinal virtues are consideration, modesty, tact, sensitivity to the needs of others, and the absence of self-assertion. Honesty, truthfulness, consistency, and candor mean nothing. The same principle determines all practical acts. The child learns to do what the adult expects from it, not to follow any inherent principle or sense of morals. Distortions and after-rationalizations are clearly preferred to objective descriptions. Possible skepticism in the receiver of the message is quickly neutralized by the short average life span of the population. Carleton summarizes the prime imperative of Melanesian culture as follows: Act and speak toward people the way they really want you to act and speak, not the way they claim to want you to act and speak.

One is tempted to remark that this is the exact opposite of Kant's categorical imperative. Does this represent the natural, original psychological *ur*-condition of our species, the primary functions of our brain and language? Can't we observe the same phenomenon in our own world as soon as we look behind the facade? Hasn't the same principle always been employed by people who've been forced to live under dictatorships and totalitarian ideologies? And doesn't it play an important role—if less fatal in terms of its consequences—even in our democratic everyday existence? Haven't we erected an entire network of judicial, scientific, and social mechanisms in order to keep these natural tendencies under control?

Carleton chooses the sexuality of children and adolescents as the main example of his third paradox. In most Melanesian cultures children participate in sexual activities with their peers and also with adults. It is regarded as a normal, lustful game. Carleton uses the word "sexual" but his diaries leave no doubt that he means homosexual activities, which are regarded as a natural stage of development. They are practiced by practically all teenage boys and are later without problem replaced by the socially regulated heterosexual activities of the adult men.

Not without a certain amount of irony Carleton points out that explorers, whalers, traders, missionaries, and other Westerners have always, without openly admitting it, appreciated sexual contacts with native children and adolescents. While doing so, they often simultaneously preached strict Christian morality.

Where is the paradox? From the point of view of the natives there is none. The Western behavioral pattern which Gajdusek criticizes deserves the forthright word "hypocrisy."

Time and again Carleton states in his diaries that sexual behavior in New Guinea displays as many variations as the languages and the cultures at large.* He reminds the reader that New Guinea is the world's second largest island with a population of 2.5 million inhabitants and is a kaleidoscope of 400 cultures that are in part very diverse. Each culture speaks at least one separate language. Together with the Melanesian islands, New Guinea has 700 different languages—fully a fourth of all the languages in the world. Any description thus only characterizes a handful of tribes, and one must be careful not to make generalizations.

In many of the highland cultures there are special houses for the adult men, who never sleep in the houses of their wives. They have sex with their wives in wooded, fairly private gardens in broad daylight. Some cultures practice heterosexual promiscuity already in early puberty, while in others regard this as the age to get married. The Fore tribe, which Gajdusek has explored in depth, and other tribes in the western highlands practice heterosexual abstinence during their teen years. The Etoro and Anga tribes are known for their prolonged and practically exclusive homosexuality among teenagers. When the adolescents are old enough to get married, their marriages are arranged by the older generation. Often sisters are "traded" between boys who have grown up together in the same male dwellings. This worked fairly smoothly until Western ideas were introduced through the schools and through missionary work. The natives try to adapt to our system, their norms change, and their original cultural pattern is concealed. Within a few years everything has changed beyond recognition.

Here we recognize Carleton the scientist, the mapmaker, the storyteller, and the analyst. But where is the man? We shall look for him a bit later. Two paradoxes remain.

---

*D. C. Gajdusek, in *Health and Disease in Tribal Societies*.

Gajdusek's fourth paradox, like the second, starts with our need for an ethnic identity, our wish to constantly re-experience the language, legends, songs, dances, myths, and food of our ancestors. Despite these bonds we can frivolously abandon everything for insignificant practical or economic advantages or for whatever happens to be "in," including commercially stimulated fashions. What's old and genuine can easily be exchanged for superficial glitter or hollow substitutes. The motives may also be political. Carleton mentions the lingual re-orientation in Java as a particularly drastic example. The island's 60 million inhabitants have abandoned "one of the most dramatically nuanced, refined, and poetic languages ever developed by man" for an artificial, esperanto-like language, Bahasa Indonesian, which was created by a committee over the course of a few decades and is mainly based on the unwritten Malay language of the basars. The purpose of the switch was to strengthen the grip of the Indonesian state over the extensive archipelago's many nationalities and lingual groups. But instead of choosing one of the natural languages, as in many other countries with similar problems, a synthetic language has been created that is no one's mother tongue. In this way the children have been robbed of their ability to speak with their grandparents. The same situation often arises within American or Australian immigrant families, but in this instance it happened within the home country. The population has also been made to change their written characters twice; first to the Latin alphabet during Dutch rule, and then to a simplified, de-Dutchified script during the 1970s. Every school book, map, calendar, and phone book in the vast nation had to be replaced.

Gajdusek has chosen a case which is very complicated politically and historically, but there are several examples closer to home. The commercial popular culture of TV, video, beer, and Coca Cola has spread over large parts of the world, and in doing so it has replaced with an assortment of clichéd knick-knacks countless traditions, languages, and songs that for thousands of years have expressed people's sorrows, joys, worries, desires, and hopes. Only some of the threatened cultures are sufficiently conscious of this process and determined enough to withstand it. Can, for example, the pristine moonlike landscape of Iceland, full of troll's magic, continue to protect this small nation's ancient culture from the filthy hurricane of commercial trash?

The fifth paradox is the most consequential in terms of practical matters, since it involves the relationship between the West and the developing countries. Carleton's comments are particularly significant thanks to his extensive and profound experiences on both sides of this divide. His unhesitating readiness to live under very primitive conditions and remarkable talent for establishing good personal relationships enabled him to receive direct firsthand information like no one else. In addition, his recurrent visits and especially his contacts through his adopted children have provided him with a particularly nuanced picture of the course of events when isolated communities change through Western influence. He has also received intimate knowledge of official Western attitudes through his long-standing membership in the committees of the World Health Organization (WHO) and the World Bank that provide aid in the areas of medicine, education, hygiene, and provisions.

Our Western world seeks rational solutions. We want to concentrate on the problems that we consider objectively most acute and extensive: poverty, illiteracy, outdated and ineffective methods of farming, famines, the high rate of infant mortality. Some of these problems are possible to solve on principle, but cannot be treated effectively for political or organizational reasons. We're particularly incensed when food, medicine, or the elementary medical technology that is generally available in the developing countries fails to reach needy recipients in remote villages. Repeated requests from impoverished countries for ultramodern equipment, such as the latest X-ray diagnostic or radiotherapeutic apparatuses or even entire educational hospitals, strike us as irrational or absurd. Modern laboratories that can identify micro-organisms in the drinking water with great taxodermic exactness may seem unnecessary when demanded by countries where the drinking water is regularly polluted by sewage. We usually emphasize that the most advanced medical and technological resources can't fill any useful function in countries that lack all necessary infrastructure. We prefer to try to raise the living standards of the poor, improve their level of education and medical care so that the entire population can benefit. We don't feel protective of the political leadership, the rich merchants, or the relatively well-educated professional groups. We don't empathize with wealthy, well-established ethnic minorities in other countries. We neither can nor want to empathize with the feelings of inferiority experienced by the elite in the developing countries when they meet with our Western representatives in the United Nations, the WHO, or at various international conferences. The thought that these often very well-educated politicians and experts don't necessarily share our desire to save "simple" human lives in their own back yard appears totally alien to us. But this is the way it often is.

The Indonesians have never forgiven the Dutch for only wanting to teach them how to educate their illiterates and organize their medical schools so that the sick could be treated by domestic doctors, while in fact retaining the worlds of law, engineering, banking and finance, business, and politics for themselves. The Indonesians regarded this as continued imperialism. Their ambition was to take over the very areas of responsibility that the Dutch wanted to retain. Above all, they wanted to improve the economy and only thereafter deal with "secondary priorities." Education was less important to them, since the services of foreign doctors and teachers could be bought at a price. The Indonesians turned against all "degrading charity" from other states or from national and international relief organizations, religious groups, and missionaries. They weren't impressed by our Western efforts to purchase front-row seats in our own heaven or achieve a certain satisfaction in our own lives. We find it difficult to accept that this is perceived merely as continued attempts at colonial domination.

Our criteria for admission to higher studies or promotion are not regarded with respect. On this matter Western values often collide with those of the native culture. Among the many conflicts mentioned by Gajdusek are those between Indians and Fijians, Maoris and white New Zealanders, Australian natives or Native Americans and the victorious white colonizers, the French and Melanesians in New Caledonia, Tamils and Singhalese in Sri Lanka, black and white South Africans, Indians and Europeans in Latin America. Native cultures that have been allowed to develop in their own tempo according to their own natural and historical conditions have suddenly and incompletely been imbued with alien moral and religious decrees, lifestyles, and attitudes. This problem is not limited to confrontations with Western Culture. The well-known Chinese diligence, loyalty, and willingness to compete provided them with great practical advantages in Malaysia and Indonesia, where the majority culture by long-standing tradition valued wholly different characteristics. A certain conflict was therefore unavoidable. Malay culture put positive value on daydreaming and the ability to entertain. Deeper human communion is sought through trance-like ecstatic conditions where the participants temporarily willingly abandon their individuality. Tact and consideration are more important than self-assertion, social climbing, or competition. Individual success is nothing to strive for since no one's impressed by "winners." Conscious decision-making is not respected; instead foggier, undefined solutions are preferred. Unlike many other cultures, not even individual sporting triumphs or academic achievements are seen as particularly desirable.

Carleton describes these antitheses to our culture in such glowing terms that anyone who knows him as a work-addicted, incredibly productive scientist and a highly effective expedition leader begins to wonder how he can be so successful in "our world" if he's so ambivalent about its goals and lifestyles. If you read his diaries you understand that he manages only with great self-discipline and not always without a certain effort.

In a diary from 1985 Carleton describes his encounter with a prominent female scientist at an international symposium. The reader is informed that the woman is responsible for some very important scientific research and has received several prominent awards. Yet she finds no mercy in Carleton's eyes. He considers her aggressive, belligerent, pretentious, and a political hawk. One has no choice but to argue with her when meeting her, writes Carleton. She's an American chauvinist, supports nuclear weapons as a deterrent, favors high technology, and likes Ronald Reagan. She accepts a "properly calculated contamination of the environment." She is for "better people, better genes, better intelligence." She declares with absolute assurance what is right and wrong, good and evil, and which people are better than others.

Carleton repeatedly emphasizes that she's a brilliant pioneer and a prominent figure within her field. She's probably gotten good use out of her aggressive characteristics in the highly competitive area where she's been so successful in her work—and a woman needs them to an ever greater degree than a man. But her specialization has been brought about at a cost. She has no understanding of cultural diversity. Her only frame of reference is the Western value system. Her rabid anti-Soviet attitude is reminiscent of the many female bullies who held dominant positions in the Communist East Bloc. Carleton summarizes: "Men are seldom found for these roles. This lady is the prototype of an aggressive, dogmatic, self-righteous woman who constantly wants to read the law to anyone who is less informed or in an inferior position. I was fairly amused at meeting such a perfect copy of a Communist commissar in rabid anti-Communist guise."

Carleton, if anyone, is able to see our world from many diverse cultural vantage points simultaneously. He needs no visa when crossing the borders between our world and the Stone Age, between his life as a researcher and his own Melanesian extended family, between a warm sense of companionship and the deep solitude which he also constantly seeks and keeps returning to. The five paradoxes are only an example of his constant attempt to articulate what he sees. He's forever occupied with analyzing complex connections and battling stereotypes. Sometimes, in a low, melancholy voice, but one void of sentimentality, he remarks on the fleeting, changeable quality of life.

While in Buenos Aires in the 1980s he writes in one of his journals:

"I wonder how many days, weeks, months I can keep myself intellectually stimulated, emotionally satisfied, and 'content' without feeling any pressing need of my home, family, and friends in America. I write to many people, but after having written I turn inward, toward myself and my brooding, my reading and my observations, and then I immediately find myself at home, happy and relaxed with my contacts with totally foreign people."

He finds us all, he finds himself in everything. But where do we find him? Shall we accept that he glides through our hands? He's much too interesting to be allowed to evade us.

SEARCHING FOR CARLETON

nè dolcezza di figlio, nè la pietà
del vecchio padre, nè 'l debito amore
lo qual dovea Penelopé far lieta,

vincer poter dentro da me l'ardore
ch'i' ebbi a divenir del mondo esperto,
e de li vizi umani e del valore;

ma misi me per l'alto mare aperto
sol con un legno e con quella compagna
picciola da la qual non fui deserto.

(The last journey of Odysseus,
canto XXVI in Dante's *Inferno*)

Not fondness of my son, nor any claim
Of reverence for my father, nor love I owed
Penelope, to please her, could overcome
My longing for experience of the world,
Of human vices and virtue. But I sailed out
On the deep open seas, accompanied
By that small company that still had not
Deserted me, in a single ship . . .

(Translation by Robert Pinsky)

Stockholm, 1990. I receive a visit from the freelance journalist Bosse Lindqvist. He's made a radio program about racism and forced sterilization in Sweden during the first half of the century and about modern colonialism. During a four-year stay in Kenya he has observed the reactions of Westerners whose privileges are threatened. Not without a certain amount of surprise he observed that the attitudes of Swedish development assistance workers in Africa were often reminiscent of those of the former colonialists, despite all claims to the contrary. These tendencies become apparent when one's own interests are threatened.

We talk about the developing nations. I tell Bosse about Carleton. He becomes fascinated and borrows a few of his diaries. After a month or so he returns them with a note:

"I'm very fond of his way of describing what he likes about a (scientific) paper . . . as if it were a work of art, a miniature portrait. Perhaps it's an example of his own wonderful mixture of science and art which his journals so vividly testify to."

Bosse is also struck by Carleton's

countless enumeration of the school boys he's met, including their names, ages, and class standing. There's something very charming about the way in which he notes all this information. In a way he writes in the manner of Linnaeus or Thunberg. He jots down each observation with the utmost care. School boys are obviously important to him both as providers of information and as company. But there's something beyond that which causes him to make such careful notes about who they are, which class they've advanced to, etc. I have a feeling that he describes people in the same way that old navigators and cartographers described land formations—partly so that future travelers will be able to find their way around these remote islands on the ocean's edge.

In a journal from 1972 Gajdusek writes about two local boys' interest in him and his interest in them. Bosse comments: "There's something almost coquettish in his descriptions of the boys' attempts to seduce him, their rivalries and the risks they take if they dare to express their interest in Gajdusek too strongly. He analyzes his relationships from an almost scientific distance, but also from a very close, human vantage point. He doesn't try to hide his childish pride at being courted."

In another journal entry Bosse observes Gajdusek's argument with the captain of the research ship *Alpha Helix.** Carleton is very critical of the captain's lack of understanding of the expedition's work, which is much broader and deeper than merely a mechanical collection of samples. Carleton believes that you must come into close contact with all people who are involved, socialize with them, stroll arm in arm. You shouldn't just focus on conducting a successful test. The nonmeasurable activities on the human level also provide invaluable knowledge. Bosse writes:

> I suspect that Gajdusek is neither fully at home in the scientific community nor in the societies in the South Seas that he loves so much. He inhabits a kind of mid-level between black and white people where very few people choose to exist. I have myself lived there during a period of my life and know what it's like to understand more than many others yet still not enough. There's a true loneliness in choosing to live at such a relatively low material standard as Gajdusek does (seen from a European perspective—but from a incomprehensibly high level from the Melanesian point of view). One's material standard obviously isn't everything, but it still noticeably limits the range of one's human relationships.

Gajdusek complains that so many of the Europeans that he meets during his expeditions lack *commitment* to the world in which they live and work.† Bosse points out the important difference between Gajdusek and most others who work in the developing countries. Gajdusek is truly involved, with everything that this entails. His ambition goes much further than to merely do a good job. He's very careful to send all of the gifts that he's promised to the many people he's met. He makes notes of all the promises he's made and how he's kept them. Perhaps his adop-

---

* D. C. Gajdusek, *Journal of a Medical and Population Genetic Survey Expedition of the Research Vessel* Alpha Helix *to the Banks and Torres Islands of the New Hebrides, Southern Islands of the British Solomon Islands Protectorate, and Pingelap Atoll, Eastern Caroline Islands.* The Gajdusek Papers, 1972.

†C. Gajdusek: *Melanesian Journal. Expeditions in West and East New Guinea, Solomon Islands, New Hebrides, Fiji, and New Caledonia, to Study Child Growth and Development, Behavior and Disease Patterns, Human Genetics, and Kuru, February 22—July 23, 1963.*

tions have something to do with this. In the Melanesian world it's customary to ask one's rich and influential friends to help one's children.

Bosse is right. Gajdusek has told me that he received many letters from Melanesia and Micronesia after his Nobel Prize. People who had met him or just heard of him had read about "the great prize." "I hear that you've become rich. Can't you adopt my son/daughter too?" many of them asked.

But Bosse's comments also prompt other reflections. Carleton's "incomplete" affiliation with his different worlds is a choice he's made and is one that is natural to him. The thought of letting his life be determined by group rules rather than by his inner impulses is totally alien to Carleton. On the surface he behaves like a polite and considerate gentleman, but he primarily runs his own race and sets his own goals. The ease with which he adjusts to the most exotic peoples and to environments that are entirely bizarre to us doesn't affect his unshakable personality, which is a key precondition for his rapid adjustment. Carleton possesses, *mutatis mutandis*, a similar "autonomy" as Ali does (see "Proteus I").

Without a firm sense of self and a strong inner driving force no person would dare to stand apart from the group as distinctly as both of my protean characters. The driving force can actually become so strong that it leaves the person no choice. The alternatives, whether enforced from without or by the inner attempts at adjustment, may seem riskier psychologically speaking than the possible counter moves of the group. The fear that drastic attempts at adjustment can lead to uncontrollable inner tensions or emptiness may be experienced as a more serious threat against one's inner balance. Being an outsider becomes a necessary evil which must be accepted.

Ali began by rebelling against his own bourgeois social class. Gajdusek's attraction to the Melanesian cultures was at first perhaps merely a byproduct of his professional involvement, but later it took on a life of its own, becoming an important part of his search for cultures that were more emotionally relaxed and genuine. Carleton's start doesn't reflect as high a degree of social indignation as did Ali's, but it displays a certain alienation from our civilization, especially from its American form. At the same time Carleton is an inseparable part of this civilization. Consequently he has always viewed his lab near Washington, D.C., as his permanent base, while even his longest journeys have remained expeditions. Most youths who grow up in Carleton's Melanesian extended family regard his Maryland house as their home. Odysseus's Gajdusekian incarnation has never left his Ithaca, however many wars he's fought in foreign lands and however many Calypso islands he's passed. He wasn't overcome by the sirens' song; he didn't need to chain himself to the mast since they posed no real danger to him. Unlike Telemakos's roaming father, Carleton understood the sirens' message and immediately saw through their seductive ruse. He always knew the limits of his curiosity, which remained firmly rooted in science. It received its richest nourishment from the deep recesses that Carleton continues to drill ever deeper into the world of the living. The kuru agent is the smallest and so far the most mysterious actor on the boundary between the living and the dead. The eager traveler's balloon continues its remarkable long-distance journey without any visible restraints, yet without ever leaving its base. Carleton's most important incarnation represents our civilization's rationally objectifiable scientific manifestation at its best. Its roots are stronger than those of the thousand-year-old sequoias in Muir Woods, north of San Francisco. But his escape is also real, it cannot be regarded as a mere sideshow. In someone less well-grounded than Carleton it could be really dangerous.

What are these images that appear from the shadows? Have I seen, heard, experienced Carleton's escape before in a more dangerous form?

Was it a ship that had cast away its hawsers, gotten rid of its anchor?

Oh yes, now I remember. First come the lines of an unforgettable Hungarian translation that I can identify without difficulty. Then I go straight to the French original:

> *Comme je descendais des Fleuves impassibles,*
> *Je ne me sentis plus guidé par les haleurs:*
> *Des Peaux-Rouges criards les avaient pris pour cibles,*
> *Les ayant cloués nus au poteaux de couleurs.*

As I sailed down along impassive rivers
    my crew of haulers left me; for patrols
Of whooping Redskins captured them and used them
    As naked targets nailed to painted poles.

J'étais insoucieux de tous les équipages,
Porteur de blés flamands ou de cotons anglais.
Quand avec mes haleurs ont fini ces tapages,
Les Fleuves m'ont laissé descendre où je voulais.

Holds crammed with Flemish wheat or English cotton
    I was indifferent to men or load;
When the shrill hubbub of my crew was silenced
    The rivers let me travel my own road.*

Arthur Rimbaud was born in 1854 in a small town in the Ardennes area of France. His father was a captain in the French army but left his family when his son was six years old. Arthur was given a strict upbringing by his petit bourgeois mother. Even as a child he was known for his violent temper. He began writing when he was ten. "Death to God" he wrote on his school desk at around this time. After a violent quarrel with his mother he finally left home. He came to Paris, was jailed for vagrancy for two weeks, bummed around Belgium for a while, but wrote poems with feverish intensity. All his poems were written between 1870 and 1873 when he was sixteen to nineteen years old. Victor Hugo called him "the teenage Shakespeare"; Paul Claudel described his poems as "the work of a wild genius rushing forth in daylight like blood rushes forth from a severed vessel." His most famous poem, the "Drunken Boat" quoted above, was written when he was seventeen and supported himself as a beggar and a tramp. The poem is regarded as the starting point of the Symbolist or Decadent movement in French literature. Rimbaud sent it along with some other poems to his older poet colleague, and later friend, protector, and lover, Paul Verlaine. He asked Verlaine, whom he didn't know personally, to read the poems, and at the

---

*Arthur Rimbaud, *"Le bateau ivre,"* translation by Brian Hill.

same time expressed his wish to live with him. Verlaine immediately invited him to come. Much has been written about Rimbaud and Verlaine's relationship. Verlaine's admirers have blamed Rimbaud for the tragedy that followed, whereas Rimbaud's fans have done the reverse. By all accounts Rimbaud was the more diabolic of the two. The French poets around the turn of the century often played at being "satanic" out of coquettishness or perversion, but Rimbaud was the demon incarnate. He represented the primal revolt against everything. He detested the bourgeois worldview, and despised France, women, and love. Only toward nature did he express positive feelings.

The relationship with Rimbaud seems to have triggered destructive tendencies in Verlaine. He'd been a fairly well-adjusted husband and father, had managed a regular job and cultivated his literary reputation. Rimbaud managed to alienate Verlaine from his wife, children, and profession and pulled him down into the world of absinthe. They escaped from Paris together, rambled around England and Belgium, sometimes happy and drunk, but more often caught in an infernal downward spiral of mutual psychological torture. Time after time they broke up only to reconcile again. The relationship ended when Rimbaud threatened to leave Verlaine for good. Verlaine shot Rimbaud with a pistol, wounding him in the arm. Verlaine went to jail and was freed only a year and a half later. He stayed calm while in jail, but when he met his former friend in Germany, Rimbaud hit him so hard in the face that he fainted. That was their last meeting.

After breaking off with Verlaine, Rimbaud spent some time in Germany, stayed temporarily in France but left his homeland for good in 1875. He hiked to Italy and earned his living as a temporary dock worker during a short period of time. Then he disappeared without a trace, and no one knew his whereabouts for sixteen years. Subsequent research has shown that he had signed up with the Dutch army but soon thereafter deserted, then escaped to Sumatra and finally to Java where he lived in the jungle for a while. After that he returned to Europe and lived the life of a hobo in various capitals. In 1880 he worked in the quarries on Cyprus. From there he went to Aden before eventually settling down as a trader of coffee and perfume in Harar in Ethiopia. He did well and European traders came to regard him as a pioneer. He soon expanded his activities to include ivory and gold. During the next eleven years he led trade expeditions to unexplored regions of North Africa and habitually stayed with the natives. His business was particularly successful in 1888–1891, and he began to be regarded as a sort of partly independent native chief. He had a palace in Harar and developed close contacts with two Ethiopian kings. After the death of Negus John in 1888, he is said to have contributed to the establishment of the Ethiopian Empire. His intrigues supporting Menelek were in line with French but opposed Italian interests.

Verlaine thought that Rimbaud was dead, and in 1886 published his poems which he had collected under the title *Les Illuminations.* They created a complete sensation in Paris. The author, who now lived in Ethiopia, knew nothing about this. In March 1891 he discovered a tumor in his knee that forced him to leave Harrar and return to Europe. The case was deemed hopeless from the start. His leg was amputated, but he died a while later after having suffered terrible pain.

The life and art of Rimbaud has always fascinated a wide range of readers. What happened to the drunken boat which has left all sailors behind?

In the poem the boat flies over the sea in the winter and in the summer, during ebb and flow, storm and wind. It never longs to see the foolish lights of the lighthouses (*sans regretter l'oeils niais des falots*). It swims forever in the poetry of the sea (*je me suis baigné dans le Poème de la Mer*), it washes away wine stains and vomit from its decks, it shatters its rudder and lets down its anchor. It's tormented by the hot sun, the eddies, the birds, and the lightning, but it sees and experiences everything!—the green azure where drowned men float sometimes in apparently thoughtful rapture; the bitter, red witches' brew of love (*les rousseurs amères de l'amour*) which ferments until it's stronger than liquor and mightier than the songs (*plus fortes que l'alcool, plus vastes que nos lyres*). It's an uncontrollably crazy journey which continues onward, egged on by the derisive cry: *Je regrette l'Europe aux anciens parapets!* (I despise Europe and its old fences!)

But still . . .

> *Mais, vrai, j'ai trop pleuré! Les Aubes sont navrantes.*
> *Toute lune est atroce et tout soleil amer:*
> *L'âcre amour m'a gonflé de torpeurs enivrantes.*
> *O que ma guille éclate! O que j'aille à la mer!*

> Truly, I wept too much. The dawns are piteous,
>   The moon is hateful, bitter is the sun:
> Bloated with love's tart wine and drunken torpors—
>   O that my keel might split, my voyage be done!

There is only one water in Europe that can arouse his nostalgia:

> *Si je désire une eau d'Europe, c'est la flache*
> *Noire et froide où vers le crépuscule embaumé*
> *Un enfant accroupi plein de tristesses, lâche*
> *Un bateau frêle comme un papillon de mai.*

> If there's one sea in Europe that I yearn for
>   it's the black chilly pool where joylessly
> A small child crouching in the sweet dusk launches
>   A boat as frail as a May butterfly.

Other waters cannot attract him. The boat which has swum in the sorrow of all waves can no longer continue in the wake of the trading ships, cannot stand the empty boasts of the signal flags, cannot float under the bridges' despicable eyes. In the peerless original version all doors are slammed shut.

> *Je ne puis plus, baigné de vos langueurs, ô lames,*
> *Enlever leur sillage aux porteurs de cotons.*
> *Ni traverser l'orgeuil des drapeaux et des flammes,*
> *Ni nager sous les yeux horribles des pontons.*

No more I'll bathe my hull in languid waters,
   Nor join the pride of pennants' pageantry;
No more I'll track the lying cotton clippers,
   Nor float where convict-ships leer down at me.*

Who hasn't wanted to run off and slam the door shut exactly like that sometimes? Has Carleton?

Yes and no. He never had any difficulty weighing anchor, he could ignore everything that happens on our boastful continents when he wanted to, he could escape civilization's despicable eyes when he felt like it. He could get drunk on the endless sea and swim in its poetry, and he could withstand the pains of the sun, the salt, and the storm. He could be just as nostalgic for the lonesome, somewhat melancholy child and its toy boat as was the lost and crazy boy genius. He despised the stupid pride of the trading ships and the signal flags just as much, but he always kept a firm hold on the rudder. He could put on the mask and pretend to conform whenever he wanted to. However many times he did cast off, he always kept the compass and returned as surely as a bird of passage. In truth he's never really moved away, no matter how often he's traveled. The tree, not the boat, is his true hallmark. If science is his firm root, then the leaves on his tree are his rich communicative network which can reach people of all ages in completely diverse cultures. They constantly vary their form and color, but there's still a strange calm about their movements.

Have I finally understood Carleton's equation?

No, Proteus has once again escaped me; something is missing. I haven't approached the trunk of the tree; I haven't made contact with the steam that powers the machinery. The hero lies before me, cut to pieces like Fumeripitsi, Lemminkäinen, or Adonis, but I lack the magic spell which can give him life.

Carleton's diaries—some forty thick volumes of manuscript—rest heavily on my shelves. They tell of his days and nights during more than

---

*A. Rimbaud: "*Le bateau ivre*," translation by Brian Hill.

thirty years in the far corners of the world. Seen as a whole they're impenetrable and unreadable. However many times I've read them, in the end I've always had to turn back when faced with this impassable jungle.

Do I dare venture out on a new expedition?

THE DANCE

Where shall I begin?

Alea jacta est—the dice have been cast. Open the diary anywhere.

Around ten in the evening on September 23, 1972, Carleton is on an island in the New Hebrides. He's familiar to the local inhabitants who know that he opens his medical practice each time he arrives. His five research colleagues are already asleep. He should also go to bed, a busy new workday awaits him. As usual he remains seated for a while on the terrace of the medical station. A kerosene lamp shines on his nimble fingers that register the day's events on the portable typewriter. The evening dance has just begun; the music is clearly audible. A group of girls have just run by amidst much laughter and tried to lure him along, but he has declined. As always, a group of boys surround him, watching everything that he does. The few who know English peek over his shoulder trying to read what he's writing. One of them notices that he's moving his body to the rhythm of the dance music while he works. The boy tries to convince him: "If your body wants to dance, you must try!" But Carleton repeats his stubborn no. In his diary he writes: "I feel the same profound shyness and repulsion toward social parties and dances today as I remember so well from my youth. I prefer any kind of work to partying. All social gatherings make me feel like an outsider. Alban [one of Carleton's local assistants] diagnosed my problem immediately and with remarkable certainty."

Two weeks later, on October 2, we find Carleton at the same place again. It's now midnight and he's just returned from the dance. This time he obviously couldn't stay away or else he came along because he felt like it. Skilled guitarists and ukelele-players have played and sung, together with half a dozen school boys. A few members of the expedition who blended in in a natural way were also there. A while later two albino boys in their upper teens arrived from a neighboring village. Albinos are discriminated against in Melanesian society, but many get by as musicians. As usual the two newcomers proved to be better singers and musicians than the local talents. All the others smoothly subordinated themselves to the boys' greater musical authority.

The feast was arranged to the memory of a villager's father who had died a month earlier. Guests milled in and out of the family's house the entire day, ate and talked until the dance began at sundown.

In the middle of this detailed description of the party, Carleton unexpectedly opens a small window:

> G and F danced a lot. D and I only participated somewhat. I'm a clumsy dancer and find very little pleasure in dancing. Now when I've passed fifty I find it hard to control my basic dislike of feasts and parties that most others find enjoyable. I felt the same aversion even at fifteen. I prefer private gatherings with one or a few people to these diffuse, socially restricted relations that I've always tried to ignore. . . . I've usually retired in the hope that one—and only one—of the many guests would seek me out in private, which indeed has usually happened. Here on this island it was S who joined me yesterday, but last night D also wanted to join. This embarrassed both and therefore I couldn't be comfortable with either one of them.

I'm strangely moved when reading this. I find that Carleton's descriptions almost exactly correspond to my own behavior when I was young. The similarities are so striking that they prompt a number of questions about both Carleton's and my motivations in our professions, our lives and our relations to other people.

I suspect, without being sure, that I may have gained a certain insight into my own reasons and motivations—which are usually well hidden even to myself—during a memorable Tuesday night at my Department of Tumorbiology in Stockholm in the early 1970s. From the mid-1960s to the mid-1970s every Tuesday night was "Nairobi night," since the only SAS plane of the week from Africa arrived with fresh tumor specimens on that day in the afternoon. An African tumor, Burkitt lymphoma, was our most important research material.* We were in a hurry to work on the material while it was completely fresh. The staff was there loyally each week and we worked into the night. But this particular night was Midsummer's Eve.

Despite the fact that the shipment contained an unusual amount of interesting material I couldn't demand from the staff that they refrain from celebrating Midsummer's Eve. With what I myself regarded as a grand and courageous gesture, I declared my firm decision to perform all the tests by myself. I'd never before handled the material directly since the specimens were always prepared by the lab assistants. My task was to read the result in the microscope, and I had felt for a while that it was high time for me to learn the craft.

The visible skepticism of the lab assistants egged on my eagerness to work. I was given reagents, instruments, and instructions, and the girls ran off with a merry "good luck!"

I was all alone in the entire building and began working in a buoyant mood. My cheerfulness surprised me somewhat, since it didn't reflect my objectively speaking fairly desperate situation. It soon became clear that I made one mistake after another. After having failed with even the simplest maneuvers I decided to peer into the microscope in the vain hope that I would, against all odds, manage to save at least a fraction of the tests. This was not the case, but it in no way influenced my good mood. I remained into the wee hours studying tube after tube, and could only confirm that everything was spoiled. At four in the morning I admitted total defeat and gave up. I was in a state of total euphoria.

While driving home that bright Midsummer's morning, I wondered how I could be so happy after having destroyed the excellent samples. The answer was obvious: I had been excused from participating in the Midsummer's dance!

---

*George Klein: "First Encounter with Africa" in *The Atheist and the Holy City*.

Why was this so important? I have nothing against other people celebrating Midsummer or other holidays. Sometimes I enjoy watching it at
a distance or on film. As long as I don't have to join in! The same goes
for dances and social parties in general. But I'd never really thought
about this until I read Carleton's diary. Our feelings of exclusion arose
at about the same time, when we were fifteen or sixteen. That was when
the boys in my class began attending dance classes. In our segregated
world boys and girls attended separate schools. Natural and relaxed
contacts between the sexes were prevented by various hypocritical but
no less paralyzing norms, and the dance classes and the parties were the
only socially acceptable venues for such contacts. My desire to meet
girls was just as strong as anyone else's, but every attempt to adjust in
order to "join in" ended with an inner defeat. I felt awkward, isolated,
and cut off from all meaningful communication. In addition I was disturbed by the hullabaloo. I can't see any clear reason for this reaction,
which has followed me faithfully through my life. The teenager I try to
see from half a century's distance had often been told that he was good-
looking and was liked by many people. Neither did I have any difficulty
appreciating rhythm and dancing, nor did the feeling of exclusion have
anything to do with anti-Semitism. Anti-Semitism was fairly prevalent in
Hungary at the time, but in our urbanized and cosmopolitan culture,
Jews, converted Jews, and various filo-Semites were not just an obvious
but even a dominant ingredient. Furthermore, I felt equally alienated at
Jewish get-togethers.

Can I see any other explanations that don't require several years of
psychoanalysis to dig up? Carleton's contrast between his dislike of parties and his positive appreciation of private contacts point in a certain
direction. As for me, I remember the chamber choir of my youth.

I was sixteen, maybe seventeen. The choir met once a week. Our
twenty-year-old musical director and conductor—who after the war became one of the leading conductors at the Budapest opera—was equally
excluded from formal higher education as the rest of us who were "of
Jewish extraction." Our choir became his main instrument for the moment. We sang a cappella, everything from the pre-classics to modern

choir works, especially Bartók and Kodály. We were a devoted group brought together by the talent and the compelling personality of our conductor. "Chamber choir night" was the high point of the week for all of us.

Girls made up half of the choir. We sang together but had rarely time to talk to one another. We worked hard and were then in a hurry to get home. But the choir arranged a party every six months in order to promote social contacts. I went there in the more or less repressed hope of making contact with one of the girls. One of them had an angelic voice, another had an open, pleasant face, and a third could raise her arm in an unforgettable way. I wanted very much to talk to one of them. No, this isn't a euphemism—I mean talk. We middle-class kids lived in a double world. Girls from good families you wanted to talk to, and, if you were lucky, dance with. The surging sexuality of the teenage boy was discreetly channeled in the direction of numerous brothels whose social regimentation and varying price levels were a mirror image of contemporary society. This generally accepted, self-evident process was never mentioned in "cultured conversations."

Despite my joyous expectation it didn't take many minutes after my arrival at the choir party until I felt as rejected, as depressed, and on a sure course toward a headache and a sleepless night as I had ever been at any other party. And of course, being angry at myself didn't make things better. Why had I sacrificed my colorful inner world, disturbed my continuous monologues, blocked my free associations? What had I received in return? Disconnected and partly inaudible fragments of conversation; unbearably loud dance music (where had the musicality of all the choir members gone?); thick cigarette smoke; conventional, quasi-gemütlich, pseudorelaxed, noncommittal friendliness; questions asked but no one waiting for the answer; eyes that focus on one's conversational partner for just a few seconds before returning to their restless search to find out who has arrived now; a casual attentiveness which mainly deals with the question of how people are dressed and who they're speaking to, dancing with, or going out with. The smooth surface of my inner lake has been shattered by a million pebbles. The waves frightened even the larger fish from their depths, and they began moving in a jagged, chaotic, meaningless manner.

But before the battle was totally lost came the command from within, clear as a bugle blow: Flee! Turn back to your solitude, to your books, to the piano, the earplugs of your soul, to the carefully restricted yet infinite playground of mental concentration! It took at least two days before the lake's surface was once again smooth and the sun dared to appear.

Only the last time that I participated in the chamber choir party did something different happen: I made close contact with a girl. After just a few minutes the eating, drinking, and noisy, meaningless party receded into an indifferent background murmur. The encounter was the start of a long relationship with partly tragic consequences which I have described elsewhere.* But there and then my continuously pleading inner lawyer received a supporting argument for his case. I'd been right. It wasn't necessary to dance. You didn't have to conform to the conventionally sanctioned ways of socializing in order to make contact with the girl whom you so longed for, whether you admitted it or not.

A year and a half later we were engulfed by the Holocaust. But neither the actual murders being committed in our immediate vicinity or the knowledge that we only had a minimal chance of survival would stop the human psychology and biology from functioning as usual. Every morning we wondered if we'd be alive that night. But except for the moments when we were subjected to acute stress we behaved as if everything was in order. My thoughts were preoccupied with my first love affair with a girl. The intense nearness and communication on all three levels—emotional, intellectual, and sexual—occupied the center of my consciousness. External events that decided whether we would live or die seemed irrelevant by comparison.

These experiences have only consolidated a behavioral pattern which had crystallized much earlier. The conclusion—never clearly formulated but rigorously followed—was that you could manage without superficial conventions and ways of socializing. It was a *quod erat demonstrandum*: a confirmation of something that was instinctively known. My permanent lifestyle became a combination of the more or

---

*George Klein: "Suicides I" in *Pietà* (Cambridge, Mass.: MIT Press, 1992).

less abstract concentration of working and a few intense and close personal contacts. What was useful during a time of war and genocide became useful also in peacetime and after emigrating to a new country. It has neither been affected by defeat nor—which is much more difficult—by success.

Can Carleton and I have been shaped in a similar way, despite all the differences in our backgrounds? I'm inclined to believe so. His flight from dances and parties, his feeling of being an outsider seem to mirror my own reactions. Work has become a companion for life, a faithful friend that leads us both into and out of solitude. Its challenges never cease to entice. The goal of our search is not another trophy which merely leads to new parties, but more work. The road leads ever onward and ever deeper into the real world of nature; it leads via small, objectively verifiable steps toward a larger complex of problems that can never be fully analyzed in its entirety. At the same time the road leads to our inner selves. But in the evening we sometimes hope that someone will come. Whether it's a seemingly remote foreigner from a Stone Age or South Sea culture, or a cultural relative—old or young, beautiful or ugly, disheveled or well-groomed—doesn't matter. And she/he will come.

EPILOGUE

In the autumn of 1990 I make plans to visit Carleton again. Is he still as intense? Or has he given in to his longing for a more contemplative and philosophical existence? I read his diary from 1986. During a short stopover in Toronto he first made some notes about the AIDS situation in the city, and then he wrote down what he had heard about his local friends, their children, and grandchildren. One of his friends was of Persian extraction. The ensuing conversation reminded him of the old Persian philosophers and poets:

> Such sophisticated writers they had, many centuries before the emergence of European literature! I must return to them! I want to study

Persian history, I'll send for all the books on the subject. . . . The thought of being able to make excursions to such intellectually exciting areas has almost convinced me that it's time to withdraw from the departmental leadership and from today's competitive neurobiological research in order to be able to devote myself to some relaxed scholarship and what really amuses me. Running a large lab is an ungrateful task. It proves self-defeating in many ways. I'm an old man past sixty, and it's time to abandon this. I feel as intellectually vigorous as I was in my teens, but I know that a certain amount of self-delusion is necessary for me to really believe that this is true. In this late stage of life one's proper goals should be contemplation, stimulating one's intellectual curiosity and excursions into literature, art, and philosophy. I am fully capable of this. I should forgo scientific competition, its politics and administration—it's a devastating waste of talent and intelligence. You can possibly afford it when you're in your thirties, forties, and fifties, but not at sixty. There are no prizes, awards, or honorary distinctions of any kind that I strive for now. I have received more than my share; no one should demand more. My emotional and intellectual self-esteem demands that I switch over to hedonistic exploitation of my curiosity and analytic ability. I should distance myself from the politics of academe both for my own sake and the sake of others. I hope that I can reach a condition of equanimity so that I can realize this thought.

I didn't believe this when I read it one year after it was written. I was convinced that Carleton cultivates an illusion that ignores his own psychological reality. How could he—man of action and problem-solver beyond compare, a flow-addict dependent upon his own inner reward—be transformed into a passive recipient of the flow-products of others that have been collected over millennia, however strongly these may speak to his poetic sense? How could he indulge in such daydreaming? However repulsive the competition and the politics may be, they're as much a part of the scientist's everyday world as the trivial frustrations of the laboratory. When has Carleton, the incomparable master of resistance and conquest, ever let himself be stopped by the one or the other?

My intuition proved correct.

✦ ✦ ✦

Frederick, Maryland, 1990. I had made arrangements with Carleton to stop by in Washington, D.C., and visit the "house" on my way to California. But I've barely landed in the United States before I'm deluged by fax and phone messages at half a dozen places telling me to please call Carleton's secretary immediately. I'm astounded by the accuracy. Carleton's assistants have called every place that I might possibly contact on my way.

The message is simple and shocking: Carleton has been in a serious car accident. It could have been much worse, but miraculously, he's gotten away with only seven broken ribs. He still wants to see me—can I come to the hospital?

At Frederick Memorial Hospital I'm met by an empty bed. Carleton is sitting at an improvised table offering orthopedic support which is already full of papers. He's writing while simultaneously talking with a Yugoslavian guest researcher. It hurts when he speaks, but his words flow forth as usual.

First he recounts the accident to me in detail. He was on his way home from the lab at one in the morning accompanied by one of his adopted sons and one adopted daughter. The son was driving. On a long, straight stretch of road they spotted a car approaching at quite a distance which swerved over on the wrong side of the road. They began signaling when they were about a mile apart. This didn't help, and the other car kept coming at them on their side of the road. Getting off the road was an impossible option. Gajdusek told the boy to get over on the opposite side of the road too. He did, but then the approaching car also switched sides, like a rabbit hypnotized by the light, and there was a head-on collision. The driver of the approaching car uttered "I must have fallen asleep" before loosing consciousness. He had suffered a spinal fracture and was now dying. Carleton had broken seven ribs while his son and daughter suffered only minor injuries.

I couldn't get a word in edgewise. Carleton cut off my awkward attempts to express my joy at finding him alive, and instead embarked on a discussion about how a person who is half asleep moves when a strong light shines in his eyes: He unconsciously follows the movements of the light. Then Carleton began telling me about everything that had happened in his lab. "We're on top of the situation!" he exclaimed again and again with the natural joy of a child and without any boastfulness. He blazed with intensity whether talking about molecular prion research or about the newly discovered kuru-like diseases in humans and animals. The developments had confirmed Carleton's predictions to an extent that far exceeded his expectations.

It turns out that GSS, the hereditary form of CJD, is caused by a mutation in the previously mentioned PrP gene. The mutation, which is inherited, increases the probability that PrP^C is transformed into PrP^{SC}. In the case of infectious transmissions in animal experiments the opposite is found, as was expected. The infectious PrP^{SC} agent can feature a mutation in exactly the same place as in the inherited form, but the mutation disappears in the passage to the next animal. This supports the hypothesis that the infected animal's PrP^C is changed to PrP^{SC} after coming in contact with the infectious form. According to this hypothesis the mutation is only a predisposing event that triggers the change in the protein's conformation which is decisive for the disease.

Are kuru and similar diseases a risk to be seriously reckoned with? Isn't it an exotic disease which has now been effectively eliminated? Unfortunately it doesn't appear that way. An outbreak of infectious Creutzfeldt-Jakob Disease (CJD) has been reported from Orava in northern Slovakia, a sparsely populated area mainly inhabited by shepherding farmers.* Twenty-two cases have been diagnosed during a fourteen-year period, of which twelve occurred during the last three years. An additional nineteen cases have been found near Lucenec, a rural region further south. The central nervous system showed the same type of degeneration as with the sporadically occurring CJD. The course of the disease was equally depressing, and the patients died within seven months of the first symptoms.

---

*Tim Beardsley, "Profile: Gene Doctor. W. French Anderson Pioneers Gene Therapy," *Scientific American* 263, no. 2 (August 1990): 33–33B.

The Slovakian kuru epidemic has caused great concern. The sheep in the area often get scrapie and a large percentage of the population comes in regular contact with the animals. The question is has scrapie "hopped onto" people. As mentioned earlier, infected prions can pass between species, but it's not an efficient process. Similar questions have been posed in connection with the previously mentioned Mad Cow Disease (BSE) in Great Britain which is also suspected of originating from scrapie-infected sheep. It's been proved that scrapie-infected mutton has been used in producing cattle fodder or as a protein addition in the geographic area in question. The possibility of human contagion is viewed with great concern.

In connection with possible ways of infection in the West, Gajdusek has coined the expression "high-technological cannibalism." Fourteen cases have occurred in people treated with human pituitary extract for various hormone deficiencies. Three occurred in recipients of cornea transplants, one in connection with a dental operation, and in at least three cases the infection could be traced to electrodes that had been inserted into the brain during neurosurgery. The electrodes had been treated with chemical disinfectants prior to use, but this doesn't suffice to neutralize prions.

Carleton is obviously in pain as he speaks, but he continues without pause if he were assigned to give me a private tutorial. Sometimes he's interrupted by very painful fits of coughing, but then he immediately continues. Fortunately the secretary enters. She's received strict orders from the boys to bring me to the "house" where they've prepared dinner. I'll return with them to the hospital later when they came to visit Carleton.

I follow the boys home. It's not the same house as on my last visit. That large, half-dilapidated, eighteenth-century building had burned down a week after the Gajdusek family had moved away. Now we're in an average suburban American family house. Two of the older "boys," who have their own families in the U.S., have returned as temporary fathers for the younger ones. The seven resident youngsters are, as before, between fourteen and seventeen. One of them is a girl, the sixth in the large group of adopted siblings.

I'm in the same warm, relaxed environment as before. The atmosphere is characterized by a natural, laconic, gentle congeniality. Will the boys talk more now that Carleton isn't here?

They don't. It's mainly the oldest father-figure who converses with me. Sometimes the second temporary father says a few words.

I ask if they've visited their biological parents since they've become Americans. Yes, the one with an American wife has done so. He had trained her for an entire year prior to the visit, teaching her some of the local language. He explained that Melanesian society treats fathers with a great deal of respect. One must watch every word one says in order not to hurt the feelings of the father or of others. The American wife spent a great deal of effort to learn the nuances. But these good intentions proved to be misguided. Twenty-two years had passed since the son left his family as a thirteen-year-old, and during that time the island had been westernized quite rapidly. The language he had used as a thirteen-year-old now seemed both childish and out-dated. He'd never learned the more forceful expressions of the adult male. Especially tricky was the usage of the many different forms of "I" and "you," which are determined by differences in age, sex, and social status. This was in itself very complicated and could only be mastered in part by a thirteen-year-old. But the language had changed even further during the two decades of his absence. The problem was solved when the son and the father agreed to speak English with one another, and so the language studies of the wife proved superfluous.

After dinner we return to the hospital. I'm invited to come along when "the kids" visit Carleton. There are no dramatic displays of affection. The kids sit or stand. Two of them sit on the side of the bed. They kiss Carleton but don't say much. At first they seem shy. I assume it's because of my presence. Then I notice a few small and warm but almost concealed smiles. They touch Carleton now and then, as if wanting to reassure themselves that he's still alive. At the same time they want to convey a message. Yes, they want to show their joy at still having him around.

I must leave, but the boys remain. Carleton works and talks at the same time. A happy family scene? Yes, if there ever was one. Can you get any further from a stereotypical family? Hardly. Has Carleton's restless search found a resting place? No, never. Proteus? Or rather: Odysseus?

Before I close the door behind me I look back one last time. Carleton continues working in his hospital chair while ceaselessly talking. The boys look at him. They smile their silent smiles now and again. I remember something Carleton has written. I look it up when I'm back home:

> Life is much too valuable to be fettered with chains, too fleeting to be lived incompletely, too impersonal to be drenched in sentimentality, too promising to be channeled, too costly to be wasted on superficialities. Intensity, depth, antithesis, change—harmony and then dissolution in death. Pain is temporary and unimportant . . . only a sign that life is not lived in the right manner. When you feel pain, you should quickly change course in order to transform the pain into something superficial or else give up the ghost! To abandon oneself to pain and live in its ramifications is a banality.

POST MORTEM

Denn wir sind nur die Schale und das Blatt.
Der grosse Tod, den jeder in sich hat
das ist die Frucht um die sich alles dreht.

Rainer Maria Rilke: *"Das Stundenbuch"*

For we are just the leaf and just the skin.
But that great death which each one has within,
that is the fruit around which all revolves.

(Translation by J. B. Leishman)

Summer 1991. After six hours of travel by car from Budapest we pass the northeastern border at Csap, where Hungary, the Soviet Union and Czechoslovakia meet. We're approaching the Subcarpathian region, which is now a part of the Ukraine. The Russian border guards are as stiff and serious as at other crossings along the long border of the still existing Soviet Union, but a few of them here speak Hungarian. A couple of unexpectedly friendly young women are in charge of some of the tedious supervision. They speak a beautiful, somewhat old-fashioned Hungarian which sounds both polite and natural—an unusual combination. Our minibus is allowed to pass together with the larger buses and we avoid the several-hours-long line of cars. The motorists are mainly Poles on their way home after a shopping excursion to Hungary. Despite the line they'll get home quicker than if they'd have tried to drive around the boxed-in, relatively narrow Soviet territory. The border which previously was hermetically sealed is now relatively open. The "pits" built for the inspection of car chassis remain, but while private cars must pass over them no border guard gets into them any more. The passport control is long and tedious compared with the West, but expeditious and gentle compared with earlier Soviet methods.

The landscape is the same as on the Hungarian side, but with a few minor differences. With joy I recognize the large haystacks, those wonderful playgrounds of my youth, which are gone from the Hungarian side. People here work with the same primitive hayforks as fifty or sixty years ago. The small villages haven't aged. The pavement is as defective as half a century ago, if it remains at all. The clay puddles bring frightened memories of soiled white shorts on the Sabbath. My unfilled desire to sleep in a haystack under an open sky is briefly rekindled. The horse stables remind me of the swift delivery of a foal I once witnessed, but the horses of today seem skinnier and more worn. The cows returning from pasture create the same dust clouds as when I followed them home during hot summer evenings, surprised at their faultless sense of direction. But the endless vineyards of my childhood are gone from the bare hillsides, which now seem ominously foreign.

I was here last in the late fall of 1942. I was seventeen years old and as usual lived with my paternal grandmother. I studied Latin, math, Hungarian history, and physics for my graduation with a certain resigned feverishness. I was determined to strive for the top grade in all subjects, despite the fact that my chances of entering any of the universities were minimal even if I succeeded. Without top honors it would be futile for a Jewish boy to even try.

Strangely enough I was completely uninterested in the war that raged just beyond our borders and that would have such an impact on our future. Like most others I didn't know that it wasn't just a question of being able to study and work, but a matter of life and death. I knew nothing of the concentration camps, located a few hundred miles from my father's village, where the Jews of German-occupied Europe were being murdered on a vast scale. Least of all did I realize that this would be my last visit with my grandmother and the entire family, and that it would be my definitive farewell, not just to most of those who were near to me, but to the Jewish population and culture of the entire region.

We drive up to the village. I had shown an old photo of my father's house to my temporary traveling companions the minute before. In my childhood it was the only house in the village with an upper story. The villagers simply called the house "The Upper Story." Don't you recognize it? asks one of my traveling companions. I say that I do but that we aren't there yet. But he insists.

Look at the house on that corner—it's the one you showed me in the photograph! No, not yet, I insist, but my words suddenly get stuck in my throat. Unemotional eyes obviously see better than my own memory-laden photo-receptors. Of course it's my father's house. It has the same form as in the photo but is shabby and run-down. All the paint has peeled off, the balcony has rusted away, and the door to my father's office on the bottom floor has been cemented shut.

Two men are conversing in front of the entrance. They speak Hungarian, like all others I meet in the village. I greet them.

Excuse me, but my father built this house. I was conceived here, I was an infant here, my father died here. I lived here until I was six years old. May I look inside?

Of course, go ahead.

Who lives here now?

No one. It's the office of the village administration.

The stairway is unchanged. I see the crack in the wall where I stuck a little paper note when I was here the last time, forty-nine years ago. I wanted to send a greeting to my adult self when he returned. The note is gone but the return visit has materialized.

We ascend the stairs. I point toward the door in the landing in the middle of the stairs: There's the famous water closet! It was the only one in the village when I was a child. It was treated with the same respect as were other wonders of modern technology.

It doesn't work, say the men from the village. It's been out of order since World War II. The village still has no running water. The toilet seat and the bowl are in perfect condition, but the rainwater tank and the plumbing hasn't been maintained.

What *do* you use?

They point to the outhouse in the back yard.

The veranda one flight up is unchanged. This is where I ran as a four- and five-year-old, always with a worried glance as I looked into the room: Is Mother crying? She was often sad. They told me it was because my father was dead. But I didn't believe it. I was certain that she was sad because I had not behaved. When she was happy, the heavens smiled.

I enter the room where she used to sit. Only the old tile stove remains. But the walls recognize me; they greet me with silent matter-of-factness. They know that I was conceived here and that my father died in this room, in the very same bed.

Half a dozen girls are at their desks, writing by hand. There, in that corner, was my bed. In it I used to fantasize about my future life. I would become a hermit. I would never have to meet or speak with anyone. Once each day my food would be hoisted up to me in a basket.

The window to the street was open during the summer nights. I can still taste the bitterness of having to go to bed while the neighbor's girl was still allowed to play outside.

Excuse me, I'm from Sweden. This was my father's house. May I look around?

In that case you must be Gyurka! one of the girls suddenly exclaims. Is your name Gyurka?

That was what my mother called me, as did the other villagers. But everyone who knew me was gassed and incinerated forty-seven years ago. How can you know what they called me forty years before you were born?

Don't you know? Your uncle, everyone's Uncle Miska was our boss here. He was number one in the entire region. We have a museum with all his medals and honorary diplomas. Our village received many citations for good accomplishments during his time and only then. He sat at this table after he was paralyzed. That was his office during his glory days. Come and look at the museum.

They all speak at the same time.

On the walls are photos, medals, clippings. In one picture a crowd huddles under a forest of umbrellas in the pouring rain. I recognize the buildings. It's the village main square, just outside my grandmother's house.

What's happening in this picture?

It is your Uncle Miska's funeral. The entire Kárpátalja* was here. There wasn't a more famous or beloved person in the entire region. It was an official party funeral; he was a Hero of Socialist Labor.

I wander among the pictures, seeking familiar features behind the aging, somewhat rounded face. Yes, it is he. My most beloved uncle. All the village children's most beloved uncle.

We simply called him Miska; we never had to say "uncle" as we had to address all other adult males. His hardware store was the favorite haunt of all children. You were always given a candy, and could do everything that you weren't allowed to do at home. You could dangle on his knee or ride his favorite white horse, all depending on your age and ability. You could play with the telephone, a still quite rare contraption, or sit by the cash register and accept payment from customers. You could hammer long nails into wooden boards, build tree-houses, play with mouse-traps or—best of all—come along to "The Mountain," the enchanted land of wine-growing.

I saw Miska for the last time in Budapest in 1945. He was the only one from his family to return from Auschwitz alive. He had seen his mother, his wife, and his only child, a two-year-old daughter who was born after fifteen years of infertility and countless gynecological consul-

---

*Hungarian name for the Subcarpathian region.

tations with Hungary's best experts, disappear into the gas chambers.
He kissed them and asked his wife to take good care of their small
daughter. Only he knew that it was a final farewell. The others thought
they were going for a shower and to receive new clothes.

On his way home from Auschwitz Miska passed through Budapest.
His older brother, my Uncle Béla, was a renowned pediatrician in the
Hungarian capital. He asked Miska to stay and begin a new life, suggesting that it would be unbearable for him to subject himself to all the
memories in the deserted village and the empty houses. But Miska refused. He wanted to live and die in his mother's house, alone with his
memories.

And he did. But he couldn't resist taking charge of the rudder. Earlier
he'd been one of the region's most popular people, regardless of which
country the village happened to belong to. He was a decorated Hungarian
soldier during the First World War. The villagers—but not Miska himself—always mentioned that he had received the rare Golden Medal of
Bravery of the First Order. During the Czech period he enjoyed the confidence of both the Hungarian population and the Czech authorities, and he
held several honorary positions, including the important assignment as
fire chief. During the last two decades of his life, when the village belonged to the Soviet Union, he was head of the village cooperative.

Before leaving the house, I look down from the balcony upon what
was once my garden and constant playground. That was where I cried
when the fox took my white doves during the night. And that was where
I was overcome by unspeakable sadness when a large boy whom I didn't
know jumped up onto my fence from the street and suddenly pissed on
me with hatred in his eyes. I was so startled by this unsuspected and unknown hatred that I almost forgot to move away. Now the fence is gone,
there's no garden, and there are no doves, only plenty of junk and rubbish. Our kitchen where my mother made me small clay ducks one calm
evening has become a kind of primitive washroom.

I leave the house and wander along the village main street, accompanied by an increasing number of followers. I recognize most buildings
and remember their inhabitants. Who lives here now?

The Jews' houses have become offices, the two largest ones serving as a daycare center and a school. Not a single new house has been built since World War II. The empty houses that belonged to those who were deported have provided more than enough room.

The synagogue has been torn down and is totally gone, as are the Jewish religious school, the rabbi's house, and the ritual bathhouse. A combined storagelike restaurant and café has been built on the site. On this street I used to walk Friday evenings, dressed in my best finery. Most often it was Miska or his brother Vili who took me to the synagogue. Afterward there was always a sabbath meal at my grandmother's house.

We enter Miska's old hardware store. It remains a hardware store, but is today only half as large, scruffy and bare. But the keepers remember Miska and his father, who founded the store. Old newspapers, documents, and letters remain from that time.

I now want to enter my grandmother's house, which was my home during the summers of my childhood and teen years. This was where I read my first great novels, fell in love with the words of poets, heard my first operas, and studied for my high school graduation.

I am let into the room that faces the square. It's still called "Miska's room" twenty-two years after his death. My grandmother used to sit by the window during summer evenings. The carved cupboard which held a small glass model of the crown of St. Stephen containing soil supposedly walked on by Franz Joseph is gone, and has been replaced by a large picture of Christ. Gone too is the bed in the corner, where I remember how my twelve-year-old self awoke in surprised wonderment from his first wet-dreams. But the simple washbowl remains, and the water is brought up from the same well in the yard.

Suddenly the door opens wide. A kindly, somewhat corpulent older woman bursts in and embraces me as if I were her long lost son. Gyurka! she cries. It's Mrs. Teri, the widow of one of Miska's employees in the hardware store, who has inherited the house from Miska. She speaks of him as if he'd been the protective friend and grandfather of her entire family, and tells how she cared for him during his last years. Then she produces Miska's photo album. Among the family photographs I find images of myself as a child and a teenager. The album also contains the snapshots of my children that I sent Miska during the 1950s and 1960s. Everything is there, carefully and lovingly preserved. While looking at the photographs I listen to Mrs. Teri's quick and cheerful cascade of words. I try to assemble in my mind a picture of my uncle during the time of Stalin and Khrushchev. But how can I reconcile the lonesome, bitter mourner with the celebrated and decorated workers' hero; how can I regard the friend of all children and the important party member as the same person?

I go for a walk with Mrs. Teri. We begin with the Jewish cemetery. We proceed on a muddy side-road and find that the cemetery is surrounded by an iron fence and seems completely grown over. The one gate is chained shut. I climb over the fence, cut myself on the barbed wire, and jump down on the other side. Deep inside the shrubbery I find the graves of my father and grandfather next to one another. Lucky they who died of illness, still in possession of their dignity and blissfully assured of their family's secure future.

When I climb back over the fence I notice a boy who is obviously waiting for me. He says that the village chairman sends his greetings and would like to meet me. A while later I'm back in my father's house. The chairman, Miska's successor, wants to show me pictures and diplomas from Miska's time in office. He translates the Russian texts for me. Some have been issued by local authorities, others by the Ukrainian government, and a few by the central government in Moscow. There are red banners and lots of pictures of Stalin and Lenin. I see Miska's name in Russian everywhere: Awarded for great achievements. Awarded for remarkable achievements. For overproduction, personal initiative, outstanding organizational ability, and for continued selfless work for others.

We browse through the large photo albums. My athletic uncle is no longer riding his favorite white horse. His body is heavy, his hair thin and gray. But what has changed most is his gaze. I see an unutterable pain, an open wound which cannot heal or be soothed. Otherwise: seriousness and order.

The abrupt, mustached, and deadly serious village chairman invites

me to the café which is located where the synagogue once stood. Flies
are buzzing around us; they don't seem satisfied with the empty liquor
glasses here and there on the scruffy tables. This was where I heard the
indescribably sorrowful and ungraspably strange, crying, whimpering,
lamenting recitation of the Jewish cantor. I now know better why he wept
when he sang, but how did he know it even then?

The village chairman insists that I taste the town's special walnut
liqueur. We toast to the future of Kaszony, but we're no longer alone. The
rumor has spread quickly. Villagers enter, they want to press my hand
and tell me about Miska. It's a choir of many voices all bearing the same
testimony: he worked day and night, he was in his office even on holidays. He arose at four in the morning, hitched a ride with the truck drivers, and then checked all transports personally. He could have sent his
subordinates like all other bosses and even people at considerably lower
positions would have done. But he wanted to check every shipment himself, regardless of the season. He knew how to get the wares through. He
was very persuasive and didn't shy away from bribing parsimonious officials if he had to. He never gave up. It was to Miska's and no one else's
credit that Kaszony became famous all over the Ukraine and, after it was
awarded the rare title of "Millionaire Village," famous all over the Soviet Union. But the model village's great accomplishments were largely
due to the fact that the chairman of its cooperative had no longer any interest in material rewards. He only wished to support others.

Didn't he want to have a new family?

No, he never thought of it. It was as if he'd chosen to remember his
murdered family every day, every minute. As if he'd decided to think
about what couldn't be spoken. He seldom talked about it, but it was always evident on his face.

The village chairman toasts me. Then he adds, somewhat sadly, Even
now, more than twenty years after his death, our reputation as a model
village lives on. But it's no longer deserved. We haven't over-achieved in
many years; nowadays we can't even live up to general standards.

Miska's old assistants try to surpass each other in their praise: If Miska
saw an old woman by the roadside when he was riding in the cooperative's

truck in rain, snow, or the worst heat, he always ordered the chauffeur to
stop, and asked the woman to sit beside the driver while he himself
climbed in the back onto the truck's flatbed. He gave away his money to
children, friends, and the needy, or in order to appease corrupt bureaucrats
and party bosses who tried to interfere with his food transports.

The village chairman has barely left before the remaining men point
out that, just as you would expect from a bigwig, he has grabbed the
most prominent office in my father's "Upper Story." He's also obtained
expensive furniture and rugs. Miska, in contrast, always preferred the
smallest room where the diplomas and awards are now kept.

I'm asking everyone who knew him the same unanswerable questions. Am I really hoping for an answer? Or do I merely want to hear my
own voice echo in the void? How could he cope with the pain? How
could he live in the house of his brutally murdered mother, in his
parental home where he had himself grown up? How could he stand remembering the Friday evenings when his murdered brothers sat around
the bountiful table with the candles and the fresh bread which my
grandmother had baked? How could he pass his own old house every
time he walked to his office and remember his wife and little daughter?

Silence. Again someone says that he lived only for his work. However many his responsibilities, he constantly sought out new tasks. He
felt best when he was overworked.

But he was always like that, I object, even before; during Miska's
and the family's best days. I remember the summers of my teenage years
in Kaszony. Miska didn't want to hear of any spare time. He was constantly involved in work or fixing something. He liked helping others,
and didn't give up until he had enticed some smiles from those he
helped. He was interested in everyone without exception: children and
grownups, Jews and Christians, strangers and relatives, Hungarians and
Ruthenians. He was always in a hurry. Only on Friday evenings would
he agree to sit down at a set table. Otherwise he literally threw the food
into his mouth. It was a family proverb of sorts that you could get an
ulcer just by watching him eat. Work was his way of life even then, and
a way born of joy rather than of pain.

What was his personal life like after he returned here? Did he have any close friends?

No, but he kept in close touch with Mrs. Teri and her family, who were his tenants and to whom he willed his mother's house. And he kept in touch with all the children in the village, of course.

Women in their thirties and forties take turns in recounting how they ran across the street when they saw him coming on the other side. He always had a piece of candy in his pocket, or money for ice cream.

One of his old assistants shows photographs from committee meetings and congresses in Kiev and Moscow. Miska seems stiff and absent, surrounded by unfriendly Russian faces. They're all sitting under large red flags, portraits of leaders, and political slogans; they seem stone dead.

How could he stomach all the party propaganda that he was subjected to? How could he keep calm at these meetings when there was work to be done back home?

He knew that all of this was unavoidable. He thought of the propaganda as just another sermon in church and turned a deaf ear.

Did he ever read books or magazines? Was he interested in world events?

No, he never held a book in his hand. And he never read the paper. He lived for the moment, keeping busy with what he set out to do. When he didn't work or sleep he wanted to be alone.

Suddenly I, too, strongly feel that I want to be alone. I say my thanks and leave. While I'm walking along the very familiar yet totally alien main street I wonder if I spoke the truth when I wrote the dedication to one of my earlier books, *Pietà*, three years before this visit could take place. The sentence flowed from my pen without me really contemplating it:

"To the memory of Kaszony, my father's village, gone forever but always near, stronger than the smells or tastes of the past, warmer than love and, unlike pain, unfading."

What did I mean by this? Is it truthful?

I'm standing at the foot of "The Mountain," the steep hill which led to our family's vineyards. There are no grapes left; everything was destroyed in the early 1950s. But to me it all seems like a backdrop. Why is the always ephemeral "now" of today or tomorrow more real than that of yesterday? The hillside in front of me is still full of vines weighed down by large, ripe bunches of grapes in light green, black, and purple. Day laborers with waxed aprons are hurriedly busy harvesting. The large baskets on their backs called *puttony*, a kind of birch-bark rucksack, are filled to the brim. Strong, barefoot men are crushing the grapes in large vats, and the juice pours through the taps. My cousins and I are running about while the workers laugh and joke with us. One or two know whose child I am and tell me that they knew my dead father. It seems strange that I, who am his son, know less about him than this man with his *puttony*.

A while later I'm standing at the soccer field by the country road, only a few hundred yards from the sometimes open, sometimes closed, but now half-open Hungarian border. To my inner eye the unkempt soccer field is transformed into a well-tended tennis court. Two thirteen-year-olds, my cousin and I, are bicycling back and forth on the dusty road. We look at the Czech guards at the carefully guarded border. We think it strange that they're here to protect our village without being able to speak our language. We don't suspect that they've been put there by the fickle wingbeats of history, or that their days are numbered. We cannot imagine that within a year the border will disappear—to our great but, we would later realize, misguided happiness. Least of all can we imagine the great disaster which five years later will annihilate our family and the Jewish population of the entire region.

Who do I notice playing tennis while I'm biking past; who gets me to stop and open my eyes wide? It's the beautiful daughter of the owner of the large estate who is playing a match with the village dentist. But he's not a real dentist. As soon as he is out of earshot, the villagers like to point out that he has less education than the ordinary dentists who are fully licensed. Consequently he may not be addressed as "doctor," although he's allowed to perform all dental procedures except surgery. There are constant whispers about him and the daughter of the estate's owner, but the whispers die down when we children come near. There's something strange about this couple which I can only half understand.

It is said that since they're living as if they were married, they're committing a great sin. Such arrangements are not permitted, or must be kept secret. But the couple seems determined to challenge public opinion, and are not at all being secretive. I look at them with curiosity, admiration, and fear. I experience a mixture of respect and revulsion against this nameless thing which seems holy and dirty at the same time.

The woman seems to notice my dreamy but also inquisitive gaze, or perhaps she can read thoughts. During their smoke break she begins to kid me about all the new thoughts that may have come into my head recently. The dentist makes an ambiguous comment to the effect that the cause of my new thoughts are in my pants. Such brazenness I've never before heard in our Jewish middle class world. The street boys can express themselves in much coarser terms, but their language was not ours. As I stand by the soccer field more than half a century later, within full view of the border guards who for the moment happen to wear Soviet uniforms, I still feel the blush which spread to the hair roots of my thirteen-year-old self. It could only in part be cooled down by the wind which brushed against my face as I hastily pedaled away from the tennis court.

Again I turn toward the main street. A while further down was the doctor's house which contained a large piano where I was allowed to practice when I was fifteen and sixteen. The doctor and his wife always had a good word and something freshly baked for me. Here on this corner I was stopped by some local boys cruising around on their bicycles. They joked with me and hinted at some activity which was disguised by the expression "using the motor." I didn't understand what they meant, but figured it had something to do with girls. I didn't like these boys; I found them vulgar and uninteresting. One of them asked me if I had a girl-friend. Only Lady Musica, I answered with pride and contempt.

My sixty-six-year-old body moves slowly along the same street which is not the same. Mrs. Teri has joined me. We look into house after house. I recognize most of them although they're dilapidated and their yards are full of trash, but the people seem alien; all the Jewish faces are gone. They look at me with kindness in their eyes, though; I am Miska's nephew and many have heard my childhood name. This is the

yard where I first witnessed a chicken being slaughtered; it was horrifying. Over there on the other side lived a sick old lady who never ventured out into the street. During the evenings she would sit at the
window and express her astonishment at my having grown so much. I
visited her sometimes, she was usually in bed. There was a strange odor
in the dark sick-room. An unfamiliar nurse was also there; she was all
dressed in white. The yeshiva, the Jewish orthodox religious school, was
located in the opposite house where I now see an empty grocer's and a
half-empty shoe shop. We were told that the rabbi was famous all over
Jewish Eastern Europe. Some thought him capable of performing mira-
cles. Religious Jews came all the way from Poland to ask for his advice
or subject themselves to his judgment in disputes.

All stores are as good as empty. How do the people survive?

They manage, says Mrs. Teri. Nothing works, but everyone has private sources. Everything is available on the black market; you can buy
and sell on both sides of the border. It's tricky, but we're used to it. If
you have an old car, you install a 100-liter gas tank, fill it with black
kolkhoz-gasoline which is usually stolen and very cheap on the black
market, line up for five hours at the border, sell the gas much cheaper
than the Hungarian price of gas, and then buy food for the entire family.
People aren't satisfied with bad food in this area. Nearby Hungary,
where they complain about huge economic problems, seems like a vir-
tual paradise. Just to think that the groceries there are well-stocked and
that the food smells good . . .

People also take advantage of differences in the exchange rate, Mrs.
Teri continues. You can exchange goods with the farmers. No one needs
to starve here—quite the opposite. We're so well off that our poverty-
stricken region with its empty groceries and eternally closed gas stations
is regarded as a land of plenty by visitors from central Russia. Truck drivers who drive east, and sometimes all the way to the Urals, return with
reports about real disasters, real famine.

No one I meet has anything good to say about the leadership, neither
the old nor the present; not the local, the regional, or the central. They
call them crooks, cheats, or incompetent fools. They say that party merits

and/or family ties have been decisive at all appointments during the entire Soviet period. The bigwigs drank and mismanaged their job while finagling great benefits for themselves. Only Miska is spoken well of. During his time there was food, and people worked for real.

THE FIRST NIGHT

I spend the night at the only Intourist hotel available to foreigners in the Subcarpathian capital, Uzhgorod in Russian and Ungvár in Hungarian. This Russified town has seen plenty of construction and investments. Most people here speak Russian or Ukrainian, whereas Hungarian is seldom heard. The loneliness of the hotel room feels more pressing than usual. I step out onto the balcony which overlooks several monotonous, quadrangular apartment barracks characterized only by the boredom they inspire.

How do you end up with a system whose total bankruptcy is now evident in country after country? As long as the monolithic party was in charge, such questions were not only dangerous but rather meaningless. But now, when the dictatorship has collapsed like a house of cards, the question is even more pertinent. How could so many who should have known better put their trust in such a system? How did they fall into the trap?

In 1948 I traveled to Sweden for the third and last time. I left Hungary for good, in the twelfth hour, just before the iron curtain descended and the country's Stalinist Rákosi period began in earnest.*

Six months after my arrival in Stockholm the Swedish Communist party celebrated some anniversary. The Hungarian Communist party was represented by, among others, András Szalai, who knew one of my Hungarian friends in Sweden, a neurologist at the Serafimer hospital. Szalai suffered from the effects of a blow to his head while being tortured in a Nazi jail. His injury caused repeated epileptic fits. My colleague gave Szalai medical treatment during his Swedish visit.

---

*Mátyás Rákosi (1892–1971) served as secretary of the Hungarian Communist party from 1944 to 1956 and as head of the party from 1949 to 1953.

One evening I met Szalai in the company of my friend. He spoke glowingly about developments in Hungary. Everything he had risked his life for as a member of the Communist underground was about to come true. The war-torn country was being rebuilt by the people and for the people. It was a time of communal work and a spirit of great together-ness. Not even in his most optimistic moments had he dared imagine that the Socialist dream would be realized and even surpassed in this manner. When he was a prisoner of the Nazis he thought that his life was over. Only now did he know what life really was, and he regretted every moment he had to spend in a capitalist country like Sweden.

"Doesn't he like what he's seen in Sweden so far?"

"No, not at all. This is a police state."

"Why?"

"There's a uniformed man in front of every restaurant who stops anyone who's had a bit to drink or who in any other way displeases him. Is this democracy?"

We try to explain the function of a Swedish doorman. "Aren't there any alcoholics in Hungary who cause similar trouble?"

"No, they're gone."

"How?"

"The workers have lost their taste for alcohol. They're spending their evenings at the party seminar instead of in some bar or restaurant. They're busy discussing the conditions of their life and their work. They know that they're making decisions about their own future. They have no time for drinking or similar childishness."

My colleague and I look at each other. Is he serious? Apparently he is. He's viewing the world through his special glasses, his interpretations are woven from Messianic dreams and wishful thinking and his frames of reference are protected by narrow blinders. This is the behavior of a True Believer. We feel a reluctant respect for such a deeply rooted faith, even if we could never bring ourselves to share it. But we're also irri-tated by our inability to budge him.

Only a few months had passed after Szalai's visit to Stockholm when the horrible news reached us: The greatest Stalinist show trial in Rákosi-led Hungary had begun. Foremost among the accused was László Rajk, the country's former minister of the interior. Rajk was a legendary underground Communist during the Fascist period. Unlike Rákosi and other Hungarian Communist leaders who sat out the war in Moscow, Rajk had braved the constant danger to his life and remained in Hungary and continued his underground work with the outlawed Communist party. Rajk had long been an irritation to Rákosi. Because of his worker and partisan background, he was more popular among the workers than the Muscovite theoreticians. Within the party they were well aware of the fact that the Communist seizure of power was mainly Rajk's doing.

During 1948 Hungary was run by a coalition government which included Rajk as the lone Communist. As the one in charge of the department of the interior, he succeeded in infiltrating the police force with Communists and their sympathizers. With the Soviet power's frightening presence looming in the background, Rajk's police saw to it that the Communist party was given a "majority" at a fraudulent counting of votes.

Despite, or perhaps precisely because of this, Rákosi didn't hesitate to strike. The point was to tarnish Rajk in the eyes of the people and the party. He was accused of having been a spy for Marshall Tito and the imperialists ever since he had been an underground Communist, and now he was a betrayer and an enemy of the people and the worker's movement. He was sentenced to death and hanged. After the fall of the Rákosi government less than a decade later, Rajk was "rehabilitated." His corpse was dug up and reburied in a state funeral. His widow and surviving family were awarded state pension. A street in Budapest was named after him, and a commemorative plaque laid down with the inscription "To the memory of László Rajk: indefatigable and fearless fighter for Socialism and proletarian revolution, faithful son of the Hungarian workers' movement."

Szalai had been Rajk's co-worker and was also one of the main accused at the show trial. During the trial he accepted blame for a long series of crimes. He confessed to never having been a true Communist but a spy from the start. What else could be expected from someone who comes from the rotten middle class? asked Szalai rhetorically during the public court proceedings. He confessed that he was unable to identify with the real problems of the workers. He had been infected with the values of Western capitalism from as early as his school years in Switzerland, which further weakened his minimal moral stature. His supposed torture and imprisonment by the Gestapo was just a ruse calculated to disguise his spying from his comrades. This was proved by the fact that he was allowed to stay and peel potatoes in the kitchen, while the other prisoners were forced to do hard labor. András Szalai confessed on all counts. He was sentenced to death and executed with László Rajk, and was later "rehabilitated" together with Rajk.

Tens of thousands of people followed the funeral procession at Rajk's posthumous entombment. One of my colleagues at the university of Budapest walked in the first row along with the psychology professor Sándor Szalai (no relation to András), who had been Rajk's party colleague and good friend. The large throng moved slowly up a hill. The sun broke through and the two professors turned around to look at everyone who followed them.

Poor Laci!* said Professor Szalai; what if he'd been here with us today? What if he'd seen all these people who've come to celebrate him? He'd have been overcome with an undescribable feeling. All of his instincts from his days as minister of the police would have been aroused. He would have commandeered a police force and ordered them to shoot at the mass of people who had gathered spontaneously, without the permission of the party.

Is this gallows humor or post-Stalinist Communist self-recognition? Resigned sarcasm or hope for a better future? Maybe contempt for such collective insanity, or anger because so many had played along without asking questions?

What kind of psychological summersault could make András Szalai first regard Sweden as a police state and then confess to a series of crimes which he had never committed? How can someone believe his own illusions of the ideal state to the degree that he refused to trust his

---

*A diminutive form of László.

own senses and not notice anything of the factual reality in front of him? How does one shut one's eyes to every obvious eye-opener? And what happens later when heaven turns to hell? How can someone who has done nothing to deserve the accusation accept being branded a traitor? Does he hope to be pardoned, or does he hope to protect his family by confessing? Or does the personal integrity of the devout Communist demand that he continue to subscribe to the infallibility of the party even if it costs him his life? Do you feel forced to retain the great illusion even at the price of obliterating your identity, spitting on yourself, and confessing to illusory crimes which lead directly to the gallows?

Many have tried to answer these questions with varying degrees of experience and insight. The riddle was given its most stirring analysis in Arthur Koestler's *Darkness at Noon.** But there probably isn't a simple answer. The powers of inquisition have varied their methods from country to country, from case to case, and from one time to another. Much must also have depended upon the personalities involved and the interaction between the prisoner and his interrogator.

A Hungarian psychiatrist who took care of some ex-prisoners following their release during the first Hungarian wave of liberalization after Stalin's death told me the following story a few years later:

The selection of the unwilling actors for the show trials followed a certain pattern. The chosen victims were religiously faithful communists of Szalai's type. As a rule they were middle-aged and held prominent but not top positions in the party. The most prominent of the accused, like Rajk himself, belonged to another category in that he was a principal target for the leader's power struggle. My source's patients belonged to the "second rank." Their "conspiracies" had been fabricated to add to the believability of the accusers' house of cards.

The ambitious but not too prominent party functionary who had been chosen as a target was usually a somewhat frustrated person. The great day when he would be able to perform some historically significant deed for the party seemed to recede further and further into the future.

---

*(New York: Macmillan, 1984).

Then, suddenly, like a bolt of lightning from a clear sky, he would be arrested without warning in the middle of the night or the early morning and be thrown into a dark, solitary cell for days or weeks without anything at all happening. Isolation breeds fear and depression. The prisoner would be constantly thinking about himself, with his blind belief in the party and its infallibility his only firm frame of reference. He would conclude: I am mediocre at best. But I might be something much worse.

The interrogator would appear after several weeks. Often he would be a fairly pleasant and sympathetic person who would be willing to listen and discuss.

The "interrogations" would begin with rather short conversations. Tell us about yourself. Where are you from? What are your ambitions? What have you done for the party? One hour per day, a few hours. No pressing questions, no bright lights at night, no torture or drugs. Here's a pen and some paper. Write down everything you know; write about yourself. Write, just write.

The prisoner would become increasingly self-involved. His head would be spinning; he would become as if obsessed. The central question and answer would come of their own accord without the interrogator needing to interrogate:

Have I done what the party and I expected of me?

No, I haven't. I'm a pitiful failure.

At this decisive moment a new thought would be introduced. The interrogator would let it unfold and flow forth spontaneously from within the prisoner, and would then only have to stand by like a gentle, experienced midwife. At other times the interrogator would be the one to call the charge: NOW YOU CAN DO YOUR PART! The party is threatened by counterrevolutionaries or revisionists, imperialists or Titoists (or whichever ideological term of abuse would best suit the leader's personal power struggle). You and I are Communists, we belong to the party elite. We can easily recognize the threats to the party. But we cannot expect the simple people to comprehend unless we provide a clear demonstration. The workers and the peasants must be given a clear message; they must know who to love and who to hate without complications. If we put on a grand spectacle we can get them to close ranks and whole-heartedly engage themselves in the struggle against the enemies of the party.

Now you can play your part! You'll be the actor. You'll blacken yourself to provide the people with a fitting target to hate. It will be a great, lasting contribution, far more important than anything you've done so far. You'll become a historical figure within the party.

Their "confession" would fall from their hearts like overripe fruit. In the most "successful" cases the prisoner would want to surpass the director. He would work out the final scenario in perfect agreement with the interrogator. The goal would be to convince the majority of the people and the party's foreign sympathizers that two plus two is five or that the earth is as flat as a pancake. Remarkably enough, this has often worked. Abraham Lincoln's famous dictum that you can fool all the people some of the time, and some of the people all the time, but that you can't fool all the people all the time remained true here as well, but it is remarkable that so many people have been fooled during such long periods by complete Potemkin villages where everything, from the first word to the very last, was an outright lie.

When one of the old revolutionaries who was sentenced in one of Stalin's show trials in Moscow during the 1930s confessed to his made-up crimes, he shouted: "I am a swine. I do not deserve the air that I breathe!" And when he was sentenced to death, his interrogator broke down in tears. Had a strong bond formed between the two men while they collaborated on their fictitious tale of crime and punishment? Had they sacrificed on the same high altar of sacred illusion while they prepared for the martyrdom of one but not the other during their talks? Had they become as involved in their play as the best of actors?

After Stalin's death the show trials have been referred to as "conceptual trials." This is an interesting expression coined during a period when the Soviets were still reluctant to call a spade a spade. Mikhail Gorbachev was the first to use the expression "deliberate falsification." "Conceptual trials" has a more elevated, philosophical ring, but the euphemism conceals a twilight world of nightmares and false confessions. The revolution devoured its fathers; weapons that should have been aimed at the oppressors were aimed at fellow comrades in arms; children reported their parents for their ideological lapses; friendship was recast as treason; love and marriage could lead to prison or even death. Individuals were crushed by a tyranny which pretended to embody an unstoppable historical process. The people were as insignificant as the grains on a dusty road.

During the spring of 1991 the Russian journalist and lawyer Arkadij Vaksberg was interviewed on Swedish radio. He was one of the first to be given access to the KGB's archives and was interested in researching Stalin's show trials. Vaksberg stressed that the scenario of the trials, which had been determined in advance, *was not expected* to have any correspondence with reality whatsoever, even though outside observers found this hard to believe. The trials were outright fabrications from beginning to end. They were formally based on signed "confessions," whose texts had been presented to the prisoner in finished form. If a story was fabricated out of thin air, why hold back: neither small nor large details needed any foundation in reality. Strangely enough the authenticity of the signature under the "confession" remained sacred in this world of deliberate falsification. Why, really? Wouldn't it have been easier to fake the signature too? Was it needed as proof of the individual's ultimate submission to tyranny? Did it fill the same function as forced genuflections and bows to religious authorities? Was it seen as a sign of surrender to a dominant power? But a signature by the signer's own hand has only very seldom saved any of the devout idealists who have dreamt of building a better society. Didn't they foresee where things were heading before it was too late?

Yes, many did, but they were systematically eliminated during Stalin's reign of terror. In his book about Stalin's chief state prosecutor, Andrei Vysjinskij,* Vaksberg remembers the old bolshevik Rjutin who wrote a remarkable document in 1932. It was discussed in private by fifteen other revolutionaries. A few weeks later the meeting was branded a

---

*Arkadij Vaksberg, *Shoot the Mad Dogs!* (Stockholm, 1990). Vysjinskij (1993–1954) conducted the Moscow "Great Purge" trials (1936–1938), which resulted in the deaths of large numbers of people.

"secret conspiracy," which helped seal Rjutin's and the others' fate. The document contained the following words:

> Because of Stalin and his retinue the party and the dictatorship of the proletariat finds itself in an unprecedented detour and is experiencing a fateful crisis. By means of fraud and slander, through countless acts of cruelty and the use of terror and under the pretense of a struggle for the purity of Bolshevik principles and the unity of the party, Stalin has, during the last five years, with the support of the powerful, centralized party apparatus, eliminated the best, tried and true Bolshevik party cadres from leading positions, established his own personal dictatorship in the Bolshevik party and in the country as a whole, abandoned Leninism, and reverted to the most reckless policies and taken the road of deranged personal whim.

According to Vaksberg, the rest of Rjutin's analysis is so on target that it might well have been written today: only the present and future tenses would need to be changed to imperfect. For example:

> The adventurous rate of industrialization, which brings with it an extraordinary lowering of the real wages of workers and office workers; the burdensome direct and indirect taxes; the rising prices and the devaluation of the currency; the adventurous collectivization aided by the campaign against the "Kulaks," a campaign with its main thrust actually directed against the mid-level farmers and the poor masses in the countryside; and finally the expropriation of the countryside through various duties and forced shipments—all of this has led to an extremely severe economic crisis, terrible impoverishment of the masses and famine. . . . Looking ahead, we can expect continued impoverishment of the proletariat . . . every form of personal involvement in the agricultural sector has been eradicated, people work only because of unconcealed coercion and oppression . . .

For today's Western reader, Vysjinskij comes across as the most despicable of all the characters in Vaksberg's book. A highly gifted, prominent lawyer, diplomat, and brilliant speaker, the unscrupulous Vysjin-skij spinelessly put his skills at the service of the corrupt system. There were no limits to his lies and distortions, and no bonds of friendship that he did not hesitate to break. He employed any exaggeration possible when, as prosecutor at the show trials, he called for death sentences for his earlier friends and comrades. Vysjinskij's language sparked a mass psychosis among the accused, who topped each other in accusing them-selves. The same psychosis affected their party comrades who sentenced them without being conscious of the fact that they would themselves be next in line to be accused. This type of language was first used at the earliest show trials in the late twenties. According to Vaksberg that was when the prosecutor

> for the first time used outright terms of abuse. It wasn't just [Vysjin-skij's] characteristically acrid way of expressing himself but outright insults which the Dramatist [meaning Stalin] perhaps hadn't directly put into his mouth, but which were undoubtedly uttered with his blessings. The prosecutor was no longer satisfied with such oratorical terms as "bandits, crooks, charlatans, and contemptuous adventurers who with their dirty feet try to crush the fragrant flowers in the so-cialist garden." He found many other pictures in the rich and evoca-tive language: "Liars and jesters, worthless pygmies, mutts and mon-grels barking at an elephant . . . insidious vandals, . . . loathsome wretches"—were some of the expressions that poured out of the mouth of the hyperintellectual chief judge and replaced the established proofs demanded by a state governed by law. No proofs existed, but the invectives created a psychological illusion that they did.

Vysjinskij's obvious goal was to stay on the side of the angels and at all costs avoid ending up on the side of the accused, which he might very well have done. He eventually died a natural death and received many tributes from Western envoys and politicians for his diplomatic skills as Soviet foreign minister. One need only remember the words of Swedish foreign minister Östen Undén, who in a 1947 conversation with the Swedish Raoul Wallenberg Committee strongly rejected the "dreadful" suggestion that Vysjinskij would lie,* to realize to what extent Western politicians let themselves be fooled by this charming and cunning but utterly criminal person. Undén's positive attitude toward Vysjinskij was shared by politicians in the United States, Great Britain, and France.

A Swedish radio interviewer asked Vaksberg how he experienced toiling in the KGB archives. Wasn't it unbearably painful to plunge into this corrupt world of shadows? "No, since I knew what to expect," he answered. Many details were new, but the rules were known. It was more upsetting to read what Western commentators at the time had to say. The KGB carefully registered all Western media comments on the trials, often for several years after they took place. The tendency of the commentators to accept at least in part the trials' fabrications, the illusion that there must be at least a grain of truth behind the facade, and the frequent use of metaphors such as "no smoke without a fire" is disheartening reading for the modern Russian observer. For us Westerners it is perhaps easier to comprehend the unwillingness or inability to imagine the uncompromising, unmerciful logic of absolute deceit.

"Nessun maggior dolore che ricordarsi del tempo felice nella miseria"—"there is no greater pain than to remember good times in misery," says Virgil to Dante in *Inferno*. One can assume that neither Virgil nor Dante would had been able to imagine another and possibly greater pain which typically besets those prisoners who have been persecuted for many years, often condemned to death, and who have then finally, miraculously been able to reach freedom in some longed-for land: the despondency of not being believed. This often happened to the victims of Nazi and Stalinist terror who escaped to the West and gave

*Rudolph Philipp, *Raoul Wallenberg* (Wiken, 1981). Raoul Wallenberg (1912–1947?), a Swedish businessman, helped approximately 100,000 Hungarian Jews escaper deportation to Nazi death camps. On January 17, 1945, Wallenberg was arrested by the Soviets in Budapest on trumped-up charges and was never heard from again. The Soviets, who later admitted that the arrest was a mistake, claimed that Wallenberg died of a heart attack in a Moscow prison in 1947, but no proof has been offered. Wallenberg is one of only two people to ever receive honorary U.S. citizenship (Winston Churchill is the other).

witness to the hell they had lived through, often in the naive hope that their story would help those they left behind. Confrontations between refugees from the former East bloc and Western Socialists who still believed in the utopian illusions which had already gone bankrupt in the refugee's homeland could be particularly nasty. The ideology's well-fed drawing room representatives of the West, protected by their full democratic rights, did not always shirk from preaching morality to those recently saved from hell. They tried to convince the refugees to put on rose-colored glasses and forget their fresh wounds.

Since I was lucky enough to have left Hungary in the spring of 1948, I myself have experienced this to only very limited degree. But I do remember a small episode from 1949. I had recently gained permission to continue my medical studies in Sweden. Hungary had been run by the Stalinist Rákosi regime for a year and a half, and the process against Rajk was in full swing. Because of our status as refugees, I and a handful of other foreign students had been accepted by royal Swedish permission as so-called exemption students. One of the students in our class was a Polish Jew, ten or fifteen years my senior. He had spent the entire war period in Sweden, but had not been allowed to study earlier. He was a confirmed Communist, and we often found ourselves in heated political discussion. But we reached a crisis with the Rajk process.

When I voiced my suspicion that the Rajk case was a show trial, similar to the Moscow trials against leading revolutionaries during the 1930s, he became very angry. Had anyone been forced to confess to crimes that they hadn't committed? This was totally unthinkable and typical capitalist and counterrevolutionary propaganda! How could you believe such nonsense? The revolution was plagued by many enemies from the very beginning, and the forces of imperialism had done what they could to destroy it. The Soviet state and the new Hungarian state acted correctly when they apprehended the agents of imperialism and got them to confess their despicable crimes. Many of them deserve the death penalty many times over. Who was I to besmirch the homeland of socialism? What did I do while the Russian armies were fighting year after year against the Germans in order to save my life and that of many other Jews?

I answered that I was in Budapest, in the shadow of Auschwitz and the deportations. I survived by pure chance.

He answered me with a violent tantrum. What kind of nonsense is that? I was in my bourgeois parental home studying. He, on the other hand, had to go to Sweden where no one wanted him. He was not admitted to the universities, and had to work in a factory. He was called "damn foreigner" so often that he had lost count. He was the one who suffered, in Sweden—not us middle-class Jews in German-occupied Hungary.

We parted in total discord, and he stopped greeting me. I have always wondered how he felt a few years later when the executed Rajk was rehabilitated in Hungary and the process against him was officially revealed as a fraud. But I also knew that ingrained wishful thinking may keep a personality fraught with inner conflict from rupturing and can be used to deny reality even when faced with irrefutable evidence. People can hold on to their religious and ideological illusions incredibly long. The question is, when has the ultimate limit been reached? What do you do when your worldview finally cracks? What has to happen to make you realize that the entire "meaning" of your life is contradicted by an increasing mass of signals coming through all communication channels and even your own senses, and when reality refuses to obey your expectations? Most people begin by denying reality, or they try to rationalize, explain and, if possible, modify it. You do everything to adjust all news to the deeply rooted patterns of your accepted truths; you treat information as a soft, malleable mass. And you can do this for quite a while. When the mass hardens and can no longer be manipulated, the veil may fall from the eyes of some. But others will even then vigorously defend their right to keep their eyes shut.

Should the moment of truth arrive in its most implacable form, for example when the entire system of power cracks, the pendulum will swing in the other direction for a large majority of those afflicted. Not, however, because they finally begin to use their own eyes and ears to draw the right conclusions, but because most of their friends and others within their cultural circle have changed their opinion. But then, if you have minimal expectations and a pessimistic view of the majority's desire and ability to examine the world and draw their independent conclusions, you must admit that this, after all, may be the best of possible worlds. Who wants solitary Japanese soldiers still fighting World War II in the splendid isolation of the jungle more than thirty years after the conflict has ended? But nothing is unequivocal. What can one say about Jossel Rackower, if you look at him without turning away your eyes? According to the true or apocryphal tale, or perhaps one distilled from many truths,* he was a forty-three-year-old religious Jew, the last surviving member of his family, who stood on the top floor of a bombed-out house in the Warsaw ghetto while the Germans were drenching the ghetto revolt in blood. He and his family had earlier defended the house by throwing Molotov cocktails at the attacking German soldiers, but by now the other family members had been shot to death, one after the other. Their bodies were lying around Jossel and he was next in line. The Germans had gone for reinforcements, and he knew that he had another hour to live at the most. While he waited for the renewed attack, with only three bottles of gasoline left, Jossel wrote a letter to God. I still love you, he wrote, whatever you do to me you will not get me to hate you. You're doing everything you can to crush my faith, but I'll show you that you won't succeed.

Who can judge Jossel in his ultimate moment? Who can argue for stricter rationalism when everyone dear to him lies dead around him, and when all he has left is his desperate dignity in the face of death and his contempt for the executioners?

I must have fallen asleep during my reverie. Someone is knocking at my door. Who can it be? I know no one here.

I open. A man is there with fresh bread and sausage from the country. I've already forgotten that several hours ago I asked for a table in the restaurant. No, it was impossible; all the tables were fully booked since several months back. But they quietly added that for a small private fee one of the waiters could bring some food to my room.

Now he's here and I bid him to enter. He speaks Hungarian. I ask how I can pay him. He looks nervously around, then whispers that he'd

---

*Z. Kolitz, "*Jossel Rachower spricht zu Gott.*" *Judaica* 4 (1983): 211.

like to ask for two dollars, but that I mustn't tell anyone that he has received them; this I must promise.

Two dollars? When I was in Moscow three weeks earlier, I wanted to buy a magnetic phone card for the only telephone at the Intourist hotel through which it was at least theoretically possible to make a direct call to Sweden. The card cost twenty-five rubles, but there were none left. Finally one of the sales people surreptitiously indicated that she happened to have one card left, but that it cost forty-three dollars in cash. I paid, but the card proved useless in helping get through to Sweden within reasonable time. In front of the hotel were rows of taxis, although it had been impossible to hail one in the street. The drivers would pick you up only if you could pay them in dollars. Half a dozen prostitutes dressed in the latest Western fashions were posted around the hotel's carefully guarded entrance, through which one was welcome only with a special hotel pass. According to my Russian colleagues they had appeared a few months ago as a "glasnost phenomenon" and only accepted customers who paid with dollars. I wanted to go for a swim in the pool of a nearby hotel. Only if you pay ten dollars, was the answer.

I look at the waiter. He's waiting for an answer and seems quite scared. I give him five dollars. He is overwhelmed and doesn't know how to express his gratitude. In his authentic, ancient regional Hungarian dialect he continues to beg me not to tell anyone, not even my traveling companions. Shall I tell him about my experiences in Moscow? No, I decide, and instead eat my delicious bread and sausage, that indestructible hymn of the farmers to their land.

The grapevine doesn't appear to be particularly efficient in the deteriorating Soviet empire. I'm in a border zone where everything has become hazy. The clocks testify to the confusion by alternating between Hungarian, Ukrainian, and Moscow time. Everyone watches Hungarian television, but also programs from Moscow and Kiev. If you want to go shopping in Hungary, you also have to consider the time factor. The number of border guards present is determined by Ukrainian time, which therefore influences the lengths of the lines at the border crossings. It isn't clear if anything is still run from Moscow, but you never know.

The fruit is ripe for the picking, the chickens have come home to roost, the wheat grain has for a long time been prepared to die, but the oriental tyranny of the paranoid dictator is only now ready to give up its breath. In retrospect it's easy to see how everything had to follow its given course. When a large multinational state like the Soviet Union looses contact with its own reality, the impending collapse becomes as inevitable as fate in a Greek tragedy. It may take a long time, but it can also occur when no one expects it, which is what actually happened. To an outside observer the unstoppable logic of the process may be difficult to penetrate. I've yet to meet or read about someone who claimed to have predicted the collapse of the Soviet Union.

But what is the next step? Will the bitter old ethnic hatreds lead to civil war? Will racism degenerate into pogroms? Will democracy emerge gradually as it has done earlier in other countries? Will free debate promote more rational solutions than what was possible under central rule? Will the rights of the individual stand up to the all-powerful state and its self-sufficient bureaucracy? Or is the idea of democracy nothing but a reverential pipe dream when confronted with the many problem-ridden nations that lack all democratic traditions? Perhaps. But how has the Scandinavian north, once one of Europe's most violent corners, within just a few centuries turned into such a calm region that many Scandinavians seriously believe that peace and prosperity is the normal state of our species rather than a rare exception which only confirms the contrary rule? If it has happened there, it may also happen here, against all odds. But why is the opposite true of Northern Ireland?

The monotonous gray-brown walls of the bleak Soviet-style Hotel Ukraine seemed fairly friendly when I first saw them, especially when I realized that this was the first time I had set foot in a Soviet hotel room without having to worry about concealed microphones. The microphones —or at least their wires—were probably still there, but were either broken or switched off. But now it seems darker and more threatening again. Am I experiencing the calm before the great disaster?

THE SECOND DAY

We continue our walk with Mrs. Teri along the main street in Kaszony. Miska's house has become a music school which is run-down and poor but teeming with playing and singing children. The former home of the estate owner is now a daycare center where one hundred and eight children whose parents work are sent from all over the region. The staff complains of the poverty and misery, but the children are alert and well-fed, and the walls are covered with brightly colored children's drawings. The large living room is filled with the small beds of many children who sleep here at night.

Once again I'm standing in front of the doctor's house. It wouldn't surprise me if he emerged with his doctor's bag and invited me to come in. The piano is waiting, the coffee is hot. But the doctor and his wife have been gone for many years. What happened to them?

They took their own lives when the gendarmes and the Germans came to get them, answered Mrs. Teri. They asked to go to their bedroom for a moment to get some essentials, and a minute later they were both dead. They knew. They weren't fooled by the ruse of relocation and labor camp. They preferred to die with dignity by their own hand, in their own house.

May we enter?

An older man with a thick shock of white hair is tinkering with his car in the yard. He speaks fluent Hungarian with a heavy accent and introduces himself as the school's Russian teacher of the past few decades. He stresses that he is neither Russian nor Hungarian, but says that his ancestors have lived in this area for many generations. He's a Ruthenian, or a "little Russian," as the Hungarians would say.

When he discovers that I know very little about the Ruthenians he immediately embarks on a history lesson. Linguistically and ethnically the Ruthenians are closely related to the Ukrainians, but they have always stressed their own identity. They differ from the Ukrainians and the Russians because of their history and their special Slavonic-Orthodox religion, which pays tribute to the pope in Rome. For many centuries the region was infamous for its strange and superstitious cults. It had almost always been dominated by more powerful or better educated peoples while many Ruthenians remained illiterate and their culture stagnant. During the Austrian-Hungarian monarchy the Ruthenians lived here as a backward, poverty-ridden minority subsisting on primitive farming.

After World War I their territory became part of the new Czechoslovakia and was allowed a certain amount of autonomy. The Czechs founded many Ruthenian schools, fought illiteracy, improved health care, and modernized the economy. In 1930 "Carpatho-Ruthenia" was inhabited by 725,357 souls. The Ruthenian teacher of Russian knows the figure by heart, but opens the book to show me the region's exact ethnic distribution: 450,925 Ruthenians; 115,804 Hungarians; 95,008 Jews; 34,511 Czechs or Slovaks; 13,804 Germans; and 12,777 Romanians. After the Munich agreement in 1938, the southern and most fertile part of Ruthenia—including Kaszony and environs—was given back to Hungary, while the rest became part of Slovakia. The Slovakian part was called Carpatho-Ukraine, which was very misleading according to the teacher. This promoted the establishment of a strong Ukrainian nationalism. After World War II the entire region was incorporated into the Soviet Union.

The teacher invites me to enter the house. A stocky babushka greets the unknown and unexpected guest with her warm, spontaneous smile. It turns out that she is Ukrainian and the teacher's wife as well as the village's pediatrician. Her Hungarian is not as good as her husband's, but her smile tells me that the children love her. Their two beautiful daughters are students at the Ukrainian university in Uzghorod. They too smile at me and their Hungarian is flawless.

The teacher knew Miska very well. He was my *haver* (pal, buddy), he says. He liked to sit and chat; we saw each other on a daily basis.

What did you talk about?

Only practical things. Miska always began by asking what he could do for me. He wanted to take care of everything.

Did he speak about his murdered family?

Yes, he often spoke about them. I feel as if I knew them all. He also talked about his few surviving family members, including you. I knew that you were doing medical research and lived in Sweden.

How could he stand living here alone?

He wasn't alone. Everyone knew him. People of all kinds cheered up when they saw him. All the villagers were like family to him. But they didn't replace his real family, the ones who were dead. He always carried them with him, along with the pain.

What do you know about the murdered Jews who once lived in this village? Do you know their names?

I know more about them than the Hungarian villagers do, who know very little. I'm writing the history of the village. But you knew many of them. Tell me about them.

We exchange stories: I, who was conceived and spent my early childhood here but who now feels as alien as a Martian; he, who comes from someplace else, but who has lived and worked here during most of his life.

What is my mission in this foreign village? What are these invisible bonds which refuse to break? My childhood? The warm and soothing eyes of my grandmother? The mismanaged houses look pensively at me, as if they had forgotten something but are not sure of exactly what. Is it history's immobile dinosaur footsteps in the petrified cliff? Or is it the ultimate, the unspeakable mass murder of an entire culture?

I am on my way to "the other" cemetery. Not the overgrown, locked-up, fenced-off one that I visited yesterday and where I found my father and grandfather buried beside each other. No, Miska is buried in the new Christian, mixed Catholic-Reformed cemetery; the only one in use when he was buried.

I walk with Mrs. Teri on one of the village's side streets. There has never been any public garbage collection here, she says. In the old days everyone took care of their own garbage without anyone noticing. Now no one wants the trouble. People throw their garbage into the street. Why bother?

How easily our social contract crumbles.

Finding Miska's grave isn't difficult. His portrait adorns the large stone which is topped by a red star, and his name is engraved in both Russian and Hungarian. There are no Jewish or other religious symbols.

Immediately beyond the cemetery is a path which leads to "The Mountain," the vineyard which was owned by my father. It's now totally bare. Here, along this road, I walked with my cousin the summer we both turned fifteen. We said that our forefathers must have walked this road three or four generations earlier, and that they had prepared the path for us. I didn't then imagine my sixty-six-year-old future self returning for a visit. At the time Miska would still be riding his beautiful white horse.

I can see the entire village from the top of "The Mountain." It's exactly the same village as half a century before. It doesn't seem alive, yet it is not dead either. It's like the dinosaurs whose tracks solidified into the rock of the cliff hundreds of millions of years ago while their DNA survive in all of us. It's like time, both measurable and impossible to grasp. The time we've helplessly lost. And time is all we have left.

Trialogue. Mrs. Teri treats me to lunch. The shops are empty but she tempts me with all the goods that this once abundant agricultural region still seems able to provide. Suddenly two people appear. They are uninvited and their simultaneous arrival is a coincidence. The Ruthenian teacher of Russian wants to show me his collection of images of my childhood village which he never knew. A young man, representing the previously forbidden Hungarian cultural association which, thanks to glasnost, has been reconstituted, wants to talk about his association's goals and activities.

A strange conversation ensues. The teacher wants to say something positive. He repeats that he's neither Russian nor Ukrainian but a "russin," i.e., a Ruthenian. He's searching for common Ruthenian and Hungarian ground, and tries to avoid divisive topics. The Hungarian makes no secret of presuming to represent the original inhabitants of the village. He is coolly polite toward the immigrated Ruthenian who has trouble finding the right words. He's careful to phrase his words in as tactful a manner as possible. Does he do it for neighborly reasons or out of personal respect for the teacher? For a moment I think that it's because of the Hungarian's awareness of the fact that the Russian empire is still run by Russians. It may be in a state of disintegration, but perhaps the bear is only wounded and can still gather his strength.

Not many minutes pass before I realize that I'm wrong. The two are united in their harsh criticism of Great Russian "gigantomania." Large tractors and bulldozers have torn across the fields and the vineyards. Everything was demolished and rebuilt while the propaganda machine heralded great promises about the emerging Socialist society and the all-embracing wisdom of the Great Leader. But everything new was much worse than what had gone before. The sloganeering about the dictatorship of the proletariat and the rule of workers and peasants turned out to be an outright swindle. What was instead created was a heaven for ingratiating, servile opportunists. The party's and one's own supposed altruistic solidarity was praised with shameless self-righteousness, while in reality everyone practiced Orwellian "double-think": say one thing but do the opposite! What you should say is dictated by the party's latest directives and by selfish interests. The overriding rule is to always place yourself on the side of the angels, whoever these may be. Only in this way can you retain and hopefully increase your privileges and those of your family. Important posts in such a society are never filled by people who have spent their time obtaining knowledge and competence within their chosen fields. The result instead is a system of self-perpetuating crookedness, where "reliability," i.e., party merits and family connections, is paramount, and where superficial sloganeering about Socialism and the class struggle replaces knowledge. A new elite emerges whose leaders' and officials' primary goal is to get rich at the expense of poor people, while they simultaneously claim to be the people's only true representatives.

This attitude prevailed throughout the Soviet Union and in Kaszony. The few who insisted on stressing expert knowledge were branded as class enemies and jailed, tortured, deported to work camps, or killed outright. Party representatives ruled supreme at every workplace; everyone courted their favors, and they were generally feared. The only thing the representatives had to do was, on the one hand, to flatter and ingratiate themselves to their party bosses, and on the other, to bully, be suspicious of and spy on their workmates and even their families and friends. They didn't have to worry about managing their regular work because no one could or dared to check up on them. Much of their time was spent strutting around the workplace with an air of self-importance, distributing small favors, and, after much fawning from below, finally signing the papers that they should have signed, according to the law, long before and without any special measures. Many were not beyond accepting indirect or direct bribes.

Why did they destroy all the vineyards?

The Michurin biologists, who were disciples of the charlatan Trofim Lysenko,* set the tone and the bulldozers followed. They claimed to know more about the earth than the earth itself and the farmers had known for centuries, but none of their predictions came true. What was planted according to their directions failed miserably; one project after another collapsed. All that remains is devastated soil on a bare hill and an impoverished population, poorer than ever before.

When your Uncle Miska was the chairman of the cooperative, the teacher and the Hungarian suddenly say in unison, Kaszony was awarded the title "Millionaire Village." It was a rare award given only to the most productive villages in the entire Soviet Union. You must have seen all the diplomas up in the office in your father's house. In those days the vineyards of Kaszony produced as much wine per year as the entire Subcarpathian region does today. Back then there was order and discipline.

Was Miska a stern man?

No, he wasn't, but everyone respected him anyway. He was different from other bosses; it was as if he lacked personal interests. Of course he no longer had a family to support, but he appears to have been the same when his family was still alive. His ambition was to create prosperity, to provide for everyone. He succeeded because of his organizational skills, but above all through his personal effort. He had the ability to approach everyone on his or her own level.

Since the Jews left us, says the Hungarian, everything here has declined. There's no leadership, no organization, no desire to do something for others or for the community. Decay, poverty, drunkenness, ineffi-

---

*Josef Stalin's favorite scientist, Trofim Lysenko (1898–1976) supported theories of heredity that denied the existence of genes and held that all parts of an organism take part in heredity. Due to his influence, Stalin outlawed the teaching of approaches toward biology that differed from Lysenko's.

ciency, and laziness characterize our society. As we like to say: After
Lenin tried to turn the workers into Communists, Gorbachev has a tough
time turning Communists into workers.

I express my surprise. What do you mean when you say that the
Jews left you? They were deported and murdered, not by the local inhabitants, but partly with their support.

The Hungarian averts his eyes. He wasn't referring to World War II
and its tragic events. He meant the handful of Jewish families who survived the Holocaust and then returned to the village, like my uncle. They
were few but very important; they had the will to work plus organizational
skills. But sadly, they have since left the village, one after the other.

Why would they want to remain? To confront constantly the shadows
of their murdered relatives? Or to breed new scapegoats for anti-Semitism? There's only one half-Jewish family left in the village. I've just
spoken to them, and they're ready to leave. They've received permission
to leave the country and are only waiting for their airline tickets.
They've been hounded by persistent anonymous telephone calls: Get out
of here, stinking Jew; this isn't your land. The voices speak with a native Hungarian accent and must therefore come from the village or its
near vicinity; calling long distance is hopeless.

The Hungarian squirms in his chair while the teacher nods in agreement. The Ruthenians have never been anti-Semitic, he says; their antipathies are mainly directed against Ukrainians and Russians. They
long for a certain autonomy, like the region's Hungarian population
does. Most Ruthenians are poor farmers who look up to Hungarians in
general and Hungarian Jews in particular. To prove that he hasn't made
this up in order to flatter the Hungarian or me he pulls out a thick
Russian manuscript that is interspersed with photographs. To my astonishment I see many familiar faces: the aunts and uncles of my childhood. I recognize their smiles, I remember how they leaned out of their
windows or saluted me on my way to the synagogue on Friday evening.

Why have you saved all this?

I want to write a history of the Jewish families in Kaszony, since
they're all dead and no one else is doing it.

Our conversation is now cautious and wary. All three of us know, as do the other villagers who have entered the room, that we're navigating dangerous waters. I begin to wish we'd drop the subject and talk about those who are present. My eyes wander over my grandmother's house where our family portraits have been replaced by simple oils illustrating Jesus and Mary. Suddenly I notice my grandmother's undamaged tile stove in the corner. Why didn't I see it earlier? The pattern reminds me of the time when I had put a small cat which I played with on its roof to see if it could jump down. It could, but only after a long period of hesitation. My grandmother happened to come into the room just when the cat jumped. She looked at me with mild reproach that stung worse than the harshest reprimand. Neither one of us said a word, but I decided never to repeat the stunt.

No, I mustn't leave the subject. The coroner must remain with his corpse, the archaeologist dig further, and the paleontologist assemble his bones. I mustn't take the simplest way out: polite, conciliatory conversation. This isn't the proper moment for good-natured superficiality.

I've just visited your cemetery. I saw a memorial which apparently was recently put up, with the inscription: "To the memory of the village's Hungarian martyrs of 1944." Why don't you write that they were Jews? You cannot have meant the later victims of Stalinism who have supposedly been given their own memorial?

This is precisely what I wanted to discuss with you, says the chairman of the Hungarian cultural society somewhat officiously. We're not sure if we should write Jew—zsidó in Hungarian—or Israelite. We thought that it would be more proper to write Israelite, but we felt unsure and therefore wrote nothing.

The term "Israelite" was a traditional euphemism from the days of the Habsburg monarchy. It was used in polite conversation between Jews and gentiles in much the same way that we avoid talking to an invalid about his disability. The word zsidó, on the other hand, was frequently used by anti-Semites and has therefore gained a denigrating tone, somewhat like "nigger" in America.

I become quite irritated. There's no reason to worry about this distinction today. It was an important part of the great tragedy of the Hungarian-Jewish bourgeoisie that the mendacious euphemism "Israelite" was accepted, even when it was used by the basically anti-Semitic Hungarian aristocracy or the minor nobility, which the Jews often despised but whose favors they were quick to court. I don't want to deny that we often rely on euphemisms in other situations. We say "pass away" and "expire" instead of "die"; we say "make love" instead of the various appealing or ugly but straight-forward words which describe the act of copulation; we say "Holocaust" instead of "mass murder." But I don't want to accept the euphemism "Israelite," not here and now. The toadying before the anti-Semites must come to an end. If I may speak for the dead, they should be called Jews, nothing else.

Everyone nods in agreement. Our mutual understanding is total. But I know that the basic attitudes haven't changed since I was last here almost half a century ago. Like many other regions in Central and Eastern Europe, the Danube basin remains, for the foreseeable future, a fertile ground for ethnic, religious, and social conflict.

Have they read my thoughts? Has some unconscious signal passed around the room? Suddenly the Ruthenian and the Hungarian strike up a chorus of mutual complaint which leads to their merciless condemnation of the Gypsies who inhabit the outskirts of Kaszony. The Gypsies prosper through the efforts of others; they live high on stolen money; they lie, swindle, and cheat. Round and round spins the merry tune. My inner ear replaces the word "Gypsy" with the word "Jew." I remember the boy who pissed on me with glowing hatred in his eyes and I remember my grandmother as she lit candles every Friday evening in this room.

Now I understand why everyone loved Miska. He never thought like this or talked like this. To him this chorus was as unreal as a priest's sermon or the propaganda speech of a party hack. Miska could communicate with everyone, regardless of their language or to which group they belonged, just as he could converse with all children. He was simply unable to classify people according to their origins. Was this why he could so easily become a gold-medaled Hungarian soldier during World War I, a fire chief and influential villager under Czech rule, and the chairman of the village cooperative under the Soviets? Was it this universality that made him a loyal Jew, a good Hungarian and a convinced supporter of the democratic system in Tomas Masaryk's Czechoslovakia?* He did become a boss and member of the Communist party during his last, Soviet, period, but my witnesses emphasized time and again that unlike other Communists he never told people what to think. He received many official Soviet visitors, and sometimes high party functionaries, and while he plied them with liquor he always remained sober. After a certain amount of alcohol had been consumed some of the visitors would inevitably begin to complain about the system, but Miska would remain silent. He regarded the situation as unchangeable. To those around him he always extolled the importance of listening rather than speaking.

Was he a man without principles who merely followed the crowd? Or was he a tolerant pragmatist who always tried to do something positive for others? This nephew, a stranger to the villagers who is nevertheless greeted with open arms thanks to the memory of his uncle twenty-two years after his death, prefers to believe the latter.

How do *you* remember your uncle? A teenager who has listened in intense silence asks this unexpected question.

Do you know that there was only one movie house when I was young, I ask the boy. It was an old storage space around the corner here with one single showing every Saturday night?

Yes, it's still there, he says. It's still the only cinema in town, but now there's a showing only once a month. Why do you ask?

Miska used to bring me and my cousins there during the summer when we were teenagers. About a minute after the film began, he'd fall asleep, and he'd wake up the moment the film was over. He came along only for our sake. When he visited us in Budapest, he would "steal" me and my cousin of about the same age away from our parents and take us to the city's best cafés that we'd only heard about before. Once there he'd let us order whatever we wanted. But this was only part of our treat. The next day we'd discover a hundred-pengö note or two in our jackets

---

*Tomas Masaryk (1850–1937) was the founder and first president of the Czechoslovak Republic.

which must have been smuggled there with the skill worthy of a pickpocket. For boys with a weekly allowance of perhaps a ten-pengö note this was a temporary entry ticket to the world of grown-up liberties. When we were older he would ask us what we wanted to do. Once I asked him to take me to a theater, and he took me to a very exciting performance of Pirandello's *Henry IV.* He bought us the best seats in the house. He then slept through the entire performance, but woke up in time for intermission when he treated me to soft drinks and cake in the hall of mirrors, where I'd never been before.

Sometimes I tried to ask Miska what his teen years had been like. He never really answered, but others in the family told me a little here and there. When he was thirteen he apparently opened up a "shop" in school. He'd buy and sell everything including school books, pocket knives, boys' caps, and toys, and became a young entrepreneur at fourteen. Now, when he was older, he wanted to treat us spoiled city kids to whatever he had saved up through his hard work.

We recognize this, says Mrs. Teri's daughter. It's just like the way he wanted to give away everything when he lived here with us.

My hosts keep returning to Miska's "generosity," but I think it's the wrong word. The entire concept is based on its opposite: stinginess, unfriendliness, contempt—these time-honored attitudes toward other ethnic, religious, or social groups as well as other social classes within one's own ethnic group. They were probably a means of survival in the multiethnic Austrian-Hungarian Empire, especially during periods of famine and pestilence, but they've become stereotypes and an end in themselves. The indoctrination of the children began early in life. Suspicion and aversion were built into the children's tales as obligatory ingredients. When I began school I soon heard of and read about dirty Romanians, murderous Serbs, and cowardly Czechs. "Educational" tales embraced proverbial "moralities" such as: "Beware of letting a Slovak into your house or you'll loose it." In first grade we sang this pretty old children's song: "Stork, stork, little stork, why is your foot bleeding? Turkish boy has cut me, Hungarian boy will cure me." The Hungarian of the stories was always good, heroic, strong, just, clean, and tender.

The neighboring peoples and the many ethnic minorities in the quilt-like empire were described accordingly except that the positive and negative characteristics were reversed. Jews were doubly victimized: both as Jews and as members of the ethnic group whose language they spoke and who frequently discriminated against them.

This environment fostered an indifference toward the problems of other groups, however difficult they might be. Less well-to-do social classes within one's own ethnic group were also treated without empathy, a pattern facilitated by the feudal social order. In some cases the class differences are still built into the language. Many proverbial phrases express subservience toward "the lords" or "the masters," whoever these may be. In literal Swedish translation these expressions appear ridiculously servile and incomprehensibly self-deprecating, but they're still in constant, natural use in the original languages. It was just as natural to feel sympathetic only toward members of one's own ethic group or social class. In its most extreme form positive emotions were even more circumscribed, encompassing only one's own family or simply certain members of it. Many of these usually wholly unconscious tendencies are still in evidence today. You're only interested in "us," never in "them." Many events during World War II that are incomprehensible to a modern observer, for example the broad indifference to the victims of the Holocaust, can be regarded in this light.

Miska's inborn immunity against these categorizations is clearly related to his communicative skills. He took as much personal interest in Hungarian farmers as in Jewish merchants and gave their children the same candy. Everyone got to play with the large mouse traps and the many other exciting objects a child can find in a hardware store. Thanks to his language skills Miska had no difficulty exchanging confidences with the Ruthenian farmers who came down from the blue mountains on the horizon. For me and most others they were strangers who came from a remote landscape, spoke an incomprehensible language and wrote with unreadable letters. Only Miska could talk with the coachman and the stable hand as if they were his own family members and without sounding tense or artificial.

THE SECOND NIGHT

I return to my dull hotel in Uzhgorod. It is Saturday evening and the hotel appears to be under siege. The guard behind the glass door who only admits hotel guests with special passes is backed up by a stocky, uniformed man. For extra security they've put a large U-shaped iron bar on the inside of the gate which makes it impossible to open unless you want to smash the large glass windows. The guards remain immobile behind the glass, their indifferent faces staring at the mass of people outside, their gaze remaining cold. What's going on? Is it a political demonstration? Or some kind of assault?

As I force my way through I notice that the crowd mostly consists of youths who are dressed up under their worn jackets and coats.

I begin to understand. It's simply the Saturday night dance at the town's best hotel. Hotel Saga in Reykavik would be no less closely guarded on a Saturday evening. The throng is the same, and the guards display the same aloof air of impassibility. But there's a world of a difference. The tall young vikings who guard the Reykavik hotel could at any time exchange places with the kids waiting to get in. Another Saturday night they may be the ones lining up outside the hotel dressed in colorful shirts and jeans or whatever they wear to go out at this particular moment. The roles are interchangeable. When employed by the police, you act the role of a policeman. When off-duty, you can dance or get drunk on Saturday night if you feel like it or if you need to for the sake of your friends. But not here. These guards serve the authorities, and they always have, and therefore they cannot socialize with the youngsters on their night off. Today's young generation does seem to be gaining self-confidence, but the situation is still fluid. Are they free now? The guards don't know. Yesterday the youths risked being arrested for "hooliganism," a serious charge which could be directed at anyone, with or without cause. You could easily have been jailed or disappeared for less, say critics of the regime. There used to be law and order, say the conservatives. The system is in its death throes but its many guards continue to play their usual roles, even though the director has long since left the stage.

I show my passport and they let me in. I cast a glance toward the over-crowded dance hall with its deafening music—or rather music surrogate. In a desperate attempt to retain some thoughts in my head and without embarrassment I apply my earplugs. The dancers don't seem to mind the noise. The smoke is thick above their heads, their faces are shining with sweat, and there's hardly any room left on the dance floor. Some girls who must have seen too many American TV-shows have dressed in silvery glitterworks, but they move like stiff marionettes on invisible strings ma-neuvered by unskilled hands. The boys are dressed in what seem to be home-sewn tuxedos or tails—so this is what was hidden under their worn coats. There is obviously nothing "fancier" to do on a Saturday evening in the provincial capital than to dance at the Hotel Ukraine.

It's like watching a crowd of tightly reined-in kindergarten kids who've been permitted to participate in a party where they don't really know what to do and where they feel shy because of the attention, the noise, and the bright lights. At the same time they seem eager to construct an adult world based on the radio waves that their electronic ears have picked up from the "real world," where people own cars, houses, and swimming pools and consume an abundance of food, and where milk and honey and whisky and beer and anything desirable flows freely from the faucets. That's where the action is, and where your life can be grand, meaningful, and exciting. I think: If they only knew. . . . But they know nothing about the outside, "real" world yet, only that they've once and for all had enough of their boring kindergarten, and want to tear down the walls and escape. . . . To where? From the line in front of my hotel to another line somewhere else, in their vain hope to get past the no-longer-existing authority or, rather, its remaining and still definitely ponderous guards.

It's difficult to look away. Where have the strong and eternal themes of nature disappeared; where is the sublime rhythm of eroticism? The contrast between it and what I see before me is as sharp as between "the apotheosis of dance," that irresistible rhythm of Beethoven's Seventh Symphony, and soulless muzak in a dull restaurant where everyone avoids everyone else and longs to be elsewhere. Who has been able to strangle the pulse which provides each one of his marionettes with a temporary feeling of omnipotent eternity? No, I cannot with best ability discern it here. Either it's been suffocated by the circumstances, or it's hiding behind the Victorian veil of the rules of this kindergarten.

What kind of kindergarten have these children and their parents attended?

What kind of déjà vu am I experiencing? Who first told me about the great kindergarten?

The First Circle. In 1950 the German radiation biologist K. G. Zimmer came to Torbjörn Caspersson's Department of Cell Research in Stockholm where I was employed as an assistant. He was the first real eye-witness from Stalin's Soviet Union that I had met. He was already a scientist with an international reputation when he became a prisoner of war and was taken to a top secret research facility in the Caucasus where he was held for five years. The entire scientific staff consisted of Russian labor camp prisoners and German prisoners of war. When I read Aleksandr Solzhenitsyn's novel *The First Circle** many years later I went from one experience of déjà vu to another. The novel describes exactly the same kind of facility that Zimmer talked about. Where Zimmer worked the German prisoners of war were treated much better than the enslaved Russian scientists. Despite his prisoner-of-war-status, which he shared with everyone else, Zimmer could support his entire family in West Germany on the salary he made. All scientists were body-searched when entering and leaving their laboratory every morning and evening. They were ordered to conduct their experiments and to pen the results into chained notebooks with numbered pages. The notebooks were collected in the evening by armed guards and locked inside a safe until morning.

The instructions for the experiments came from the commanding authorities, not from scientists. Zimmer's task was to study the distribution of inhaled radioactive elements inside the body of a rat, for example

---

*(New York: Harper & Row, 1968).

strontium and other products created by nuclear blasts. According to Zimmer the experiments were "extremely boring but important." Four decades later, and especially after the 1986 nuclear reactor melt-down at Chernobyl, one may wonder whether advanced research of this type, conducted in secrecy, may ever—even later, in more peaceful times— gain any importance in a gigantic, undeveloped country which combines advanced nuclear technology with an inferior infrastructure.

Zimmer and his colleagues regularly had to report their results to the commanding authorities, but never received any comments in return. They never knew whether their work was approved, whether the authorities were content, or if the results were useful. Instead they were regularly given new instructions without apparent connection to their previous work. Zimmer and his German colleagues felt like children in a kindergarten. They were treated fairly well, but they had no contact with the outside world and lacked any possibility of influencing their situation.

While Zimmer was in Stockholm, we received a visit by a Russian governmental delegation consisting of architects who were projecting a new medical school and led by an assistant minister of health. My chief, Torbjörn Caspersson, myself, and the architect of the Karolinska Institute were escorting the delegation. They had brought an interpreter who translated everything we said, but none of the delegation's Russian members opened their mouths during the lengthy tour. Finally we arrived at a newly built but unfurnished laboratory which Torbjörn Caspersson indicated would be used for virological research. Suddenly the vice minister of health spoke up:

"Excuse me for asking a question. I know how much trouble questions can cause. If you by any chance don't want to answer my question, for example for classified military reasons, please refrain from answering. But if I may still ask my question, I'd very much like to know how you've arranged the ventilation in this room."

We chuckled at the question and took it as an example of typical Russian paranoia. When we told Zimmer, he remained serious. It was a very good question, he said, but you have to understand why it was asked. The assistant minister wasn't at all interested in the ventilation.

He has to write a report about his trip which will go directly to the NKVD (the KGB's predecessor). In order to have something to report, he needs to find out whether our institute is working for the defense department. While the interpreter is busy interpreting, he studies his hosts' faces. If everyone laughs, he draws the conclusion that the military isn't involved. If the question is taken seriously and complicated explanations are provided, it proves that military research is being done.

Why would the NKVD or the KGB want all this information? Did they really use it or did they collect it mainly in order to keep the enormous bureaucracy busy and/or in order to remind the citizens that the secret police was constantly watching them? The latter answer is probably the best. Fear was a constant element in Soviet society from top to bottom. At about the same time as Zimmer's stay in Stockholm, an Austrian colleague arrived for a visit from Vienna. This was during the time when Vienna was divided into four sectors, each occupied by one of the four Allied Armies. My colleague's wife had a doctorate in Slavic languages and was now employed as an interpreter for official Russian visitors at the Viennese city hall. Many of her guests were high Russian officers. Being unaware of the inner atmosphere of the Soviet system she always began by introducing herself and expecting her guests to do the same. But they never did; colonels and generals never even mentioned their names. Sometimes she would ask directly, only to find out later that the name would be false. Later she noticed that the visiting Soviet officers didn't even introduce themselves to each other. When she told this to a Soviet official who had been stationed in Vienna for a long time and whom she knew relatively well, he laughed. He explained to her confidentially that you have to be careful when you visit an official Western institution since you never know which remarks you might happen to make are recorded, or how your remarks are twisted and misrepresented. The best way to avoid ending up in an unfavorable light in someone else's report—and everyone knew that everyone else had to write one too—was simply to keep your name a secret. This habit became as automatic for the Soviet officers as the various stratagems New Yorkers employ to avoid theft and assault in dangerous neighborhoods.

But if the Soviet authorities could fabricate any kind of charge out of thin air, what ends did all the reports serve?

The significance of the reports were probably more in the atmosphere of suspicion and fear that they created than in the direct information that they contained. "The party," or rather the dictator, wanted everyone to feel as if he were under constant surveillance. There are many anecdotes, but I will limit myself to two.

During the Brezhnev era the Russian biochemist and gerontologist Zhores Medvedev decided to find out through a series of scientific experiments how the Russian censorship of the mail system operated.* Being a natural scientist, Medvedev began by working out his methodology. He bought a strong glue which wouldn't dissolve when an envelope was subjected to steam—the usual clandestine method of opening letters. He then addressed fifty envelopes to nonexisting recipients in other countries, and listed himself as the sender of every one. The envelopes were carefully numbered and after Medvedev slipped in a note containing a few empty phrases in each one of them, he sealed half of them with the strong glue and the other half in the usual way. The letters were sent out and after some time they were returned rubber-stamped "addressee unknown." All envelopes that had been sealed with the strong glue were severely damaged, leading Medvedev to conclude that they had been opened.

Now the real experiment could begin. His first task was to figure out whether all of the letters sent to foreign countries had been opened, regardless of whether they'd been posted from an airport, a large postal station, or a small village. Yes, all foreign letters had been opened, regardless of point of origin. Domestic letters from within the Soviet Union were not all opened; in this case the authorities were content with making spot checks. The next question was if the contents of the letters had some measurable effect. Medvedev, who often had proved his courage as a critic of the government, wrote a number of letters by hand that were critical of the system and mailed them in the same manner as

---

*Z. Medvedev, *The Medvedev Papers: The Plight of Soviet Science* (London: Macmillan, 1971).

the previous letters. The letters went out and were returned. They'd been opened, but nothing else had happened. Next he enclosed clipped newspaper articles with the letters. Now something happened: the envelope returned with the letter, but the clipping was gone. Then he tried to ascertain whether it mattered if he included, for example, a political article, a cultural column, personal ads, or governmental announcements. It didn't matter. All printed matter was confiscated, regardless of content. Medvedev concluded that the Soviet censorship functioned in a mechanical manner, like a brainless robot.

Medvedev did encounter a less brainless phenomenon with another experiment. The two most important general magazines for science, *Nature* and *Science*, were available at all university libraries in the Soviet Union, but they always arrived almost a year late. Once, when Medvedev couldn't find on the correct page an article in *Science* which had been mentioned as a reference in other magazines, he began to wonder about the causes for this delay. He wrote a letter to *Science* in New York asking how many subscribers there were in the Soviet Union. Five, was the answer. Consequently the issues in the Russian libraries were skillfully made photocopies. Medvedev decided to find out whether they'd been censured, and if so, what had been removed.

With the help of the magazines' index and ten-year index Medvedev could reconstruct the titles of various missing articles that had been replaced by other texts—usually advertisements—from previous issues. One obvious category subject to thorough censorship was articles about the Soviet Union. But there was another type of article that was as regularly censored. I have amused myself by asking friends and colleagues if they could guess what these articles were about. No one I have asked—at least thirty people—made the correct guess, and I wouldn't have been able to pick the right one either, even though the answer is logical and makes perfect sense. The censors regularly removed the rather numerous articles which in one way or another revealed that foreign scientists had criticized their own government.

The kindergarten, the love of secrecy, imprisonments, surveillance, the cult of fear and suspicion: these were some of the expedient and paranoid methods of the Soviet reign of terror—and at least as long as the Great Leader and Teacher and his likeminded successors were still in charge, they were quite effective.

After Stalin's death the system weakened, but very slowly. Established institutions guard their turfs in all systems, even after they've lost all self-justification. The first and most rapid changes occurred in my homeland, Hungary. In the early 1970s when Kádárism* was still young, I received a letter from a close friend in Budapest, the artistic and managing theater director Ottó Adám. At this point in time Ottó was often in the news and quite well-known to the Hungarian public. The Madách theater, which he led, was constantly trying to provoke the censors by experimenting with ever bolder plays which in one way or another touched upon the nation's most urgent trauma—Stalinism, only recently deceased and not yet fully buried. You could speak relatively freely as long as you didn't touch upon the following three taboo subjects: the Soviet Union, the secret police, and Israel. Censorship was still in effect, but in a more unpredictable manner. The secret police had eased up on their methods, people no longer disappeared, and the executions had ceased, but the organization was still there.

Ottó wanted his son to study abroad. After investigating some possibilities I wanted to speak with him directly on the phone. I dialed his number in Budapest and a male voice answered. "Is this Ottó Adám?" I asked. "Yes, this is I," said the voice. "Hi, this is George from Stockholm," I began, but was interrupted after my second sentence by the voice, which claimed to have no idea who I was. "Is this Ottó Adám?" I asked again. "Yes, that's my name," the voice answered. The name is not a common one, and as I found out later, he was the only one registered in the phone book with this name other than my friend. "Is your phone number 125 . . . ?" I asked and mentioned the number that I had just called. "No, not at all," he answered. "My number is 437. . . . You've dialed the wrong number." "But I can't have misdialed to that degree," I

---

*Kádárism was the relatively liberal reform Communism that characterized the Kádár regime.

protested. "The numbers are totally different, and besides, you have the same name!" "It's not my fault," he said with irritation, and hung up.

I tried again, dialed the same number and got the same man on the line. Now he was really angry. He didn't understand either, but he was not interested and had better things to do. He hung up again.

I called the international operator in Stockholm and said that I had tried to call someone in Budapest but had reached a different person with the same name and a completely different number. She'd never heard of such a case. I then asked her to help me make a personal call. After a while she called me back saying that the same thing had happened to her; she'd dialed the number but reached a completely different number although the person had the same name.

I got suspicious. I stopped calling and instead sent a telegram with the text: "I'm trying to call you, but transcendental powers are stopping me from getting through."

I immediately received the following telegram in reply: "Yes, but they're transcendental powers set in motion by evil people."

A few months later I visited Ottó in his Budapest home. He laughed at my story. All our conversations are registered, he said. The telephone in front of us on the table registers everything that happens here—even now. They hear every word you and I say. Often we hear clicking noises during our conversations as if a tape recorder was being started or turned off. I'm regarded as a person capable of influencing public opinion. All such people's telephones are routed straight to the secret police. The day you called some idiot must have misconnected the wires so that your call to me came in through some tape recorder but was then re-routed to the only person in the catalogue with the same name.

But how can you speak so freely about all this if our conversation is being recorded?

What we say is of no importance; we can say whatever we want. No one cares, and I doubt that anyone will ever listen to our conversation. If the authorities decide to kick me out, they can do so in five minutes without listening to anything. This entire spying apparatus was set up under Stalin, but even then the main point was to keep fear and suspicion alive rather than to actually collect information. Today this system is a fossil, but it keeps a number of people busy who otherwise would have nothing to do and can neither be fired nor transferred to other positions.

What happens to a system encumbered with an enormous bureaucracy which collects, reports, and records countless conversations but never uses them? In all likelihood the bureaucrats themselves realize that their work is meaningless. Add the secrecy to the absence of modern computer technology and one can only expect that their archives are in tremendous disorder. My suspicion has recently been confirmed within my own field.

Like all statistics on disease in the Soviet Union, cancer statistics were classified. Soviet cancer epidemiologists—of which several have held important international positions at the World Health Organization in Geneva and were well informed about cancer statistics from the rest of the world—were as uninformed about cancer statistics in their own country as were their Western colleagues. The Soviet Union was a white spot on the map.

Now the information has been made available and the Russian epidemiologists have immediately dug into the archives to uncover all the information that they've unsuccessfully tried to obtain for many years. It simply wasn't available anywhere! Only fragmentary, incomplete, and unsorted reports were available. This mindless secrecy has prevented not just the information from scrutiny but it had also concealed those who collected it. The entire point of collecting data was lost, due to the total absence of criticism, questioning, and inspection which is a necessary part of any democratic system. Instead of inquisitive scientists eager to study the material in order to draw conclusions or to test hypotheses, the system produced soulless bureaucrats uninterested in work or in testing whether their collected data was complete or even representative. They apparently hadn't even made the effort to insure that the information was stored in an ordered way. A Russian cancer epidemiologist told me that he and his colleagues now had to start from scratch, as if the earlier, very expensive organization and its many years of work simply hadn't existed.

Man has the ability not just to adapt to outright absurdities, if those in power so decide, but also to regard absurdities as a natural state of affairs. In the early 1960s, when the first Russian scholarship students were let out to study at American research departments, a Polish-American colleague of mine had two Poles and a Russian working at his department during the same period. The Poles despised the Russian according to their traditions, but they also feared him. The Russian was happy to have two comrades from the "Socialist bloc" close by. He told them a few secrets, for example about his obligation to visit the Soviet embassy in Washington, D.C., every week in order to deliver his report about everything he'd seen and heard. The Poles faithfully reported to their fatherly compatriot, the American boss.

One day the Russian cheerfully told the Poles that he'd gotten hold of an important secret which surely would be appreciated in Moscow. He'd been called in to see the boss, but the man wasn't in his office. The Russian happened to see a stenciled folder on the boss's desk and quickly peeked at it. It was the official American polio statistics, obviously a top secret document. He wrote down the most important figures in great haste. Now he really had something to report!

The folder that he'd happened to see was a statistical periodical available at every library and every microbiological institution. It contained no secrets whatsoever. But then, how could the Russian have realized that?

A constant theme of Soviet society was that the secrecy surrounding the gathering of information about health issues—or, for that matter, the collection of data in general—was more important than to solve the issues at hand, for example the health problem of Soviet citizens. There were many variations on this theme but common to all was that a higher priority was given to the system than to the citizens, as if one would prefer the package to its contents. Throughout the Soviet medical and health care system, political control was more important than the professional search for knowledge, experience, and solutions.

The consequences of this mentality were ghoulishly evident after the Chernobyl disaster. One of the doctors flown in by the American billionaire Armand Hammer to save victims of radiation told me how the doctors' work was constantly impeded by officials whose only job was to keep foreign journalists away from the medical team. Their task was not, as they claimed, to insure calm working conditions for the doctors. The first difficulties arose even before the medical team left the United States when they were told that the doctors weren't allowed to bring their own nurses and lab assistants despite the fact that Hammer was willing to pick up the tab. The reason wasn't specified at first, but after they arrived in the Soviet Union they found out that every member of the medical team was watched by about ten Russians who ensured that the doctors only spoke with people who were "officially approved." There simply wouldn't have been enough overseers to keep a watch on the technical staff as well!

Even when the medical team was hard at work the authorities put a higher emphasis on secrecy than on the efforts of the doctors to save the lives of as many as possible of those stricken with radiation poisoning. The doctors were given infected, dusty rooms rather than more practical spaces in the hospital's routine labs, and their pleas for rapid practical rearrangements were rejected with the explanation that they first had to ask the authorities in Moscow for permission, and that it would take weeks, even months, before they could expect an answer.

How and to what extent have doctors and scientists let themselves fall into this trap? According to my own limited experience, most of them adapted to the authorities' demands no matter how political and irrational they were, and only a minority kept their integrity. During the last weeks before I finally left Hungary in late 1947 and early 1948, when the Communists who had gained power through a sham election were in the process of consolidating their positions, an interesting spectacle was in progress before our inexperienced student eyes.

Between the two world wars one of the most brilliant clinical directors in Hungary was Professor Istvan Rusznyák, a converted Jew, highly intellectual central European, brilliant lecturer, and reputable diagnostician with a charming personality. During the half-fascistic Horthy regime* Rusznyák was, despite his Jewish origins, made professor of internal medicine and head of the clinic at the University of Szeged—a very unusual appointment. Immediately after the end of the war he joined the Communist party.

Rusznyák's lectures were very popular among us students since he was one of the teachers with the ability to really inspire. An hour's lecture on tuberculosis would reach far beyond the medical aspects of the disease, which he would begin by summarizing in a correct but succinct manner. After stating that the details could be learned from any textbook, he would proceeded to discuss tuberculosis as it's been portrayed in art and literature. Thus Hans Castorp's tuberculosis in Thomas Mann's novel *The Magic Mountain* became as important to some of us as the actual case histories. Some of the students devoured the novel and the textbook on internal medicine with the same eagerness. We experienced the two as mutually complementary and felt doubly stimulated.

Rusznyák's well-reasoned, sharp-witted, and articulate lectures were very different from the rhapsodic and unpredictable but no less fascinating lectures—if one may call them such—of the other professor of internal medicine, Imre Haynal. Each time the bell at the university's second clinic for internal medicine summoned the students to the lecture hall, no one knew if the head of the clinic would be present. Half an hour could pass before an embarrassed associate professor appeared saying that Professor Haynal was absent, for reasons unknown. Then the man would conduct a boring, ill-prepared lecture. The pace picked up when Haynal finally arrived, even if he would appear only ten minutes prior to the end of the appointed lecture time. With Haynal anything could happen: a spectacular medical demonstration, a combination of intuitive diagnostics with precise data, or free associations about anything under the sun. At times the professor could be cruelly ironic at the expense of incompetent interns or ignorant candidates, or he would deliver a partly jocular, partly incisive homily about the absurdities of life.

---

*Vitez Nicholas Horthy de Nagybanya (1868–1957), a Hungarian admiral, was elected regent of Hungary in 1920 and overthrown in 1944.

Whatever Haynal did, it was never boring. He himself would declare that "Sometimes it's a circus, sometimes a lecture. You'll never know which in advance. Most of you are here to see the circus, and a circus is what you'll get. But sometimes you'll learn something too."

Perhaps we did. But what was most fascinating was the contrast between Rusznyák's and Haynal's attitudes toward the recent but not yet fully consolidated Communist seizure of power. Before and during World War II Rusznyák was a widely respected and sought-after physician for members of Hungarian high society, including its faction of anti-Semitic aristocrats. Haynal, who, in contrast to Rusznyák, was of old Hungarian stock, was appointed professor at the university in Kolozsvár, the most important city in Transylvania. Kolozsvár was returned to Hungary after the Munich agreement (one of Hitler's tricks by which he lured Hungary into the war) and retained until the end of World War II. It was only after the war that Haynal and Rusznyák became directors of Budapest's and the country's two most important university clinics for internal medicine. Transylvanian students recounted how the Hungarian Nazis had ravaged the University of Kolozsvár just after the town had been returned to Hungary. Marching from one lecture hall to another they violently harassed and evicted all Jewish students. Such behavior was a clear violation of the university's autonomy; according to an old but still existing law each university professor had the sovereign right to permit or forbid any outside person—including the representatives of the state—to enter his institution.

Haynal was a highly decorated officer from World War I and still kept his service weapons at home. He carried a special title before his name—*vitéz* in Hungarian—given only to soldiers who became known for some particularly distinguished achievement on the battlefield. It had the ring of an aristocratic title and actually means "valiant." Feudal Hungary had a mania for titles. The title *vitéz* was rare among people with university degrees and was usually carried by its bearer with a great sense of pride. Haynal never used it during normal circumstances. But when the anti-Semitic students marched up to his clinic he confronted them in front of the gate, aimed his service revolver at the demonstrators and proclaimed the following words, which became legendary:

"I, Vitéz Imre Haynal, will personally shoot anyone who attempts to enter my clinic without my permission."

Nobody dared to enter and the Jewish students were left unmolested.

Although it took two and a half years before the Hungarian Communists seized power after World War II, the Yalta agreement had already assigned Hungary to the Soviet sphere of interest. Because of his early entry into the party immediately after the war and his great prestige as a medical doctor, Rusznyák attained a key position among party intellectuals. He was elected to various important committees and became a member of parliament. He was later appointed General Secretary of the Soviet-Hungarian Cultural Society, then President of the Academy of Science, and finally, a member of the highest executive body of the Communist party. It was a strange career. Rusznyák had always belonged to the upper bourgeoisie and had never broken black bread with the workers, either figuratively or literally. His magnificent villa was filled with a valuable art collection to which he kept adding. It was astonishing to observe how this inspiring interpreter of Thomas Mann absorbed without qualms an ideological vocabulary totally alien to his basic liberal beliefs and pronounced humanist background.

Just before we left Hungary in 1948 Stalinism became a force to be reckoned with at all universities, schools, and workplaces. The guardians of purity appeared everywhere in various guises. At the initiative of the party representative, who was often a lab assistant, janitor, or student, some university departments introduced a mandatory weekly "hour for self-criticism." Each participant had to stand up and "confess" that he or she had lapsed in "revolutionary vigilance." The internationally renowned, elderly professor of pharmacology, Béla Issekutz, was obviously very unpleasantly affected by being the center of the spectacle when his turn came. After some hesitation he told everyone about his "cowardice" when hadn't dared to interrupt a conversation which he'd overheard between two men in the street who had slandered the People's Republic and its leader. The professor regretted his sin of omission and promised to reform. The party representative expressed his displeasure at this timidity and cautioned all members of the departmental staff to be wary of the self-indulgent bourgeoisie which would never learn from its mistakes.

One of the last days before we passed through the narrowing gate to freedom we attended a lecture by Haynal. It was a wet day in February. The professor was late and the students were getting restless. Some reverted to elementary school behavior and began to pelt each other with paper balls, while others tried to study or flirt with the girls. The clinic assistants shuffled nervously in their seats and didn't dare commence the lecture without specific instructions. A quarter before the end of the lecture when everyone had abandoned hope, Haynal burst in dressed in rubber boots, a scarf, an overcoat, and a hat. He tossed his hat and coat on a chair but kept his boots on, and immediately began to speak as if he was merely continuing a monologue in progress.

The danger with us professors, said Haynal, is that we know more about one small segment of knowledge than most of our fellow creatures. Once we've become authorities within our respective fields, we're seldom contradicted. There's a risk that we may be misled to believe that we're better informed and more capable in every field than others. I'm a complete idiot when it comes to math, but now I've finally read a small book of thirty pages which I've understood. Therefore I'm inclined to view myself as the world's greatest mathematician even though I'm the same idiot as before.

One of my colleagues is well aware that he's an excellent person in his field. You're quite welcome to criticize his professional ideas if you wish; he'll accept it in a positive spirit. But try expressing anything other than praise for his amateurish painting, and it would be a sure way of gaining an enemy for life! (We were well aware of who he was referring to, as in the following examples.) Another colleague regards himself as an outstanding violinist even though he's just a mediocre dilettante, and one of my closest colleagues presumes to understand politics. Despite his bourgeois background he's rushed to join the most radical workers' party and offered his support to people who want to tell me what I should think. But I cannot respect a person who wants to tell me what I should think. Such a person is simply not a person of intellect, and it's meaningless to talk to him. If he dismisses my views and criticizes me for refusing to accept the thought control that he advocates, I'll think of him in the same way that I think of this large hole in my trousers—Haynal displays his tattered garment. It just doesn't interest me. We all knew that he was talking about Rusznyák and perhaps a few like-minded colleagues.

Eva and I had been in Sweden for a year after the Communists had seized power in Hungary, when visiting student colleagues told us about a large New Year's Eve party at Rusznyák's clinic of internal medicine. Among other things a small comic sketch had been performed which opened with Rusznyák's secretary sitting in front of her typewriter playing the role of herself. The other roles were acted by interns in costume. The secretary typed on her typewriter. A large, bulky man in worker's clothes appeared, saying "I'm the secretary of the iron workers' union. I'm looking for Comrade Rusznyák who's an honorary member of our association. I want to ask him to give a speech." "Please sit down," said the secretary politely. The next visitor was a well-dressed gentleman who was looking for General Secretary Rusznyák. He was on a courtesy visit from the Soviet-Hungarian cultural society. "Please take a seat," said the secretary in a pleasant tone of voice. The next visitor came to speak to Rusznyák the Member of Parliament on behalf of a parliamentary committee. Then a civil servant from the Academy of Science arrived looking for President Rusznyák, followed by the Party Secretary who wished to speak to his party comrade Rusznyák. The secretary was in a sunny mood and couldn't have been more polite to all of them. But then a very ill-looking man appeared on crutches. "What are you doing here?" demanded the secretary, now irritated for the first time. "I'm looking for Professor Rusznyák. I'm ill and have to speak to a doctor." "What impudence!" scoffed the secretary. "Go to the clinic immediately!"

That was the end of the small sketch. Rusznyák sat in the first row and laughed heartily. He was very flattered.

During the next several years Rusznyák was appointed to several more posts, awarded a succession of medals and elected to a number of committees that were increasingly important, at least by name. A brief moment of truth arrived during the Hungarian uprising of 1956 when Rusznyák was

demoted from all honorary posts and confronted with the students' anger.
But they never wished to hurt him seriously, like they wanted to punish the
infamous and brutal university rector who was a professor of pediatrics.
This man was a representative of the regime and had seriously damaged
many people. He escaped being lynched only by going into hiding. He finally surfaced when the Russians had shot the town to pieces and appointed a new Communist marionette regime. Rusznyák kept a low profile
for a while but succeeded in keeping many of his earlier honorary posts,
among them the presidency of the Academy of Science.

In 1960 when the Karolinska Institute celebrated its 150th anniversary, Rusznyák appointed himself the official representative of the Hungarian Academy of Science at the festivities in Stockholm. We met him
at a reception, and Eva asked him what he was doing. He answered that
he was building a new ten-story research department. What are you going
to do there? I'll be its first director. Will you leave your clinic then? No,
why should I? But what will you have the time to do at the new research
department? I'll take my lunch there. Just that? No, I'll also meddle in
everything happening there; I'll have a finger in every pie, as the Americans say. Is this good for you? Oh yes, it's very good for my vanity.

We laughed. It sounded funny, unpretentious, and jovial, but I felt a
certain irritation. I decided to ask an unpleasant question:

"What has happened to Professor Haynal?"

The purpose of my question was not to obtain information, but to hear
his answer. I knew perfectly well what had happened to Haynal. A few
months after the Russians had crushed the uprising and the hated rector
had been reappointed to his post, he received a medal for "heroic acts
during the counterrevolution." The decision was read out aloud during a
meeting of the faculty. Haynal couldn't control himself: "Are you a hero
who sat on your crap house during the length of the revolution?" he
shouted. This was too much for the ambitious, party-appointed rector.
Haynal's choice of an unsuitable colloquial word for outhouse in front of
the discreetly amused faculty didn't help things. Six hours later Haynal
was fired from his post as professor and head of his clinic. His private practice prospered immensely, but his academic career was definitely over.

"What happened to Haynal?" I insisted, when Rusznyák pretended not to have heard my first question. He was irritated, but kept his mask of pleasant collegiality.

"He scored in his own goal," he answered with a soccer term.

"How do you mean?"

"He quarreled with the rector. It was idiotic. I can understand a person who fights for his beliefs and I can respect him even if I don't share his opinions. But Haynal caused trouble for the sake of trouble, in a meaningless way. I cannot respect that."

I asked Rusznyák if he knew how a professor can be fired in Sweden. No, he didn't know and wasn't interested.

I persisted. A professor in Sweden can be fired only when a court has found him guilty of criminal charges.

"What's the difference? A court is an authority. Haynal was fired by the authorities. The details may differ, but it's the same principle."

I could hardly believe my ears. Couldn't this highly intelligent person, my admired and respected teacher, differentiate between a legal process and the administrative firing of a person without a legal defender and no possibility to appeal the verdict?

I didn't have time to think of a relevant answer to Rusznyák's question before he went on the offense:

"What would happen in Sweden if a professor began disseminating Communist propaganda at a faculty meeting?"

"It wouldn't happen," I answered.

"Of course not," said Rusznyák, "since Communists cannot become professors here."

Now I was really angry. I began to explain the appointment procedure: Candidates are appointed on the strength of their scientific merits, and all documents, including the expert opinions, are available for anyone to read, including the candidates themselves. If a candidate feels that he's received unfair treatment, he or she may appeal.

Rusznyák wasn't impressed. He seemed impatient and abrupt and obviously wanted to leave. But first he stated that he didn't believe in the system that I was describing with such conviction. A system where appointments are decided by factors other than political and personal considerations? It's impossible; such a system doesn't exist.

Our conversation ended in mutual irritation and was never resumed. But for many years I was haunted by this thought while looking around the table in faculty meetings at the venerable Karolinska Institute: If what happened in Hungary had happened here, who would have become Rusznyák? And would there have been any Haynal?

AUTOPSY REPORT

Lo giorno se n'andava, e l'aer bruno
toglieva li animai che sono in terra,
da le fatiche loro; ed io sol uno
m'apparecchiava a sostener la guerra
si del cammino, e si de la pietate
che ritrarrà la mente, che non erra.

(From Dante's *Inferno*, Canto II)

The day was on the wane, and by and by
the lengthening shadows freed from earthly chores
all creatures in the world; now only I
stood in the dusk, gathering every force
to face the journey and the agony
I'll now rehearse, not straying from the course.

(Translation by Tibor Wlassics)

I have begun my homeward journey. The border at Kaszony is still closed to foreign visitors. Mrs. Teri's son-in-law is driving me in his old Moskvich which rattles as if it's about to fall apart. It's been through a lot. It's been across the Ural mountains and by the Black Sea. It carries an extra 100-liter gas tank in order to bring cheap Russian gasoline—if it's available—to Hungary. The profit when sold is enough to support an entire family on the Soviet side for a month.

I ask that we drive past the "baths" of my childhood that is now called a "sanatorium." It's become a place of recreation for those approved by the authorities. I am told that there are presently children from Chernobyl there suffering from radiation sickness.

The buildings with the old-fashioned bathtubs are just barely different from the way I remember them. A large group of children are dancing in a ring, their eyes sparkling with happiness. Are these the children from Chernobyl? No, everyone speaks Hungarian.

I ask one of the nurses about the Russian children. Good Lord! The Hungarian kids don't want to play with them or even eat with them. They're in a special building a bit away from here, with their own nurses. We never see them, and we don't want to either.

Here we go again. The children of the rulers, who have been injured through sloppiness or incompetence, are hosted but ignored by the proud children of a small, insignificant, oppressed minority. These children should be happy to be accepted here!

The railway station is unchanged and looks exactly the way it did in my childhood. I am silent, and so is my driver. Here time has stood still. Very few trains pass by and grass grows between the tracks. I feel the need to just stand here for a while. It is still, completely still, as by a grave. A mass grave where no one rests.

After an hour's drive we join what seems like an infinite line of cars at the Hungarian border near Csap where I rendezvous with my original traveling companions and their car. But now we cannot get through the line and have to wait for five hours. The ditches and the fields on both sides of the road are an open latrine with human excrement in all shapes and sizes, the guano of waiting motorists. Trash piles, stench, dust, and sweat bear witness of the large number of totally inefficient passport controllers doing their best to delay the passage of tourists of whose currency their own decrepit economy is in such dire need.

What did this border look like in my childhood? And what happened here much earlier? Why would the present or the future be more valuable than the past?

A few years ago I met Israel's then minister of the interior, Dr. Yosef Burg. Among other things he was known for his encyclopedic memory.

Where are you from? he asked me. I'm born in Budapest, I answered. Yes, but where did your father come from?—The Jews in Budapest were originally from the countryside.

You can't have heard about my father's village, I answered. It's called Kaszony, a small village in the Subcarpathians.

He thought for a while: Is this its full name? Has it always had this name?

Not really; it'a a simplified form. Before World War I the village's name was Mezőkaszony.

I knew that I'd heard the name before, said Dr. Burg. A very famous rabbi lived there who founded a large religious school which was famous throughout the region.

He took down the Jewish encyclopedia and immediately found the village and the rabbi.

I felt ashamed. When I thought more about the matter I remembered that I'd heard of the rabbi in Kaszony, but I had never bothered to look into the matter.

While waiting at the border and unsuccessfully trying to find an area somewhat free from noise and stench and also a safe distance away from our car and the less than enlightening, tourist-type conversation of my traveling companions, I open a few books about Kaszony and its environs that I've brought along but not yet had the time to read. One of the books has been assembled by a New Yorker from Kaszony named Joseph Eden (Einczig), who had survived the Holocaust.* My eyes latch onto the first photograph with the village's large square. There, outside Miska's hardware store, the village elders used to sit during warm summer evenings. They laughed and joked with us children or they spoke about "the good old days" of the Habsburg monarchy before World War I. They never talked about anti-Semitism. We children hardly knew about it.

Franz Josef's rule was very kind to Kaszony. The village was a trade and administrative center for twenty-seven smaller villages that sold

---

*Joseph Eden, *The Jews of Kaszony, Subcarpathia* (New York: J. Eden, 1988).

their farming products and made their purchases here. The stores were mainly run by Jewish merchants.

During World War I all able men had to serve in the Hungarian Army. Jews and non-Jews were treated alike. In Eden's book I find a list of forty-one Jewish men from the village who fought in the war. I see my father's, Miska's, and their middle brother Vilis's names on the list. Fifteen of them never returned. After the war the monarchy was first replaced by a liberal republic and then by Béla Kun's short-lived Communist regime, which was followed by an even shorter Romanian occupation and then Czech rule. The artificial border established by the Trianon peace treaty cut through the outskirts of the village, exactly where the Soviet border is today. Two-thirds of the "satellite villages" were cut off, and the vineyards that were so essential in providing jobs for Kaszony were divided. It was an impractical border. In the recurrent summer train rides of my childhood, the train from Hungary passed the border at Sátoraljaujhely where everyone had to get off to have their suitcases carefully inspected on both sides of the border. You had to count on at least a few hours' wait at the border crossing.

When I began high school in Budapest at the age of ten, I was given a school cap. Wearing the cap outdoors was mandatory until graduation eight years later. It therefore felt very strange to be told sternly to hide the cap before we reached the Czech border. The Hungarian crown of Stephen on the cap was a forbidden symbol in Czechoslovakia. On the other hand, Czech and especially Communist symbols were strictly forbidden in Hungary. Friendship between the two countries was out of the question. A "cold peace" reigned between them.

Just after the First World War Kaszony had 2,500 inhabitants of whom five hundred were Jews. The Jews belonged to two very different categories. Our family and its closest circle of friends dressed like non-Jews and spoke Hungarian. The arrival of the Sabbath on Friday evening in "our" synagogue was mostly attended by similarly dressed, Hungarian-speaking men. I only knew a few of them, but everyone knew me: I was "the son of Henrik Klein." Respect for my father was as natural as the sympathetic and sometimes sorrowful looks that the sight of the fatherless boy elicited.

Right next to "our" synagogue was the Orthodox temple. The black hats, the curled locks around the ears and the long kaphtans belonged to another world that was totally alien to me. Two or three young Orthodox students, called *bochers*, used to dine in my grandmother's house. They ate in a special separate small room and spoke Yiddish, which I didn't understand. I had as little contact with them as I had with the town's non-Jewish families. But my grandmother and Miska could speak with them without any problems.

There were also great social differences between the various Hungarian-speaking Jewish families who were comparatively assimilated. From Eden's book I learn that about 20 percent of them didn't own anything, not even the houses in which they lived. They supported themselves through unqualified physical labor. It was an unsure existence strongly dependent upon market fluctuations. Many of them were often in need of welfare handouts, which were provided by the Jewish congregation or by wealthier Jewish families who were eager to do *mitzvot*, meaning good deeds. About 65 percent of the Jews ran small shops or workshops, and most of them owned their houses. Qualified professionals, whose private economies were completely dependent upon the general standard of living, belonged to this group. The third and smallest Jewish group consisted of rich businessmen, landowners, and the few doctors, lawyers, and pharmacists who were regarded as "intellectuals."

The Orthodox rabbi in Kaszony, or *Kaszonyer Rebbe*, hailed from a famous rabbinical dynasty. In the world of religious Hassidim the rabbi is comparable to a prince, but his authority is not founded upon his lineage but upon his knowledge of Judaism and his ability to give advice in all possible matters to the members of his congregation. Most famous was Rabbi Yosef Halevi Rotenberg, who led the Orthodox congregation in Kaszony between 1897 and 1911.

His *yeshiva* was known throughout the Jewish Orthodox world, and he is still regarded as the father of Hungarian Hassidism. During the Jewish holidays Kaszony was filled with Hassidim who came to listen to his sermons, ask for advice, or receive his blessings. He wrote two widely quoted books, he often fasted, and he donated to the Jewish welfare funds all of his belongings that he didn't need for his simple household. His successor continued the tradition. The last rabbi followed his congregation to the ghetto in the nearby city of Beregszász, where he was nearly beaten to death when he asked one of the guards if he could keep a cheap watch in order to keep track of his prayer schedule. His life ended in the gas chambers of Auschwitz, as did the lives of most Jews from Kaszony.

Young Zionists began their activities in the Subcarpathian region in the early 1920s. They won a certain following among the youth, but the majority of Jews viewed them with suspicion. The assimilated Jews couldn't understand why someone would want to move to sandy, poor, hostile, and warlike Palestine when Jews led such a good life in Czechoslovakia and Hungary. The religious Jews regarded it as an abomination to speak of returning to Jerusalem—something they longed for in their prayers—before the Messiah had arrived. They were also very negative toward the religious indifference displayed by the young Zionists and their "profane" usage of Hebrew, the holy language of prayer, for ordinary conversation. Despite all this, Central Europe's only Hebrew-speaking high school was founded in the city of Munkács. It eventually became one of the best schools in the entire region.

I knew a family with eight daughters, of whom the four oldest couldn't speak a word of Hebrew while the four younger ones spoke it fluently. The father, a pious but not extremely religious Jew, had promised the rabbi that no one in his house would be allowed to study Hebrew. When the fifth daughter, who was a Zionist, refused to accept this, her good father built a small separate cabin in the yard so that his daughter would be able to study without breaking the father's promise to the rabbi. Her younger sisters followed her example.

Reluctantly, I skip to the last part of Eden's book. Between 1938 and 1944, 774 Jews lived in Kaszony. Five hundred of them were deported to Auschwitz, where 401 of them, including 109 children, were murdered, while ninety-nine survived. Of the remaining 274, 122 able-bodied men ended up in the Hungarian army's slave labor camps for Jews, as early as one or a few years before the deportations. Fifty-seven died there, and sixty-five survived. Fifty-two were in Budapest under their true or assumed identities, and of these forty-four survived—myself among them. Of the thirty-one who were in some other part of Nazi-occupied Europe only five survived. Twenty-six died in Kaszony of natural causes before the German occupation in 1944. All forty-three who were in Palestine, in the United States, or who served in Allied armies, survived.

Altogether 256 of the village's 774 Jews (33 percent) survived the Holocaust. Joseph Eden has followed the whereabouts of these people as closely as possible. Ninety-six have moved to Israel, seventy-five to the United States, forty-one to Budapest, twelve to Czechoslovakia, while fourteen remained in the Subcarpathian region. The rest moved to other countries.

AMBIVALENT BORDER CROSSING

Finally we're allowed to cross the border. Upon meeting the first Hungarian border guards I'm at first overwhelmed by a feeling I've experienced previously. I was on my way home from Leningrad with my young family, and we practically embraced the Finnish border guards when we crossed the border after only a two-hour drive. Like then, all my negative feelings are directed toward the Russian uniforms and the stony faces of the guards. But after only a few minutes' drive into Hungary I develop a more balanced view. In 1945 my life and the lives of many Budapest Jews were saved from sure death by soldiers in Russian uniforms. During the same period soldiers in Hungarian uniforms helped the Nazis to carry though their industrially organized mass murder. My sympathies and antipathies don't always agree with the autopsy report.

Why did the Hungarians help the Nazis? Why didn't they resist, and why were they so indifferent?

Like other countries in Eastern and Central Europe, Hungary has a long tradition of anti-Semitism. Its intensity, reach, and practical consequences varied strongly during different periods but it was always present in one form or another. In the middle of the nineteenth century a legal process in the little town of Tiszaeszlár sparked outright pogroms.

A Hungarian girl was murdered and the Jews were blamed. The anti-
Semites' perennial claim that the Jews had used her blood in their bread
was widely believed. The judge presided over a correct legal process
which concluded that the murder was a criminal act which had nothing
to do with the Jews. But this failed to placate the agitated crowd—in
much the same manner as the repeated legal substantiation that the infamous "Protocol of the Elders of Zion" is a fraud perpetrated by the
czar's police has failed to dissuade today's anti-Semites in their persistent use of this "document" in their campaign to "prove" that the Jews
are part of a worldwide conspiracy set against the rest of humanity.*

The process in Tiszaeszlár and the resulting pogrom was just the visible tip of the iceberg of the many-centuries-old habit of blaming social
problems and unwanted political upheavals on the Jews. Poverty, capitalism, Communism, the lack of goods, and the defeat in World War I
were equally useful for this purpose. During my teen years in Budapest
the Hungarian Nazi journals often introduced new words in order to en-
rich their meager vocabulary with fresh anti-Jewish slogans. It didn't
matter that the words were contradictory—logic has never been a cor-
nerstone of anti-Semitism. "Judeoplutobolshevik" was one of the more
magnificent constructions. The Jew was a plutocrat, meaning a capitalist, and a Bolshevik at the same time. If you're likely to laugh and dismiss this as a dusty historical curiosity, you only need to listen to the
contemporary Russian anti-Semitic Pamyat-movement or to the local
radio station in Stockholm which calls itself Radio Islam.†

The at least ostensibly "respectable" anti-Semitism that dominated
during my youth in Hungary and until the German invasion on March
19, 1944, was of a different stripe. Béla Kun, who led the failed Communist regime in 1919, was of Jewish extraction. The victorious counter-

---

*First published in Russia in 1905, the "Protocol of the Elders of Zion" was said
to be the secret minutes of the First Zionist Congress. The document, which has since
been proven false, purported to reveal Jewish plans to dominate the world.

†The station broadcast vicious anti-Semitic propaganda for several years until its
producer, Ahmed Rahmi, was convicted of fomenting racist propaganda and the radio
station was closed.

revolution under the leadership of Admiral Horthy displayed clear anti-Semitic tendencies. Horthy wasn't a rabid anti-Semite, but many of his officers were. Many thousands of Jews were killed during the "white terror" that followed the change of power. During my childhood a decade later, people would mention the red and the white terror as if they were talking about a particularly cold winter or hot summer: It just didn't seem too serious. Only much later did I realize the brutal truth. Obviously, our parents wanted to protect us children from facts that were too unpleasant. This may have contributed to our lack of preparation for the shock of 1944. Our non-Jewish countrymen's broad indifference to our fate was a bitter surprise.

We should have known better. In 1920 Hungary was perhaps the first country in the world to introduce an official "numerus clausus" against admitting Jewish students to the universities. Only 6 percent of the students could be Jews. Despite this the Jews continued to dominate Hungarian cultural life until the Second World War.

When the Subcarpathian region was occupied by the Hungarian army after the Munich agreement in 1938, the "first Jewish law," which had been introduced in Hungary earlier the same year, was immediately enforced there as well. No professional category would allow more than 20 percent Jews. The next year the "second Jewish law" was implemented, which decreased the highest proportion of Jews allowed in the professions and in business to 6 percent. This law redefined the category "Jew" to include even those who had converted to Christianity after 1919, which increased the number of "Jews" by about 100,000. Many were fired from public and professional positions in law, journalism, banking, and the world of theater and entertainment.

The numerous Jews were allowed to continue working freely only in the field of music—all because of a one-man resistance movement. The man was no one less than Béla Bartók. Bartók, who came from an old Hungarian family in Transylvania, declared at an early stage that he could only differentiate between good and bad musicians and refused to adopt any other grounds for judgment. But he was active with more than words: In accordance with the "Jewish law" the government wanted to

establish a so-called professional chamber for musicians, from which
most Jews would be excluded. Only chamber members would be allowed
to continue their professional work. This was an effective way of quickly
reducing the number of Jews and had already been applied in all other
qualified professions. Bartók's refusal to accept membership in a proposed musical chamber halted the entire process in the musical world.
To fire Bartók from his position as professor at the Academy of Music
and to stop playing his works, which would have been the result of a professional chamber without Bartók, was simply unthinkable. There was
no choice; the founding of a musical chamber had to be put off until a
later date. As a result, Jewish musicians were allowed to continue—
until the later point when Bartók was under so much pressure that he
found it wiser to leave the country rather than collaborate with the
regime. Bartók wasn't the only one to oppose the regime, but the total
number of people who resisted was very small.

The third "Jewish law," which was modeled after Hitler's Nuremberg laws, was put into effect in August 1941. One of its decrees outlawed marriage and sexual relations between Jews and non-Jews, as defined by the Nuremberg laws.

All this was a relatively innocent introduction to what was to follow.
When Hungary joined Hitler's war on the Soviet Union in 1941, 35,000
"foreign Jews" who lacked proof of Hungarian citizenship were detained.
Of these about 20,000, who were mainly from the Subcarpathian region,
were deported. Between 14,000 and 16,000 were shot dead by German SS-
troops, Ukrainian militias, and Hungarian troops in September 1941 at
Kamenets-Podolsk. The rest were deported about a year later to Auschwitz
and other extermination camps in Poland. Hungary's able-bodied male
Jewish population was treated according to a special law introduced in
1940. They were transferred from the regular army and its reserve to military work camps. They were supposed to serve for two years, but most were
forced to stay until the end of the war, if they survived for that long. At first
they were dressed in uniform with a yellow arm band and ordered to build
or repair railroads, bridges, roads, and airports. About a year later their
uniforms were taken from them and they had to wear their own civilian

clothes with a Hungarian army cap and the yellow arm band as a sign of their military status as second-class citizens. At some units the Jewish workers were treated well, but since the war dragged on and took a continuous turn for the worse for the German and Hungarian armies, their number decreased. The Hungarian soldiers that supervised the Jewish slave workers became lords with unlimited power over life and death.

On the Eastern Front far beyond the borders of Hungary, or in Yugoslavia, the soldiers often abandoned their inhibitions and freely vented their own frustrations. Those who enjoyed being cruel or felt a strong need to dominate used the defenseless slave laborers as their objects of torment, especially during the Russian winter, which provided many sophisticated methods of torture. The prisoners were ordered to keep the roads passable, repair damaged vehicles and cannons, clean up mine fields, unload ammunition, dig trenches, and build fortifications. Sometimes they were forced to clean out minefields by simply marching through them. They were also ordered to retrieve the bodies of dead soldiers that had fallen between the German and Russian lines. If the commanding officer thought that they hadn't worked hard enough, their small food rations would be withdrawn. Sometimes their food would be stolen by the Hungarian guards. But beside these cruel but rational acts from the point of view of the military commanders, the defenseless slaves were also used for purposes of "recreation." Some tormentors would order the the Jews to swim in the icy rivers in the middle of the Ukrainian winter and then climb up into trees where they would be tied until they had been transformed into "ice statues." There is hardly any cruelty born from the mind of a pervert which wasn't realized in one platoon or another. If there was a sadist among the officers, the guards would often outdo one another in terms of cruelty, trying to come up with ever-more-refined methods of torture in order to make their comrades laugh.

After the great losses in the Ukraine, especially at the battle of Voronezj, where 140,000 of 200,000 Hungarian soldiers from the Second Hungarian Army were annihilated, and in the forced retreat which followed, the slave laborers died like flies. During the last year of the war and especially after the German occupation of Hungary in

March 1944 many of the higher officers who were in charge of the slave
laborers were replaced by fanatical anti-Semites. Malnourishment, disease, and organized and unorganized mass murder took its toll. About
50,000 of the military slave laborers had died before the war's end.

Poet Miklós Radnóti was one of the slave workers murdered by a shot
to the neck because he didn't have the energy to continue during one of the
forced marches. His body was thrown into a mass grave. When the grave
was opened after the war, his body was identified. In his pocket was a sheaf
of poems that he'd been working on until his last day. Along with the poems
was a note in which Radnóti asks in Hungarian, German, English, and
French that anyone who finds them kindly forward them to a friend.

Peter Zollman has translated the last five poems:

Eröltetett menet—Forced March

He's mad who when collapsing   will rise to march again,
a walking heap of torment   bends ankles, knees, the brain,
with secret wings to help him   he is back on the way,
the ditch is so inviting   but he's afraid to stay,
and if you ask the reason   he will perhaps reply,
at home his wife awaits him   and wiser ways to die.
But poor man is deluded: at home, above the house
the ashes fly in circles,   a scorched wind comes to browse,
the wall lies flat in silence,   the plum tree had to shear,
the night back home is tousled   in restless, shaky fear.
If I could still believe it   that it's not merely dream:
my home and all the good things   I hold in high esteem,
if only! . . . On the cool porch   just as it used to be
the jam cooled in the jam jar   to tease a bumble bee,
the late summer were basking   in sleepy semi-shade,
the apples in the soft breeze   nakedly, slowly swayed,
and Fanni's blond hair greeted   before the tawny hedge,
and shadows slowly doodled   a lazy, lacy sketch,—
but wait, there may be hope yet!   the moon is strangely large!
Oh friend, don't leave, just call me!   and I will rise to march!

(Bor, Yugoslavia, September 15, 1944)

Razglednica I

A raging cannon-thunder rolls from Bulgaria,
it hits the ridge and lamely falls in our area;
the men muddle with beasts, carts and thoughts in muddy maze,
neighing the highway shies back, the moon's mane is ablaze.
I live in this mad turmoil but you are permanent,
a still light, deep in my mind, star on my firmament,
and silent like the angel marvelling at the fall,
or glowworms in a dead tree on their sepulchral crawl.

(In the mountains, August 30, 1944)

II

The houses and the haystacks are on fire
a mere six miles away,
and poor folk sit scared, smoking in silence
on the edge of the hay,
while here the pond still drapes its lacy flounces
on bathing shepherd girls
and lambs still drink the clouds and lick the water
to frill the fleecy curls.

(Cservenka, October 6, 1944)

III

The oxes' muzzles drip with bloody slaver,
the men's urine is brown with bloody traces,
we stand in knots, the stench is hard to bear.
Above us dreadful death blows in the air.

(Mohács, October 24, 1944)

IV

I tumbled next to him, his body turned
and tightened like a string about to go,
Shot in the head.—This is how you will end,—
I breathed,—just lie rigid from top to toe.
The fruits of patience bloom when death appears.—
Der springt noch auf,—sounded above me.
A sludge of gory mud clotted my ears.

(Szentkirályszabadja, October 31, 1944)

For Hungary's civilian Jewish population the Holocaust began after the German invasion on March 19, 1944. At this time there were 760,000 Jews in Hungary, of whom 232,000 lived in Budapest and 100,000 in the Subcarpathian region. The clustering of the Jews into the ghettos and the deportations to the extermination camps, especially Auschwitz, commenced in the Subcarpathian region only a few weeks after the German occupation on April 7, 1944. The action was lead by Adolf Eichmann himself, in close cooperation with László Endre, a fanatical Hungarian anti-Semite who was an under-secretary in the department of the interior.

The Jews in Kaszony were roused early in the morning and were given only a few minutes to pack a few changes of underwear and shirts per person plus food for two weeks. They were first rounded up in the synagogue, then body-searched and robbed of their clocks, money, and valuables. Then they were driven to the brick factory in Beregszász which was used as a temporary detention camp. Everything was done in haste, and the Hungarian police and the German units including Eichmann's Sonderkommando carried out the action with great brutality. Orders were enforced by beatings and kickings. The situation in the brick factory was intolerable. There were no sanitary facilities whatsoever, and the food ration amounted to a pound of bread for five people and two cups of soup per person and day.

The most Jewish of the cities in the region, Munkács, offered some resistance. The Germans immediately executed twenty-seven leading Jews, among them the entire leadership of the Jewish congregation. The orthodox Jews were ordered at gunpoint to destroy the interior of their large synagogue. They were then body-searched by the guards in order to ensure that they hadn't hidden pieces of the Torah or something valuable. If such were found, the victims were violently brutalized, and often beaten to death.

The circumstances in the brick factory in Beregszász were so horrible that the deportation trains felt like a liberation. But this illusion didn't last. Between eighty and one hundred people were pressed like sardines into each cattle car, with a few buckets their only sanitary facilities. The cars were sealed. Hungarian gendarmes escorted the trains to Slovakia, where the SS took over. Every attempt at defiance, including resistance to the sometimes very sadistic body-searches, were immediately punished by death. The Hungarian papers were totally silent about the deportations. Officially the Hungarian satellite regime denied any mistreatment of the Jews.

Immediately after their arrival at Auschwitz some of the deportees were ordered to write postcards postmarked "Waldsee." They were told to write only that they had arrived at a labor camp and were in good health. Our family in Budapest received a few of these. The point of this exercise was to calm fears so that the Jewish population would submit to the ghettoization and the deportations without trouble.

According to the testimony of the SS-colonel Dieter von Wisliceny at Nuremberg altogether 550,000 Hungarian Jews were murdered by the Nazis during 1944. The Germans executed 450,000, the Hungarians 80,000, and 20,000 died from disease, suicide, or in accidents. The figures agree with the those provided by Hungarian Jewish leaders.

EPILOGUE

On my way home I am once again in the autopsy room at the pathology department in Budapest. Forty-five years have passed since I spent one of my life's most hectic work periods here. The year was 1946, and the war had ravaged the land. It had ended almost a year earlier, but people were still cleaning up among the ruins, trying to rebuild or at least assemble boards, pieces of tin, rocks, and rags into some sort of protective structure that would hold while they waited for the reconstruction and hoped for a better order. But many were fearful, and justly so.

I was, at this time, happily unconcerned, with no time to worry. All of my twenty-one-year-old energy was focused on work. I had recently become a junior instructor at the department of pathology, and viewed my existence as both exciting and important. There was a rich supply of corpses and few pathologists, and I'd been given what during normal conditions would have been the unthinkable responsibility of being in charge of the autopsies. My earlier teenage over-sensitivity to blood and disease had vanished. The autopsy room was where I encountered The Great Adventure. Every corpse was a new riddle which was at least potentially solvable. I tried to follow the advice of one of my teachers: Try to imagine the uncountable possibilities of human life and its bodily functions; try to imagine the pathological course of events which has occurred in each person you encounter in the hospital bed or whose body lies in front of you on the autopsy table. Never think that you've found the only solution or that you've understood all connections. Be content when you know that you've been able to pose the proper questions. These are often more important than the answers that you think you can find.

This was good advice. The possibilities were given by the laws of biology and pathology. Reality was like the marble block of Michelangelo that contained all possible statues within it. The artist's task was to sculpt one of them. But not even the most skilled coroner can be compared to Michelangelo. The body and its illnesses have been sculpted by life itself. The coroner's goal is to learn as much as he can about the sculptor's technique in order to provide as careful a description as possible.

Almost half a century has passed since then. My hands, once so used to conducting autopsies, have now tried to examine a different cadaver. They've touched the corpse of a people and a culture that is my own. Has the coroner been able to provide an adequate description?

Probably not. I haven't even opened the corpse—not for real. I've made a visit and written a report.

About what?

About three tombstones I have found. About the memory of those who, in the words of Paul Celan,* have dug a grave in space where there is plenty of room. About the ash gray hair of my grandmother, and my little cousin's golden hair. About all those who soared like smoke up into space, all those who were given a grave among the clouds where there is plenty of space. I have seen the room and the bed where I was conceived and where my father died. This was the room where I dreamed as a five-year-old about my future life. I found a number of diplomas written in the Cyrillic alphabet, in a language I don't understand. I have seen a very familiar although somewhat changed face under shrieking, frightening, foreign red flags. I have wandered in the valley of death where I sought the shadows of the dead in vain. They had become part of me, they were within me, inside my children and my grandchildren.

> *The corpse remains without an autopsy.*
> *Kaszony is gone forever but always near.*
> *Stronger than the smells or tastes of the past.*
> *Warmer than love.*
> *Unlike pain, unfading.*

---

*This and the following sentences refer to Paul Celan's poem *"Todesfuge."*

WHEN TIME STOPS

Da neigt sich die Stunde und rührt mich an
mit klarem, metallenem Schlag:
mir zittern die Sinne. Ich fühle: ich kann—
und ich fasse den plastischen Tag.

Nichts war noch vollendet, eh ich es erschaut,
ein jedes Werden stand still.
Meine Blicke sind reif, und wie eine Braut
kommt jedem das Ding, das er will.

Rainer Maria Rilke: *"Das Stundenbuch"*

With strokes that ring clear and metallic, the hour
to touch me bends down on its way:
my senses are quivering. I feel I've the power—
and seize on the pliable day.

Not a thing was complete till by me it was eyed,
every kind of becoming stood still.
Now my glances are ripe and there comes like a bride
to each of them just what it will.

(Translation by J. B. Leishman)

T he Dutch-German border, 1954. Our small, green Volkswagen rolls into the front yard of a country inn. We're on our way home from a congress on cellular biology in Leiden, but when we saw the long line of cars on their way toward Germany we decided to take a coffee break.

We've barely sat down when we hear Swedish voices from a nearby table. A few colleagues from Lund are also on their way home from the congress. They invite us to join their party. We talk about the congress, sip some coffee, and express our shared hope that the line of cars will get shorter. One of my younger colleagues goes over to take a look at the inn's selection of slot machines. I pass him on my way to the men's room. He's playing a simple machine called *Baby Face*, where you're supposed to hit certain targets by maneuvering small metal balls with two knobs. I'm overcome by a childish desire to try a round.

I've barely begun playing when I notice that I'm much better at maneuvering the balls than my colleague. He's quite surprised. Then he praises me, saying that I should change profession. My self-confidence increases. I sense that I have a certain talent for playing Baby Face. After a few more minutes I've convinced myself that I'm a genius at Baby Face. Soon the others gather around me and we begin to compete. I beat everyone. There's not even a good second best.

I don't know how long we're playing for. I have lost all sense of time and am completely immersed in the game. Indeed, I'm filled by an intense sense of happiness. Just before I started to play I was worrying about our one-year-old child, whom we'd left behind with a young Norwegian couple on an island way out in the sea. I was also feeling uneasy thinking about the long drive ahead of me, and about all the grant applications that I would have to write. My uncertain future as a scientist was looming like a dark shadow over me. But now these problems appear remote and insignificant. Gone is my fear of failure, and my persistent awareness of life's impermanence and the vanity of everything seems suddenly unimportant. My active and observing selves have merged, and I've become a complete person within myself, uninterested in the events of the world and unconcerned about the future. I want to remain in this state of concentration, I want to enjoy its sense of timelessness and euphoria while focusing on my "task."

Stockholm, 1987. Someone who has seen me on TV or read about my seemingly eccentric habits has mailed me a *Newsweek* interview with the Hungarian-American psychologist Mihály Csikszentmihályi in which he's discussing a psychological condition that he calls "flow."

My correspondent has hit the nail on the head. My inner sirens go off and all my warning lights are blinking: this is highly relevant! I immediately wrote to Csikszentmihályi and asked him to send me a few of his articles. It was certainly worth the trouble. I was particularly impressed by a lucid overview.*

As soon as I read it several different flow experiences came to mind. My episode with Baby Face I now remembered only as a curiosity. Csikszentmihályi's examples cast a clearer light on the phenomenon: the mountain-climber perched on the side of a steep cliff in a precarious situation which he fully masters; the ballerina executing a perfect pirouette in the air for a few seconds; the brain surgeon seated on the same chair for eight or nine hours while performing a complicated operation under the microscope—the operating room nurse and the assistant have to be relieved several times, but the surgeon remains at his task without pause; the sophisticated safe-cracker who is pulling off a well-planned job. They all experience the same sensation of timelessness and euphoria—flow—while concentrating on their tasks. In principle there's no difference if the condition lasts for hours or for just a few seconds. Their consciousnesses are altered in a similar way. The examples I've just mentioned have the same psychological starting point: You meet a meaningful challenge or take on a demanding task which you have a reasonable chance of managing or solving. The nature of the task and its moral or utilitarian value are not important per se.

According to Csikszentmihályi, flow occurs when the challenge and your ability to meet it are in balance. Tasks that are too daunting cause

---

*M. Csikszentmihályi, "Reflections on Enjoyment," *Perspectives in Biology & Medicine* 28 (1985): 489–97.

anxiety and worry. If your ability greatly exceeds the challenge, as so often happens in the daily routine of life, you're easily bored. Experienced people are adept at avoiding boredom by increasing the challenge. A professional chess-player who has to play against amateurs can, for example, play blindfolded or take on ten opponents at the same time.

Reading Csikszentmihályi gave me one déjà vu experience after the other. I realized that I often employ similar flow-increasing tricks myself. During long-distance flights I travel in splendid isolation behind a psychological wall of well-fitting earplugs. With my dictaphone in hand I leap from one adventure to the other, my mood varying between euphoria and short periods of deep sleep. Unlike many of my fellow passengers who have "relaxed" during the journey—with or without the aid of alcohol— but who arrive tired and irritated, I arrive rested and alert. After many years of practice I can find just the right challenge to get me to concentrate at varying degrees of weariness even in fairly hopeless situations.

One summer Sunday afternoon some time ago I arrived at JFK airport in New York City. The line snaking its way to passport control was longer than I had ever seen or could even imagine. It was very hot and people were as tightly packed as a can of sardines. I was carrying two heavy briefcases full of paper. It would obviously take more than an hour for me to pass through. The hopelessness of the situation was made worse by my bad conscience. Since several weeks back I had been procrastinating in order to avoid my most dreaded but also most necessary task: applying for an extension of a grant from the National Institutes of Health in the United States. The grant was extremely important for the economy of my research department. I felt a paralyzing displeasure toward this task from which I couldn't learn anything but which needed to be performed with great care in order to get us the continued funds in spite of the increasing competition. I knew that I had to repeat what I'd said and written in many other contexts, but the text had to be much more condensed and polished than my ordinary articles. The text had to be organized according to specific instructions and within strictly defined limits, otherwise it wouldn't be considered. The plans had to be tailored to the specific tastes of the committee members. The outcome is always uncertain. More than a dozen people vote through a secret ballot. The applications are graded according to a scale where one is the top score and five the lowest. A score of at least 1.5 is necessary in order to stand a chance. When applying you are thus constantly haunted by the sordid specter of meaninglessness: am I wasting my one and only life on an assignment doomed to failure from the start? During the normal workday's relative freedom of choice you're constantly seeking increasingly pleasurable tasks, more or less unconsciously. But a passport line offers no freedom of choice. The thought of the passive wait and my nervous focus on the line's snail-like movements felt unbearable.

Suddenly I was struck by an impulse of grumpy determination: while sweating profusely and intermittently kicking my heavy bags before me I put in my earplugs, pulled up my dictaphone and began dictating. My inward-looking gaze, which didn't meet anyone else's, and my self-chosen deafness surrounded me with a protective double shield. The reactions of those around me seemed remote and irrelevant. At first they appeared amused by my eccentricity. Then they seemed surprised that I didn't give up. After a few minutes my behavior was accepted as part of the landscape. The indifference of the people around me further strengthened my shield and facilitated my concentration. I observed with surprise that the great distaste which had earlier prevented me from proceeding with my application was disappearing like scattering clouds on a summer's day. My concentration catapulted me from the boredom of the wait into the welcoming world of my own thoughts. Suddenly I was quite enticed by this unexpected opportunity to think through my research plans in peace and quiet, undisturbed by my other interests, and then be able to articulate them clearly. Suddenly the venture's uncertain outcome didn't seem to matter. The activity which I chose only as a way out of the boredom of waiting in line had become interesting in and of itself, regardless of its result.

I stood in that line for almost two hours. I was drenched with sweat when I reached passport control, but the outline of the application was ready. I wasn't at all tired. Instead I felt euphoric because of my "victory" and was more than ready to devote myself to my American evening. About half a year later my effort proved successful: we received the grant. I don't know if my obvious flow condition during the writing of the application had contributed to the outcome. Csikszentmihályi's articles later informed me that texts written in a state of flow are more successful than stylistically and topically comparable texts written without any sense of joy. I will return to this.

My unprepared but successful struggle with the line at the airport was no exception. I had unconsciously but consistently cultivated similar practices during many years. As soon as I am able I tend to combine two or more boring or disagreeable activities. Strangely enough my boredom isn't doubled—instead different distastes have a tendency to neutralize one other. I dictate letters while driving my car, I correct manuscripts while riding my exercycle, I exercise while trying to learn a new language through audio cassettes, and I shave while reading fiction or dictating a text. My friends and acquaintances extol my efficiency. But it has nothing to do with efficiency. Of course you get a few extra things done, but this is not my primary goal. Escape would be a better description. More or less unconsciously I try to escape from everything that can disturb my concentration and thereby block the way toward my joy of life. It's a constant steeple-chase through numerous barriers and bottlenecks, past morning depressions, past conflicts among the staff, past boring, repetitive routines, and last but not least, past the deathly catches of social life. Conventional empty conversations make me panic. Many forms of passive "pastimes" and "relaxations" that other people enjoy depress me. The "general view" of how life should be lived doesn't interest me. As soon as I feel passive or inactive, I feel an irresistible urge to alter my situation so that I can get going with my own activities. I'm painfully aware that my behavior can antagonize some people. But when I weigh the possible negative reactions and their consequences against my acute mental suffering, my desire to escape and my love of liberty usually wins out—unless they're blocked by my unwillingness to hurt someone I definitely don't want to hurt.

Csikszentmihályi first developed the concept of flow in connection with his observations of a group of male art students whom he watched painting and sculpting every day.* Some of them obviously enjoyed their work. Their painting or sculpting seemed like the most important thing in the world to them. They forgot about the outer world when working. But as soon as the paint was dry, they stuck their canvas in some corner and promptly forgot about it. These students didn't expect to become rich or famous. And unlike most other students they never spoke about their plans. Their foremost motivation was neither money nor recognition. What was it?

According to the psychoanalytic school, artistic activity is based on a "sublimation" of the instincts. It's regarded as a symbolic expression of the artist's repressed desires. This explanation doesn't agree with Csikszentmihályi's observations. The artist's interest in color and form doesn't appear to be a surrogate for something else. Why would he keep searching for ever greater challenges, why should he strive to improve his skill if his real motivation were to satisfy his comparatively simple sexual needs? Young artists who haven't yet completed their psychosexual adaptation can sometimes have such needs, but they're the exception. The labor of the devoted artists has evolved into a positive, joyous force in itself. In psychological jargon the work produces its own *autotelic reward*. The word comes from the Greek "auto," which means "itself," and "telos," meaning "goal." The psychological term refers to an activity which is satisfying in itself. The activity isn't primarily performed to achieve some goal or obtain some advantages—it becomes its own goal through the feeling of happiness that it creates. Playing the stock market in order to make a profit is no autotelic activity. But if you play the market in order to improve your ability to judge tendencies and forecast the future, the activity can be autotelic. The actual monetary reward may be the same in both cases. Educating children in order to turn them into good citizens is no autotelic activity. But our enjoyment of spending time with them can be. This distinction is important. A person who is involved in autotelic activity is devoting his attention to the activity itself. He who doesn't is focusing on its effects.

---

*M. Csikszentmihályi and I. S. Csikszentmihályi, eds., *Optimal Experience* (New York: Cambridge University Press, 1988).

The experience of realizing one's goals and the feeling of being in charge of one's life produce a stronger motivation than external rewards, which can have the opposite effect. Csikszentmihályi quotes an extensive selection of psychological literature which shows that being suddenly rewarded for a spontaneous, joy-filled activity can actually lead to a loss of interest.

After his original study of the art students, Csikszentmihályi and his followers have examined many other categories of people who have voluntarily spent a large portion of their time with strenuous tasks without receiving any particular reward. A study of more than two hundred experimental subjects included amateur athletes, mountain climbers, dancers, basketball players, chess champions, and composers. The "holy trinity" of the flow experience, concentration, timelessness, and euphoria, could arise in connection with all of these activities, but also during ordinary work.

There are many border areas between flow and other psychological phenomena. Sudden, temporary liberation from established social roles at a carnival or an office party can create a euphoric feeling of togetherness. There's also a close connection between flow and the psychology of playing, and between flow and mystic or religious experiences. Our Western flow-creating activities are more directed toward competition and control than equivalents in the East, but the dynamism of the experience and the feeling of euphoria is identical in all cultures. Flow is an experience as common to all humans as laughter and weeping. The experience of flow is more hidden, however, since it doesn't manifest itself in any outward signs or typical body language. This is why we're often totally unconscious of it and its psychological and sociological consequences.

In Csikszentmihályi's anthology *Optimal Experience*, psychologists from different cultures reported large differences between the frequency and intensity of the flow experience in different people. These could in part be explained by environmental differences. The degree of stimulation experienced on the job, domestic responsibilities, and social roles were some of the relevant variables.

Large individual differences were also found between people who lived under similar environmental conditions. One student in a school class seldom or never experienced a state of flow, while another experienced flow 30 percent of the time. Some examined housewives were "in flow" a maximum of 4 percent of the time during the registered period, while others could reach 40 percent. Poor, hard-working peasant communities are seldom characterized by flow. But there are important exceptions even here. Some peasant communities have found ways of making everyday life exciting, challenging, and enjoyable. Della Fava and Massimi described a large family clan of forty-nine people encompassing three generations in Val D'Aosta, and the small village Samperye in Val Varaita, where people worked seven days a week from early morning to late into the night but experienced flow in connection with almost everything they did.* The difference between work and leisure had been erased. Everything they did was necessary and was therefore experienced as meaningful. Everyone could choose among several alternate activities. They were traditionally used to enjoying everything they did. Anxiety and boredom were kept away by constantly learning new skills through which they could influence or control their environment. The older people who had grown up in this environment stated that they had never been bored. But the younger generation had begun to display signs of listlessness and boredom.

In the same volume Richard Logan described his studies of people who have survived long-term isolation and loneliness, for example political prisoners. The ability to "realize oneself" within an inner world of thoughts and without mulling too much over one's own identity had a positive survival value. Mulling over the injustices of the world had a negative effect. One can adopt the same attitude when faced with the trials of everyday life. Narcissistic, self-centered people have a hard time seizing the moments they could use to develop their skills, especially when they've already gotten used to a lifestyle that alternates be-

---

*A. Della Fava and F. Massimi, "Modernization and the Changing Contexts of Flow," in *Optimal Experience*, pp. 266–82.

tween anxiety and boredom. People who are used to controlling their own world of thoughts do much better. They put a high value on their own effort and ability to concentrate even in situations where no one else attributes any value to this. Self-centered people are likely to see themselves as marionettes controlled by external factors. If you have a sense of being in control of your situation, you're also motivated to constantly strive for new solutions. There is also a clear link between flow and self-respect. Flow experiences increase your self-respect, and a stronger sense of self facilitates the experience of flow. The "marionettes," on the other hand, are in constant need of external recognition since they cannot identify with their activity.

When and where is this personality difference established? Kevin Rathunde found that teenagers whose parents strive for and encourage clarity, concentration, involvement, challenge, and freedom of choice within the family environment find it easier to achieve flow and do so more often than their friends whose parents lack these characteristics.* One can therefore speak of flow-enhancing or autotelic families. According to Kobasa and his assistants, adults with a sense of self control and commitment coupled with a good ability to meet new challenges quickly and flexibly are not only better motivated but also healthier and have a better resistance against stress.† Happy those who've grown up in families that have taught them to enjoy life through their own activities!

The everyday social environment is not particularly bent on stimulating people to invest the mental energy needed to learn new skills. The border to the unknown is most easily crossed by those who enjoy the act of transgression. A mathematician who enjoys sitting alone in his abstract world is constantly in the process of development. His colleagues who become bored or anxious in their loneliness become arrested in their development. Mathematic talent is not enough in itself. The same goes for writing. Reed Larson studied the subjective condition of a group

---

*K. Rathunde, "Optimal Experience and the Family Context," in *Optimal Experience*, pp. 342–63.

†Kobasa et al., "Type A and Hardiness," *Journal of Behavioural Medicine* 6 (1983): 41–51.

of high school students while they were writing essays and compared his findings with the evaluations of the essays by a literary critic.* Students who felt that the assignment was boring wrote boring essays. Frightened students expressed themselves in a disconnected manner. Students whose imagination was activated by the choice of subjects and who enjoyed playing with ideas and with the language wrote essays that captivated the reader's attention.

Csikszentmihályi's dissertation from 1963 on the art students mentioned earlier has been followed up by his doctoral student, Jane Kerley (quoted by Csikszentmihályi). In 1986 Kerley tracked down some of the original students. None of those who were dependent upon appreciation and external rewards during their student days had continued to produce art. Those who became artists came from the original "flow group." This can be related to the careers of most artists. They are generally forced to suffer a series of lean years before achieving enough recognition to make a living from their art. Those who are dependent upon external rewards tend to change profession during the lean years. If they remain within the field of art they may become ad illustrators or art dealers. Only the strongly motivated, whose main reward comes from their work, go the full distance. Vincent Van Gogh is a typical example.

Flow plays an important role also in more usual types of work. Industrial leaders are often totally uninterested in the subjective experiences of their employees while they're working. But if they're convinced that enjoyment can increase productivity, they may become quite interested. However, if flow-promoting activities are stressed and rewarded because of their utility, this may counteract the inner euphoric reward which is the very driving force in autotelic people. This can easily change the balance between externally and internally motivated people. This, in turn, can change the sociology of the activity. Something of this kind may have occurred in certain highly rewarded areas of modern science.

Young children are constantly searching for flow. The obvious euphoria of play, without any thought of practical usefulness, is a clearly

---

*R. Larson, "Fear and Writing," in *Optimal Experience*, pp. 150–71.

autotelic activity. When and why do we forget this as we grow up? Is it a necessary part of our social adjustment, our metamorphosis into law-abiding and productive citizens? Is it related to our sense of duty, our desire to do something useful? Perhaps. But we cannot escape our fundamental psychology.

CAN EVERYONE EXPERIENCE FLOW?

Many people can experience flow: poets, scientists, and chess players; strong, alert adolescents on motorbikes; pivoting ballet dancers; and bank robbers during the perfect heist. But what about the weak, the sick, the old, and the rejected? Can they move from a state of meaninglessness to a positive sense of life with the aid of the flow mechanism?

I asked Csikszentmihályi if it's possible to use flow in psychotherapy. Yes, there were a few psychotherapists who had made attempts in this direction. One of them had been interested in "completely burned out" schizophrenics who have spent many years in mental institutions, and on whom the doctors have long since given up. These patients had lost all contact with the outside world and felt constantly miserable. Prospects for stimulating them to flow were slim, but some were open to Csikszentmihályi's beeping apparatus with its recurring questions (to be described shortly). The psychiatrist just wanted to find out if there were any moments when the patients felt less miserable than usual, and, if so, what had happened just prior to these moments. One woman who had been regarded as completely burned out and uninterested in her environment felt less unhappy for a short while each time she had trimmed her nails. When asked gently if she wanted to try to trim other people's nails she became very interested. She was so skilled at trimming nails that she could be trained to become a manicurist, first as on a trial basis but then increasingly for real. Her training was a great success. After a while she could be signed out of the hospital. Today she runs her own manicurist salon.

The flow mechanism is open to just about anyone. Are there any inner limitations? Csikszentmihályi mentions poor ability to concentrate and self-centeredness as the most important obstacles. If you've gotten used to observing everything that happens around you, you can easily end up in a condition of chronically hampered attention which may close the entranceway to flow. The *self conscious*, who are continuously concerned about the impression they make on other people and who therefore constantly guard their own behavior to avoid mistakes, easily shut themselves off from flow experiences. The same applies to *self centered* people who value everything in relation to concrete, useful goals. They can miss out on self-rewarding, more or less nonuseful yet concentrated activities that can create a feeling of euphoria. People who live under really difficult circumstances don't necessarily miss out on flow experiences. Eskimos can sing and tell stories in their icy north. They have created their own art and mythology which can give meaning to their lives.

But the fight against exterior limitations should not exceed a certain limit. The desire of many South American indian tribes to survive and multiply was literally crushed during the harsh and degrading oppression by the Spaniards. The "Muselmane" of the concentration camps who had given up all hope had no escape routes left.

Csikszentmihályi's many examples show that the flow experience is open to anyone who doesn't suffer from these limitations. It doesn't require high intelligence or education, a good income or a certain social status. A stable family situation is not a necessity, nor is help from others. The one prerequisite is a stubborn ambition to meet new challenges. Happiness doesn't come from thoughtless hedonism but from mastering meaningful challenges by using our own skills.

Thanksgiving Friday, Connecticut, 1991. I have just finished my daily swim in the YMCA pool in Greenwich, which is my unfailing medicine against transatlantic jetlag. There are few visitors this early in the morning, especially on a half-holiday like today. Two men arrive as I'm getting dressed, one from the sauna and the other from outdoors. They greet each other in a friendly manner, like old swimming pals.

"Are you working today?" asks the older one, who appears to be in his fifties.

"Yes, believe it or not," says the younger, who might be thirty-five. "But only because I want to get away from home. The wife is a pain in the ass. I wonder how many guys go to work today just to get away from home. Actually," he continues with some hesitation while pulling on his swimtrunks, "I like my work pretty well. It's nothing special, but it is kind of interesting, you know?" He sounds like he is making an excuse, as if he has just confessed to a weakness. "Right now we're computerizing everything—it's really exciting!"

The older man mumbles in agreement. In a matter of minutes they're involved in an animated conversation about computers.

I'm in my son's house where we've just finished our holiday meal and are now "relaxing." My effort to get my grandchildren, six and eight, to leave the TV set by suggesting various joint activities are totally unsuccessful, although I usually succeed at other times. They have sucked onto the screen like octopuses to a cliff. Should I lecture them about the inactivating effect of TV? I realize that all such efforts would be doomed from the start. I don't stand a chance against the overpowering force of this medium. I would only loose my own good spirits.

I withdraw to my manuscripts, at a safe distance from the noisy TV. I put on a compact disc with Mozart's *Requiem.* What a wonderful oasis! I look up Csikszentmihályi's chapter describing his comparative studies of flow experiences in the workplace and during leisure time.* More than one hundred fully employed men and women participated in the experiment. They were made to carry a small receiver that beeped at various random moments eight times per day during an entire week. Each time the beeper went off they were asked to answer a few written questions. Their answers indicated what they were doing and how they felt at that particular moment. They were also asked to assess, on a scale of one to ten, to what extent they experienced their current activity as a challenge

---

*Mihály Csikszentmihályi, *Flow: The Psychology of Optimal Experience* (New York: HarperCollins, 1990).

that prompted them to use their skills, and what approximate portion of their total capacity they might be using to meet that particular challenge. Whenever the challenge and the person's use of his or her own abilities exceeded that person's average level for the entire week, the subjective condition was registered as flow. This is a liberal definition. If the researchers had only registered flow at its peak level, less than 1 percent of the answers would have been accepted as such. But according to the definition in question, 33 percent of the 4,000 answers indicated flow.

There was a clear correlation between flow and the subjective condition of the research subjects. While they were busy with a stimulating assignment they felt stronger, more active, more creative, better concentrated, and more motivated than at other moments. The most surprising result came from the comparison between work and leisure time. Flow arose much more often during work, which was defined as a moment when the test person wasn't merely at his workplace but was actually working. This distinction is important, since the study also showed that the subjects spent an average 25 percent of their work time in social conversation, with private telephone calls, or just daydreaming. In all, 54 percent of the answers that were given at moments when the test person was actually working indicated flow, compared with only 18 percent of the answers given during leisure time. Fully 82 percent of the leisure answers reported the lack of any challenge. The subjects weren't using any particular skills at these moments. They were reading the paper, watching TV, having friends over, or attending dinner parties in someone's home or a restaurant. As many as 52 percent of the answers given during leisure time were registered as "apathy." The people felt passive, weak, bored, and dissatisfied. Only 16 percent of the answers given at work indicated apathy.

There was a certain difference between people with different types of work, but there was no difference in principle. People in prominent positions were in flow 64 percent of the time while working, while subordinate workers only registered 47 percent. But even the factory workers indicated flow more than twice as often when they worked (40 percent), as compared to their time off (20 percent).

All answers indicating flow reported a positive subjective condition.

In the cases where the challenge was particularly high and demanding of the skills of the test person, he or she experienced a definite sense of euphoria. This feeling of happiness was described in the same way by people in prominent positions and by factory workers.

The paradox became evident when the experimental subjects were asked about their wishes for the future. Since most of them had unequivocally stated that most of their positive experiences occurred during work and only a smaller part during leisure time, it might have been expected that they would desire more worktime and less time off. But the opposite was true. Even those who felt best while working desired less work. Those who were often in a sour mood during their leisure hours wanted even more time off. Some of them said that they had high hopes for their time off but easily became apathetic and depressed when their leisure time actually arrived.

What is the explanation of this paradox? Csikszentmihályi suggests that most people base their pronounced opinions about work and leisure time on the dominant cultural stereotypes instead of on their inner signals. They dismiss their own subjective experiences and conform to the "general point of view," which proscribes how you "should" experience your reality. According to the stereotype, work is a necessary evil, a burdensome infringement of individual liberty, if not an outright insult.

Csikszentmihályi doesn't accept the general view that you have to "relax" in order to "recharge" for work, sometimes several hours per day, even if you don't enjoy the rest. All psychological experience points in the opposite direction. Low motivation for work doesn't usually depend on physical or mental fatigue. Dissatisfied workers complain less often about heavy workloads or low salaries than about monotonous routines, lack of diversity and stimulation, and personal conflicts. But even those who enjoy their work often tell others that they regard it as a waste of mental energy. They dismiss the positive experience from their "inner balance sheet" since it doesn't contribute to their "real" goals. Those who find work monotonous rarely realize that they should try to increase the diversity on their own and in ways that make better use of their abilities.

Wasteful use of leisure time is another major problem. Many people panic when they're left alone with the responsibility to use their own time. Unstructured time that doesn't provide any tasks for their mental energy seems worse to them than the time spent doing alienating work. When the much-coveted increase in leisure time finally arrives, many of the recipients don't know what to do with it. They become more passive, irritated, depressed, and weak. Passive relaxation, for example watching TV, alleviates the problem to some extent, but the viewer remains weak and nervous. The ancient Greeks were fully aware that leisure time couldn't be enjoyed in itself, but had to be continuously cultivated through meaningful activities. In the early 1930s the American sociologist Robert Bark wrote: "It is in the improvident use of our leisure, I suspect, that the greatest wastes of American life occur."

The vast leisure industry pretends to offer enjoyable experiences. But instead of stimulating people to use their physical and mental resources it cajoles them to stare at famous athletes displaying *their* abilities in enormous sport halls. Instead of playing music we listen—often fairly absent-mindedly—to great virtuosos playing *their* music on faultless records. And instead of testing our abilities to create some form of art, as we used to do when we once lived in caves, we attend exhibitions where we admire paintings in proportion to the fame of the artists and the monetary worth of their work. We do our best to avoid all risks in our everyday lives but spend many hours watching actors pretending to be involved in risky adventures. Such diversions can fill out our "empty moments" but they remain bleak surrogates compared to the mental satisfaction that we can reach by concentrating on challenging tasks. Somewhere deep down we know instinctively that we must develop our personality through our own activities and that passive entertainments don't lead anywhere. But in Csikszentmihályi's words, we waste "the equivalent of millions of years of human consciousness" each year. The products of popular culture are the parasites of our psyches. Unreal as they usually are, they pretend to mirror reality; they absorb our mental energy but provide no strength in return. They leave us more fatigued and dejected than we were before. Their real purpose is to generate profit for others.

Some of the greatest utopian novels of our century have in a masterful way described the consequences of man's increasing passivity. The apparently benign, hedonistic development of consumer society has been given its most ironic description in Aldous Huxley's *Brave New World*. The book was written in 1932 but is now more topical than ever. Its ideal citizens are imprinted as infants in order to develop the right ambitions for their particular social class, and in order to be content with their lot they regularly take a drug without side effects called Soma which renders them satisfied and easy to handle. George Orwell's nightmare with the outdated title *1984* is a perfect description of the Stalinist kindergarten with its constant supervision, its propagandic distortions of all fact, and its secret police that tortures its prisoners in the windowless "Ministry of Love" in order to extinguish their last vestiges of individuality.

Are there any similarities between the effects of consumer society and the efforts of communist dictatorships to render their consumers and subjects more passive?

In the spring of 1965 I traveled to the Soviet Union for the first time. I was to participate in a symposium on cancer-immunology at the Black Sea. At the Moscow airport I and one of my Swedish co-workers were met by a young Russian colleague whose name we knew from his published articles and who was quite familiar with our work. He drove us to our hotel. We happened to arrive in the middle of the festivities celebrating the twentieth anniversary of the victory over Hitler. The road from the airport was lined with flags, banners, and large images of Marx, Engels, and Lenin plus a few smaller ones of the present-day leaders. Immense neon signs proclaimed all kinds of slogans. We asked our Russian colleague to translate. They were the usual tributes to the Communist party, the leaders, Socialism, the five-year plan, and even Soviet science. When our colleague noticed that we were quite overwhelmed by this mammoth display and the constant repetitions, he asked with surprise if such tributes weren't displayed at comparable anniversaries in Stockholm. We got such a good laugh that we risked insulting our Russian host. But he was only surprised. He'd never been abroad and imagined that the entire world worked like the Soviet Union.

A few weeks later when I traveled from JFK airport into Manhattan it struck me that perhaps our merriment had been a bit thoughtless. The road was lined by the countless advertisements of market society. You were continuously enticed to buy a large number of products that you didn't need. I was aware of the astronomical difference between Communist dictatorship and free commerce, between freedom of speech and censorship, between a system based on justice and human rights and one based on political decisions and an arbitrary lack of justice. But if the two systems had anything in common it was this: the tendency to transform man, selected by evolution for his high level of activity, into a passive receptacle of indoctrination and/or entertainment.

What is the situation among us scientists? Do we constantly experience new flow experiences in our laboratories and at our conferences?

SCIENCE AND FLOW

Australian Sir MacFarlane Burnet was one of the most influential scientists in the fields of virology and immunology in the mid-1900s. When he retired from his professorship in Melbourne in 1965 he was his country's most internationally renowned scientist and one of its few Nobel Prize winners. An international scientific conference was held in his honor centering on the thymus gland and its lymphocytes. At the farewell ceremony he delivered a speech in the presence of Australia's governor general, members of the government, scientists, journalists, and a large general public. Burnet spoke in his characteristically introverted manner, his eyes half-shut as if he were meditating. It wasn't an act; Sir Mac was no poseur. The two deep lines above his nose gave proof of his intense concentration on his chosen topic: what forces motivate the scientist in his work? This was exactly the way we used to see Burnet each time he speculated, boldly and often mistakenly but always in an inspiring manner, on how or why cells or viruses behave the way they do. He was always as intensely focused when talking to a single person, discussing with a group, or lecturing in front of a crowded auditorium. His searchlights

were pointed inward, looking for the answer within his own consciousness. Now he had found this:

The general public and its political and mass media representatives usually assume that scientists are driven by the desire to produce practical and useful results. Sometimes there's also talk about
curiosity as a basic motivation. These factors are certainly important,
but the truly creative scientist is above all driven by the pleasure he
takes in his work. This is more important to him than the practical
objectives of his work or its importance to his career. It's also important for the quality of the work. The delightful excitement of the creative scientist is essential for the unbiased exploration of natural
phenomena, an exploration that doesn't benefit from the side glances
that inevitably accompany any goal-oriented activity. Taking pleasure in one's work creates the best basis for producing results that
are true and therefore potentially important.

Burnet's speech was delivered many years before Csikszentmihályi's definition of flow, but his conclusions are in line with the psychologist's results showing how the achievements of students increase in proportion to their enjoyment of their work.

When similar thoughts are put forth by less prominent scientists—which seldom happens—they usually provoke irritation. Does
he mean that public money should be spent to allow scientists to play
and amuse themselves? But Burnet's speech wasn't a plea for funds.
He merely observed that only by playfully enjoying one's work can
one create and maintain the mental energy needed to produce imag-
inative and novel scientific results.

Scientists who have experienced the joy of creativity readily
agree with Burnet's conclusion. Yet some colleagues in that great hall
in Melbourne were slightly embarrassed. Hadn't Burnet betrayed
their innermost secret? What accusations could they expect after
this? A barrage of pies in the faces of a spoiled "elite" hoping to be
paid for their hobby?

Nothing of the sort happened at the time. Burnet's unquestioned
authority enabled him to reveal the carefully concealed truth.

How did he gain his great authority? Not through his experiments. I first met him in Torbjörn Caspersson's laboratory in Stockholm in the early 1950s, when I was a young assistant professor. Just prior to our meeting I had set up our new animal section for inbred mice. Burnet dropped by for a visit and my boss asked me to show him the mouse rooms. During the walking tour he wanted to know what a certain green marker on the cages stood for. Vaccination, I answered. Against what? Against mouse pox, ectromelia. That's funny, said Burnet. Your vaccination is based on the only practically useful discovery I've ever made.

That's right—how could I have forgotten? Vaccination against mouse pox had been developed by Burnet and Frank Fenner a few decades earlier. The procedure is valuable for scientists who experiment with mice, but is otherwise of no practical use.

Why would a man whose one useful discovery is vaccination against mouse pox attain such grand international eminence?

Burnet was primarily a theoretician and a rich source of new ideas. He received his Nobel Prize for a theory—immunological tolerance—that was later confirmed by experiments made by Peter Medawar in England, with whom Burnet shared the prize. This time Burnet's theory proved true, but in other cases he's often been mistaken. Strangely enough his mistaken theories have been as influential as his correct ones, if not more so. One of his virologist colleagues describes Burnet's method like this:

Sir Mac conducts an experiment with five eggs over the course of five days. From the result he builds a theory. Instead of writing a customary article about his findings, he summarizes all his thoughts and associations in a thick book which leads to an unconventional hypothesis, articulated in fairly categorical and provocative terms. Some readers are stimulated, many are irritated. Then five hundred scientists use 500,000 eggs over the course of five years before Burnet's theory is completely disproved. But in the meantime a new science has emerged. At this point Burnet himself has lost all interest in the matter and turned to another field that he approaches in a similar way.

Burnet's method may appear eccentric today, but it followed a certain tradition in the English-speaking world where renowned scientists would construct grandiose theories based on their own observations or those of their fellow scientists. Modern molecular biology works in an entirely different way. It has been said that it is based on 99 percent perspiration and only 1 percent inspiration. Every scientist must develop his own tricks to manage the voyage between the Scylla of anxiety, when everything fails, and the Charybdis of boredom, which looms menacingly during the endless and monotonous routines of experimentation. Flow experiences are rare, and the few oases of playful, pleasurable involvement in one's work must be cultivated carefully. The conditions are best in so-called creative environments when the give-and-take between different scientists with the right personal chemistry can create great joy or—when things fail—great despair.

More than a quarter of a century has passed since Burnet's farewell lecture. The Walter and Eliza Hall Institute which he founded and led during several decades is still the most outstanding biomedical research institution in Australia and one of the foremost in the world. How has the creative environment been preserved and renewed?

Burnet was succeeded by his disciple Gustav Nossal, who has paid tribute to Burnet's tremendous influence on his generation but who works and thinks in a completely different way. In his parting speech to Burnet at the 1965 farewell ceremony Nossal emphasized that the post-Burnet department must emphasize technology and teamwork. In so doing he put his finger on the two main shortcomings at Burnet's institute. Sir Mac was more interested in ideas than in the minutia of patient experimentation. Ideas can be important enough, especially when formulated as clearly and in as provocative a manner as Burnet was capable of, but experiments are the true life substance of biology. Another problem was that Burnet was quite introverted and rather shy. He made no major efforts to encourage cooperation between different individuals and groups.

His successor has fulfilled his intentions in a remarkable way. Sir Gustav Nossal, one of the leading figures of modern immunology, is of Austrian-Jewish heritage but has spent his entire scientific career in Australia and the United States. Unlike Burnet, he is an extrovert who takes great interest in people. His personal and professional style of communication combines a fairly cozy Central European attitude with a strictly disciplined Anglo-Saxon work ethic and manner of expression. In his own research Nossal has mostly dealt with the question of how and when the cells of the immune system learn to distinguish between the proteins of its own organism ("self") and foreign proteins ("non-self"). The second leading researcher at the Institute, the laconic and sometimes playfully sarcastic Australian Donald Metcalf, has taken on the seemingly impossible task of identifying and purifying the signal substances which the cells of the hematopoetic (i.e., blood-producing) system, use to "speak" with each other. Chemical signals of this kind can prompt a certain type of cell to divide while others are ordered not to multiply but "mature," meaning the development of more highly specialized functions. Nossal's enthusiasm and Metcalf's skepticism became the pivotal axis around which the institution has revolved since Burnet's departure. The flabbergasting developments of modern molecular biology have not taken these two practical biologists by surprise, as they have many others. Metcalf has managed to purify a vast array of signal substances and isolate their genes. They may prove useful in the treatment of severe anemias and certain leukemias.

Nossal has recruited the research team of Susanne Cory and Jerry Adams to the institute. Cory and Adams, a married couple, had earlier studied the rearrangement of antibody-producing genes during lymphocyte development. These rearrangements take place at the level of the DNA and create an enormous multitude of antibodies within each individual. The antibody-genes play a veritable Monte Carlo game in our lymphocytes. They randomly recombine their code letters within certain "hypervariable" areas. As a result, different lymphocytes carry different antibodies on their surface. When a foreign protein comes in contact with a lymphocyte that carries an antibody which happens to feature the right combination—meaning that it fits the protein in the manner of a key fitting a lock—it stimulates the "correct" lymphocyte to divide. This rapidly increases the number of lymphocytes that can produce the anti-body directed against the same foreign protein. Other lymphocytes, those that haven't hit upon their matching protein within a certain lim-ited period, commit "programmed suicide": they break down their own DNA and die. This puzzling game explains the "foresight" of the im-mune system, i.e., its ability to produce antibodies against chemical substances that have been synthesized by modern industry and that our species has never before come in contact with.

Lately Cory and Adams have been mainly interested in "cancer genes," meaning growth-regulating genes that can contribute to tumor development after they have undergone certain mutations.* Before the Australians began working in this field, mutations of cancer genes had already been identified in many tumor types. It has also been showed experimentally that the mutated genes can transform normal cells into cancerous cells in test-tube cultures. Cory and Adams went one step further. They inserted similar pathologically active cancer genes into newly fertilized mouse eggs, which were then implanted into the wombs of female mice that had been prepared for pregnancy. The implanted eggs developed into vigorous mice. All of their cells contained the in-serted gene which was called a "transgene." The mice were fully normal to begin with, but after a few months they developed tumors at a high rate (up to 95 percent). Which type of tumor the mice developed de-pended on the exact nature of the inserted gene. Each transgene was connected with an "enhancer," a kind of switch sequence that could ac-tivate the attached gene whenever it found itself in the cell type where the enhancer normally worked. The enhancers had been borrowed from normal genes that were active in the normal tissue that was of particular interest and that the experimenters wanted to imitate. Cory and Adams have used the enhancers of the antibody genes themselves that can work in all antibody-producing lymphocytes. The "construct," i.e., the cancer

---

*For a more detailed discussion about cancer genes see the essay "The Tale of the Great Cuckoo Egg" in George Klein, *The Atheist and the Holy City*.

The Australians were next to last on the list of lecturers. A more un-favorable situation was hardly thinkable and the audience seemed totally bored. But after Susan Cory's first sentence everyone was wide awake. This wasn't a repetition of the same tune. The long-distance guests from down under had obviously crossed some frontier in their research without having applied for a proper visa! The usual "me too"- or "I was first with this or that"-type of talk was strikingly absent. Instead Adams and Cory produced unexpected results that connected logically to the existing body of knowledge. An intense sense of delight spread through the audi-torium, robbing the windowlessness and the stuffy air of their soporific power. Suddenly it felt as if we'd been moved to the center of the action. Adams and Cory's lecture was followed by an intense discussion. The last lecturer could, undeservedly, lap in a sea of enthusiasm.

The conference by the Dead Sea, which was about cancer genes, began in a completely different atmosphere. The Ein Gedi kibbutz is lo-cated on a small hill above the majestically calm, thick-flowing, salty waters. The bare, jagged mountains of red and brown are reflected in the viscous, metal-smooth surface and rendered dreamily obscure. Leop-ards and mountain goats live in their caves. The biblical hero David supposedly hid out in one of them when the jealous King Saul wanted to have him killed.

This area, which is located at the lowest altitude on our planet, is the chosen sight of a yearly international conference series on cancer named after the great Jewish medieval philosopher and physician Mai-monides. This is the fifth annual conference. We're all together fifty par-ticipants, thirty from Israel and twenty foreigners. In the morning we convene in a small conference room to listen to each other's talks. Whenever we feel like it we can supply ourselves with coffee and the kibbutz's delicious pastry. Our presentations are informal and are often interrupted by questions. There is a prevailing intensity and excitement in the air. It's difficult to know whether this is mainly due to the intense focusing on the scientific problem or to the unusual environment. Re-gardless of which is the cause and which the effect, the fact remains that we all feel exhilarated and involved.

Our afternoons are free for archaeological outings or other adventures. Herod's mighty fortress Masada, where the entire Jewish garrison and their families committed collective suicide in the year 73 after having held the Roman army at bay for three years following the fall of Jerusalem, is visible against the southern horizon with its three artificial, steplike plateaus on a mountaintop above the Dead Sea. From the fortress you can look down on the Roman army camps below or at the ramp that the Romans built in order to storm the fortress and which convinced the besieged garrison that they were doomed. You can walk around the large water cisterns—their supply of water could have lasted many more years—or look at Herod's once luxurious steam baths or his bakery. If you're interested in religion you can inspect the synagogue or the ritual bath where the measurements strictly adhere to Jewish law.

North of Ein Gedi are the Qumran caves, ancient home of the Essenes, a Jewish sect whose religion and philosophy is regarded as a precursor of the teachings of Christ. Bedouin shepherd boys found the Dead Sea Scrolls in these caves. If you've already seen the archaeological sights you can visit the sulphur bath at the Dead Sea or lounge by the large swimming pool, alone or in informal discussion groups. Those in good physical condition can climb up the steep mountains or visit "David's Spring," a water-rich oasis in the middle of the desert landscape. After dinner we reconvene in the conference room and continue our discussions until our eyes can no longer stay open.

The foreign participants who are visiting the area for the first time have perhaps expected a regular convention, possibly spiced with some special tourist attraction on the side. Most scientists live a fairly monotonous life. They work hard at their labs and move within their own world of thoughts with its special language. Many of them prefer to socialize with their colleagues regardless of how stimulating or boring, cooperative or competitive these may be. Their "leisure time" is mostly spent reading literature or writing manuscripts and intricate and time-consuming grant applications that are decisive for their research. During their recurrent trips to various conferences they see mostly airports and conference facilities. Nights are spent in sterile hotel rooms where you may either suffer from or enjoy your solitude while preparing for your next encounter with your competitors. Some go out and "enjoy themselves" but then pay the price of struggling to stay awake during the next day's lectures.

In Ein Gedi everything was different. We were on an active, vital kibbutz in the middle of the wilderness. We were surrounded everywhere by large trees, abundant verdure, and magnificent flowers. On our way to the conference area we passed the school house, the kindergarten, and the small family houses. We took our meals in the communal dining hall and thus didn't have to cope with the paid smiles and cold eyes of a dull hotel staff. In the mornings you would meet young mothers driving their children to the "children's house" in supermarketlike carts. Someone was practicing the trumpet behind a window. Walking around the grounds you had to negotiate irrigation hoses and playing children, puppies, and kittens. The air was clean and dry, the wind and sun constantly shifting over this strange "sea" which in the kibbutz's folk songs is called Jam Hamavet, the Sea of Death, instead of the official Jam Hamelach, the Sea of Salt. You can afford to joke about death when you're smack in the middle of flowering life.

The subjects of the scientific conference seemed newer, more interesting and more alive than at regular conferences. The territorial signals, the "here am I, I've come before you" cries, were as good as gone or were at least severely muffled. Our sometimes dormant but never completely repressed fascination for the astounding solutions that evolution has found to facilitate the adaptation of living organisms to their environment had woken from its winter sleep. That marvelous wonderland of our scientific youths suddenly seemed to have forgotten its fall from grace, its long lost virginity. The Australians' research sparked great interest here too, but so did many other contributions. Even the familiar was seen in new colors and nothing seemed obvious anymore. As established articles of scientific faith were questioned and "classic" concepts were torn to shreds, the gray dullness of everyday competition was swept away. Everyone felt like a child at an exciting playground.

The atmosphere reminded me of the conferences of my youth at Cold

Spring Harbor or the many Gordon conferences in idyllic college environments in New England. The intellectual world of modern biology
would be formed and formulated in the dining hall or at the beach where
young students could easily mingle with the field's legendary founding
fathers. An excellent place to indulge in the free play of thoughts was in
the sun on the jetty. During relaxed walks the differences in age and academic status were quickly forgotten and one could ask and speak freely
without worrying about whether it was appropriate. There was a sort of
"communal flow" in the air at these meetings, as there was in Ein Gedi.
The individual euphoria of "I can do it" was supplemented with the even
more unexpected and joyous feeling that said "we can do this together,
our thoughts are fertilizing each other, we don't have to be afraid to make
fools of ourselves or be robbed of our ideas—this is exhilarating!"

On our last night in Ein Gedi there was a farewell party. It turned out
that our small group of scientists harbored hidden talents for acting,
magic tricks, music, and song. The members of the conference lampooned
each other and themselves in roisterous abandon. Susan Cory, normally of
strict, polite, and correct Anglo-Saxon manners, appeared as a large os-
trichlike bird. It was identified as an emu, the alphabetic combination of
which corresponds to the immunoglobulin enhancer mentioned earlier
that was a part of her molecular constructs. A serious German professor,
who at first had seemed chained to his formal academic demeanor, was a
great success as a hen in this biological pantomime. His Cantabrigian colleague acted the role of the ambitious young molecular biologist. Pointing
to a long series of slides he called everything visible an artifact, while in-
sisting that the empty space where nothing was visible contained important but alas too poorly developed signals.

The collective euphoria ended naturally the week after the conference. It didn't take many days of being back home to sink back into the
routine of everyday life. But the memory of the euphoria remained as a
promise: this is possible; it must be possible to create it anew!

Is it possible to create and maintain an innovative, cooperative, and
joyful laboratory environment? Can the meeting of minds around a
shared set of problems, the excitement of discovery, and the joy of un-

derstanding bridge the dark canyons of competition, envy, and personal conflict?

Modern biology emerged from a small number of creative environments. One of the most interesting was at the Pasteur Institute in Paris during the 1950s and 1960s. The Nobel Prize-winning French trio of 1965, André Lwoff, Jacques Monod, and François Jacob, were at first ignored by the French academic establishment. Their work received much more attention on the international scene. During the 1940s and 1950s biology had begun to be transformed into an exact science as it turned out that micro-organisms offered great opportunities for rapid and exact experimentation on a large scale. They also realized, after a long period of doubt, that bacteria follow the same elementary genetic laws as the cells of higher organisms. It was a rare moment in time when lack of respect for established dogmas constituted an important resource. "We were biochemists without a license," Monod said later. Despite their status as outsiders in France, or perhaps because of it, the group around Lwoff and Monod worked in an atmosphere of absolute devotion. The youngest of the three, Jacob, joined the group as a student five years after the end of World War II. In his view the most important ingredients of the environment were "enthusiasm, clear and critical thinking, nonconformity, and friendship."*

Jacob was hired only after having for a long time stubbornly pleaded with the then fifty-year-old group leader André Lwoff. Around Lwoff there was a "remarkable atmosphere, a warm and open spirit, life and imagination." Lwoff advised Jacob to forget about his formal merits, prompting "Experiment! The rest will follow by itself." Lwoff knew what he was talking about, even if his advice was as unique as the man himself. He never obtained the proper formal credentials in France and although he was known all around the world he held no particular formal position in France. He conducted many of his experiments on his own and wanted to "know" the organisms with his fingertips. Lwoff lavished the same loving care on his amoebae, bacteria, and tissue cells as on his

---

*François Jacob, *La Statue Interieure*, edited by Odile Jacob (Paris, 1987).

co-workers. To the young Jacob he was a grandseigneur from another century. Lwoff treated him with "heartwarming kindness," first as a continuously encouraging "patron," and later also as a driving force and a laudator. It was a very unusual father-son relationship in the scientific community which later turned into a warm friendship between peers.

Unlike the empiricist Lwoff, who, with Latin precision, derived his conclusions from his experiments, Monod was a master of logic who could think up complicated and surprisingly often correct solutions to problems without leaving his desk. According to Jacob, Monod had a special sense of the interplay between theory and experiment.* He could formulate crystal-clear hypotheses and plan experiments in order to prove or disprove them. "He had the ability, otherwise mostly found in poets, to see signs that others couldn't see." But, as is so often the case with such strong personalities, Jacques Monod contained several rather contradictory individuals within himself—at least two, even if you only speak of Monod the scientist, writes Jacob. The first, whom he calls Jacques, was warm and generous, interested in people and ideas, always accessible to his friends—a man with a strong sense of self-criticism, a rigorous logician with broad insights, who could pose the most relevant questions. Jacob calls "the other individual" Monod, a dogmatic, self-assured, and domineering person who was constantly looking for admiration and publicity, always ready to make value judgments in black and white, and who had an unpleasant tendency to lecture his colleagues about what their work really meant and dismiss their arguments as "complete nonsense." Jacques could cast aside all of his priorities in order to help a friend in a tough spot. Monod could turn a friend into a lifelong foe with just a few words. In private conversation one met Jacques. In front of a larger audience one was often forced to encounter Monod. Working with the first was an "exceptional pleasure." Talking with the other could be a traumatic experience.

About a decade separated each of these three unusual, very dif-

---

*François Jacob, *Origins of Molecular Biology*, edited by André and Agnes Ullman (New York: Academic Press, 1979).

ferent but still very compatible gentlemen. Lwoff was born in 1902, Monod in 1910, and Jacob in 1920. Many gifted young scientists, especially from the United States, were drawn to their laboratory. Jacob has described the lab from this period—with the many colorful Americans, the constant seminars where everyone was simultaneously an actor and a listener, the pyrotechnical display of ideas and personalities, the tense intellectual duels and relaxed beer nights, the discussions that "bounced back and forth" between science and theater, bacteriology and the music of Bach—altogether a completely different world from the commonly imagined humdrum research environment. It was a world of curiosity and imagination illuminated by the joy of the unexpected. It could spark the deepest passions and the coolest logic at the same time. Personal relations were as complicated as at a royal court, with Monod the evident monarch. There was a constant struggle for intellectual domination, yet the youngest and most inexperienced student could be given the chance of a lifetime. If the student was François Jacob, he could silently build on his experiences from the war when he was one of de Gaulle's most decorated soldiers in Africa. He decided to employ the same careful planning, great stubbornness, and all-out attack on all fronts. And he won. One of his most important insights came suddenly during a movie he went to see with his wife. He suddenly realized that the same biological mechanisms were at work in regulating the degradation of sugars as in controlling the adaptation of a bacterial virus (bacteriophage) to its host cell. He remembers the moment as a rare intoxication of insight, combined with a feeling of deep loneliness. His wife couldn't understand why this idea was so important, and not even Monod realized it the next morning but was all the more enthusiastic the following day.

Creative environments of this kind are fairly rare and relatively temporary. Someone has calculated their average life-span to about fifteen years (allowing for large variations in both directions). Sir Hans Krebs, the great biochemist, has compared the creative environment to an enzyme: it works fast and with great precision, but is vulnerable to very small amounts of poison. It isn't hard to imagine which types of poison

would destroy such a creative environment: competition, personal conflicts, political meddling, and "structural rationalization" can ruin the
excitement of discovery and destroy the joys of friendship and free communication. It may also happen that the shared motivation is extinguished when the originators of the creative atmosphere disappear from
the scene. But no one who has experienced the enchantment of the
"functioning enzyme" will ever forget the timeless intoxication that
arises when creative people in a friendly environment, alone or together,
focus on the same problems. Some of them can re-ignite this enchantment at other places and in other shapes.

A FRONTAL COLLISION BETWEEN THE FLOW CONCEPT AND TWO MORALISTS

Together with an Israeli colleague I pay a visit to eighty-five-year-old
professor Yeshayahu Leibowitz in Jerusalem. It's my third visit with him.
Leibowitz is a legendary figure in Israel—a last polyhistor, philosopher,
national monument, and *enfant terrible* all in one. Most of all he resembles a prophet from the Old Testament. Many speak of him as a *nevi
zaam*, an angry prophet. His academic distinction is so overwhelming
that you at first refuse to believe that such a learned man exists. To the
general public he is best known as a difficult political character. Leibowitz wasn't seduced by the exaltation during the Six Day War.* The
very next week he angrily demanded that Israel immediately return all
of the occupied territories, except for Eastern Jerusalem.

---

*On June 5, 1967, less than a month after United Nations peace-keeping forces
had been removed from the area, war broke out between Egypt and Israel and two days
later with Jordan as well. Within four days the entire Sinai Peninsula, the Gaza Strip,
East Jerusalem, and the West Bank had been captured from Egypt and Jordan by Israeli soldiers, who then stormed the Golan Heights on the Syrian front. A UN-sponsored
ceasefire went into effect on June 11, 1967, but by that time Israel had greatly increased its territory, as well as its Palestinian-Arab population.

Leibowitz started out as a professor of inorganic chemistry, but has also taught extensively in many other subjects. His lectures in neurophysiology were for many years among the most popular at the Hebrew University in Jerusalem. His popular science lecture series about "body and soul" continue to attract large group of listeners from wide circles. He holds six or seven doctoral degrees, but these fade in importance next to his encyclopedic knowledge, which eclipses Academia. He is widely renowned as an expert in theoretical philosophy. He has written all the chapters about Russian literature in the Hebrew encyclopedia—Russian being one of the many languages he has mastered fully. But he is no superficial popularizer as you would suspect. He is respected and to a certain extent feared by the foremost experts within every field that has engaged his remarkable mental powers.

But Leibowitz also has a few additional qualities that you may not expect to find in such a learned man, at least not in combination. He's a religious orthodox and a radical political activist at the same time. He obeys the numerous religious laws to the letter. He follows all proscriptions on diet and prayer and never breaks the many prohibitions connected with the Sabbath and the holidays. He visits the synagogue at least twice a day. If you speak to him about philosophy, the names he most often mentions are Kant and Aristotle—he speaks of "Aristo" as if he were quoting an old friend. His skeptical outlook gives an outright agnostic impression. Asked why he finds it necessary to obey all the old religious rules so meticulously he only offers the laconic reply: "Because it is the law." Everything can be subject to discussion except the religious law, which is only to be followed. To the letter.

Leibowitz's political standpoints follow from his moral principles. "We have always been the people of the Book and the Spirit; we must not let ourselves be turned into wardens, policemen, and occupants," he says often and with emphasis. During the war in Lebanon he published a full-page ad in the largest papers where he urged the Israeli soldiers to refuse duty in Lebanon—an act which according to Israeli law can be regarded as criminal incitement. After some discussion the authorities refrained from putting Leibowitz on trial. Did they feel something of the same respect that made it possible for the prophets to expound their angry message in the Israel of the Old Testament?

Leibowitz listened quietly to my tale about Csikszentmihályi's studies and his concept of flow. His lean, pale face reflected a stern intensity which I recognized from earlier public and private discussions. He is loading his guns, I thought. When I had stopped talking he politely inquired if I was finished. His comment followed immediately after my affirmative answer. It was as short as it was unambiguous: "BLOODY NONSENSE!"

To be on the sure side he repeated the same two words three more times. Then he added, "I don't understand what you are talking about."

My colleague made a bold attempt:

"But isn't it so, Professor Leibowitz, that many people have boring jobs? An employee at the post office who performs exactly the same chores day in and out without developing her own abilities may feel a need to be involved in new activities that put greater demands on her ability?"

"I don't know what you're talking about," Leibowitz repeated angrily. "She has that kind of job because she has *chosen* it. She does it to get her salary."

Suddenly he turned to me: "Why are you an honest man and not a thief?"

"I don't know," I answered. "I assume it's because of my upbringing, my family, and the rules I learned as a child."

"Nonsense," said Leibowitz, this time without invoking the blood. "You have *chosen* to be honest. I'll give you three examples. A politician knows that he'll be elected if he lies, but that he'll lose if he speaks the truth. He chooses to speak the truth. Why? Because it is his volition. A businessman knows that he'll win a million if he lies, but not if he speaks the truth. He chooses to speak the truth. Why? Because it is his volition. A youth knows that a girl will sleep with him if he lies, but not if he speaks the truth. He chooses to speak the truth. Why? Because it is his volition."

My colleague and I both contemplated what Leibowitz was saying.

We began to realize that an angry prophet who thinks in terms of categorical imperatives and invokes the threat of apocalyptic disasters unless the sinful inhabitants of Ninive, Sodom and Gomorrah, or modern-day Israel mend their ways, cannot accept the notion of flow or other psychological concepts based on personal satisfaction. We retired like chastised dogs. But it was perfectly clear to me that Leibowitz is a flow addict himself, regardless of his opinion in the matter. He has no understanding for people who are bored since he's never bored himself. The life of this eighty-five-year-old is as full of activities as that of a hyperactive teenager during his best moments. When he isn't reading, writing, or reciting his strictly scheduled prayers he receives visitors eager for his opinions. Most are content with listening in order not to elicit the wrath of the prophet. But even if you're subjected to the full brunt of his wrath, Leibowitz is as genuinely warm and polite when the badly bruised visitor is being treated to a cup of tea or—if he dares— when he asks for a return visit.

Leibowitz loves the fight. He's always ready to stuff his long, bony frame into small, shaky cars and travel for hours on bad roads in the most pressing summer heat or during the most intense downpours to a little kibbutz in Galilee or a village in the Negev desert—but never to a settlement on the West Bank or on the Golan Heights—in order to give a lecture or participate in a debate. He's as energetic and engaged when he's addressing a thousand listeners as when he's speaking to only half a dozen. No group is too small, no distance too great.* He's the natural op-

---

*Leibowitz's "flow addiction" can be further illustrated with the following: In 1993 I had invited him to our Maimonides Conference on cancer. He was to speak on Maimonides' concept of God to the largely agnostic group of scientists. He was driven from Jerusalem in a tiny car. Before his lecture he was seated in the kibbutz dining room on the same type of uncomfortable chair as everyone else. Thinking of his age, I was slightly worried and asked whether he wanted to rest (*lanuach* in Hebrew). As if woken from deep meditation, he quipped angrily: *"Me ma lanuach?"* From what should I rest? He had not yet worked, so there was no reason why he should rest. His lecture was followed in breathless silence by the group of scientists, most of them non-Jewish. While listening, I realized that I had never heard such a silence. Leibowitz's voice went down sometimes to the faintest pianissimo, only to hit the listeners with a sudden fortissimo that felt like a whip.

ponent in all debates. He takes aim at his opponent's weak points and then proceeds with a merciless attack. He usually gets the last word in all debates because he is more stubborn, more persistent, and more categorical than his opponent. This attitude is said to have been characteristic of Leibowitz's original cultural environment which was destroyed by the Holocaust. Religious Jews from Riga and Lithuania were often called *mitnagdim*, "the oppositional." They originally opposed Hassidism and its rabbinical cult, which was dominant among Polish religious Jews. The great hassidic rabbis are spiritual princes. They're revered by their followers, their interpretations are normative, and they serve as absolute judges in legal disputes. This authority is based on the rabbi's knowledge and his strict, often very plain way of life. "A cult of personality," Leibowitz said contemptuously when I asked him about the Hassidim. His short and drastic choice of words reflect the classical view of the *mitnagdim*. The "oppositional" are convinced individualists. Each one of them is alone with his God or with his superego, if you like, although Leibowitz would probably never accept a psychological terminology. They engage in a constant discussion with Him and thus frequently end up in violent quarrels. One is inevitably reminded of the name Israel—"he who wrestles with God"—a name which, according to tradition, Jacob was given after his nightly row with the angel that made him limp for life.

Leibowitz the flow addict who doesn't know what boredom is cannot understand how anyone can act according to the views or authority of others. During his eight decades he has probably never looked up from his own flow. He's always so involved in tough disputes with other people—and above all with the god that he probably doesn't believe in but whose laws he follows minutely—that he is as unaware of his flow as the fish is unaware of the water around him.

My close friend, the German molecular biologist Benno Müller-Hill* didn't care for the flow concept either. At first Benno saw no dif-

---

*I have earlier written about Müller-Hill and his research on the Nazi scientists and doctors who prepared and/or actively participated in the extermination of Jews and Gypsies during World War II. See the essay "Ultima Thule" in Klein, *The Atheist and the Holy City*, and the essay "The Ultimate Fear of the Traveler Returning from Hell" in Klein, *Pietà*.

ference between flow and enjoyment or libido. Even after he realized that the words weren't equivalent, he found the "hedonistic aspects" of the flow concept repugnant. The strong emphasis on taking pleasure in one's work and life as a way out from conventional passivity and apathy, available to everyone, is worthless in his eyes unless it is supplied with strong moral reservations. He couldn't accept an instrument that can be used for good or bad, not even as a psychological concept free from value judgments. Had not many of the Nazi murderers committed their crimes with a devotion similar to Csikszentmihályi's description of flow?

Yes, they probably had, even if I don't want to go so far as another friend, the immunologist David Weiss in Jerusalem, who suggests that the deeds of the Nazis may have been an example of collective flow. By all accounts many of them performed their loathsome work as a routine job. But Josef Mengele's devoted "research" on defenseless people was often performed in a state of flow, as we know from the description of his pathologist, Miklós Nyiszli.* But the kitchen knife can also be used as a murder weapon, even if we normally use it to cut bread. Must we not describe the world as it is, even when discussing a psychological phenomenon? The euphoria of the experience can compel good, evil, and morally neutral deeds. It is desirable that joyful and moral activities should coincide, but we are what we are, no matter what the moralists prefer. Besides, what should we say about moral systems in other cultures that don't correspond to our values? Our women wouldn't accept the religious fundamentalist view of women in patriarchic cultures. If you're raised in a democratic society you won't accept the ideologically masked "moral concepts" of totalitarian dictatorships that are in reality centered on power and discrimination. But the flow mechanism is the same in different cultures. Australian aborigines and African tribe-members experience flow just the way we Westerners do, and describe their condition in analogous terms. Our psychological reactions are much older than our moral systems.

I share Benno's rage at the Nazi murderers, regardless of whether or

---

*Miklós Nyiszli, *Auschwitz, An Eyewitness Report* (New York: Seaver Books, 1986).

not they carried out their deeds in a state of flow. But—banish the thought—what would have happened if Hitler had won the war? By now the Holocaust would already have been carried to its "final solution." Eleven, not six million European Jews would have been killed, according to the careful planning of the Wannsee Conference. Would the murder of "undesired" ethnic groups have continued with the same natural ease as the slaughter of animals for meat production?

Our evolution has made us into group beings. We're dependent upon each other's support and appreciation. Our greatest happiness and our deepest sorrow stem from our relationships with others. Long-term loneliness easily leads to depression, even if some of us must be alone during certain periods. Therefore "moral behavior" becomes a relative concept. Its prohibitions have been defined by the nation or the religion or ethnic group to which we belong. Our identity and our self-respect is dependent upon our own group's positive assessment of ourselves. Hitler's "Thousand-year Reich," which lasted for twelve years, defined the Jews and the Gypsies as subhuman and ranked them with pests. Thus their extermination was regarded as a positive measure, sanctioned by society. Doctor Mengele and the other murderer-physicians had a "clean conscience." They had accepted the ideology and worked within it. Some of them probably used flow mechanisms in their work, just like anyone might. If my moralist friends want to discard the flow concept for this reason, it's like the married man in the old story who found his wife in bed with his best friend, and so proceeded to throw out the bed.

Let's take a look at some less desirable forms of flow.

DESTRUCTIVE FLOW

Csikszentmihályi's list of prime examples of flow contains not only the mountain climber, the microsurgeon, and the mathematician, but also the safe-cracker performing a well-planned heist. Collective flow experiences in dynamic groups are not limited to science or art, but also occur in the fields of war and crime. Visionary politicians have attempted to instill group flow in wide segments of their societies, but the results were not what they expected. Mao Tse Tung's dream of the "eternal revolution" let loose the destructive demons of the cultural revolution, and Ben Gurion couldn't stop the transformation of the pioneer Israeli state into a rather ordinary bourgeois society by launching the project devoted to making the desert bloom.

In 1978 Israel's legendary General Moshe Dayan was interviewed on Swedish television. When asked how young soldiers reacted to the war, his one eye lit up. But war is so exciting!—he answered with his famously brutal but disarming sincerity. The startled interviewer obviously expected an answer more in line with Swedish norms. This man should be shot, said an American guest researcher in the lab the next day. But Dayan was no war-mongerer. He worked to improve relations with the Arabs, and among other things created the "open bridges policy." He merely told it like it was. Hadn't the interviewer read the history books? Didn't his grandfather ever talk about the joy with which so many nations plunged themselves into the First World War, fully convinced that they might win it?

As soon as a war gets stuck or turns disastrous those who were previously so belligerent quickly sober from their intoxication. Finally only the ruins remain. Death, that mighty field marshal who surveys the dead on both sides with the true victor's absolute indifference of Mussorgsky's *Songs and Dances of Death,* is the sole victor.

How often does one reach for the euphoria of various flow experiences in order to flee the monotony of existence by creating a new challenge? Isn't it mostly bored teenagers who vandalize telephone booths or smash shop windows on New Year's Eve? And why do talented people create computer viruses that destroy the hard work of many others?

How often, in the past, were duels fought for similar reasons? Which role did the flight from boredom play at Hitler's frenzied mass meetings? Why do people enjoy attending bullfights in Spain and cockfights in Bali? How can one explain the violence of rampaging soccer fans?

Optimal Experience, the conference volume on flow mentioned earlier, contains an article by the Japanese psychologist Ikuya Sato on the

death-defying Japanese motorcycle gangs called *bosozoku*. Despite
being constantly hounded by the police these daredevils continue to
tempt fate and challenge the general public. During their "runs" they
drive at speeds of forty to seventy miles per hour with their motors
roaring at full volume through heavily trafficked, speed-restricted
streets in Tokyo and Kyoto. They paralyze traffic, cause accidents, and
have made a sport out of thwarting and fooling the police cars. Each year
about eighty to ninety *bosozoku* kids die in traffic, about 1,000 are severely injured, and between 6,000 and 7,000 are arrested for "collective
behavior that is dangerous to the general public." But the activity continues and is actually gaining momentum.

Sato has found no support for the previously widely accepted claim
that this dangerous game is caused by "frustration" or family problems,
nor does his research support the notion that the speed freaks are
dropouts bent on showing off and gaining the recognition that they
lacked in school or in the workplace. But he's found a clear link between
the adolescents' own description of their experiences and the following
description of flow by Csikszentmihályi:

"During the condition of flow one activity follows the other according to an inner logic which does not demand conscious control.
Everything flows from moment to moment like an interconnected unity
and one has full control over one's actions. The borders between the
person and his surroundings, between stimulation and response, and between the past, the present, and the future are erased."

The *bosozuko* drivers isolate themselves from their everyday lives in
good time prior to each run. The word they use to describe the special
atmosphere during the countdown to the start, when a crowd of youths
gather with their vehicles, connotes "feast" or "carnival." Their sense of
belonging reaches an explosive pitch with the sudden, overpowering
roar of the engines from which the mufflers have been illegally removed,
the persistent honking and the blinding glare of the strong headlights.
This contrast with their normal, gray, boring life creates a unique experience that the youths cannot describe, but only suggest with gestures,
facial expressions, and guttural sounds. During their run they don't care

how they're perceived by outsiders; their "observer role" completely evaporates. Their bodies move automatically, without need of conscious control. The kids convey a sense of merging with the entire world: "You burn like a fire; you're completely paralyzed; you feel very, very high; all sense of time disappears."

All *bosozoku* kids that Sato interviewed were aware of the danger to their lives, and each one remembered a friend who had been killed. But they also regarded the danger as a necessary requirement for the entire experience. They voiced their contempt for helmets, leather gloves, boots, and other forms of protective gear. Some of them drove with their arm or leg in a cast from an earlier accident, but still refused to don any protective gear.

Despite the fact that the *bosozoku* members often boasted to their friends about the risks they took, it was evident that risk-taking wasn't a goal in itself. The danger was only interesting to the extent that it tested their skills. A danger which couldn't be mastered was without interest. The awareness of the danger was transformed into self-confidence during their drive: I am competent, I am the master of my situation. Fear—the reflection "how could I do this?"—arrived only after the run was through.

Their game of hide-and-seek with the police increased their feelings of power and competence. Fleeing from pursuing police cars was simply the most exciting activity imaginable!

Sato remarked that it's difficult for the kids to "be seen" in the crowded, ethnically homogenous Japanese cities where most people work hard. The kids are each like a drop in the human sea, and are therefore denied any confirmation of their individual identity. *Bosozoku* opens the way to *medatsu*, to be seen, which is not the same as self-assertion or prestige, flash and glamour. The difference is that *medatsu* doesn't presuppose that the actor and his audience share the same basic values. It only means that the actor is taken notice of, in either a positive or negative way.

Sato has also made a comparative study of the motorcyclists and other categories of people who are intensely involved in their tasks. All experimental subjects were asked to rank their enjoyment of various activities. Mountain climbers, chess players, composers, and ballet dancers gave top ranking to the moments when they could put their ability and their experiences to maximum use. The *bosozoku* youths valued friendship and togetherness highest, and ranked making full use of their own abilities in fourth place. Prestige and glamour ended up in last place among all those queried. Competition also received a low score. The direct enjoyment of the activity itself ended up in second place among mountain climbers and chess players, but in third place among motorcyclists, who ranked emotional release in second place.

Thus, most important to the *bosozoku* driver is his dramatic acting out of a heroic role in front of an involuntary audience and the connected sense of belonging to the group and communal joy. Unlike the subjects in the other flow categories mentioned, he can't experience the same joy when he's driving alone. This is an important difference compared with, for example, the mountain climber. Both use their skill in a disciplined way, but the *bosozoku* experience cannot be planned and controlled by the single individual in the same rational way as mountain climbing. It's characterized by several more uncontrollable factors. The sense of danger is common to them both, but mountain climbing demands sustained concentration and a much higher level of intellectual and physical skill. The mountain climber assigns high value to creative solutions but has no sympathy for unnecessary risk-taking or relying on coincidence. You become a mountain climber or a chess player only after a long process of maturation based on your individual struggle with the challenge. The motorcycle-driving of the *bosozoku* gangs, on the other hand, is a group activity where the details are decided by leaders who needn't use more than a modest ingredient of intellectual skill. Herein lies the limitation of *bosozoku* and in other forms of play. The large risks are not in proportion to the low intellectual challenge. Most kids quit when they realize this, or when they're no longer content with capturing the attention of the viewer but prefer instead to be accepted and perhaps admired. The pleasure of their runs decreases rapidly and they move along to other activities.

This ties in with Csikszentmihályi's view of the evolutionary value of the flow experience. Flow doesn't constitute a primary need for survival or reproduction, he says, but its independence of cultural background, age, and social status demonstrates that its function is as fundamental a function of our nervous system as language. When we're fully involved in an activity which demands that we mobilize a large part of our total ability, we feel an elation which we want to experience again and again. But this can only occur if we keep increasing the challenge. Thus the flow mechanism contributes to the organism's development toward an ever greater potential of knowledge and competence. In Csikszentmihályi's words: "Through the experience of flow evolution tricks us into developing further."*

Is flow merely a variation on the broad evolutionary theme that the survival of the individual and the species must be assured through pleasure? Does it fill the same function as the delicious taste of healthy edibles, the orgasmic reward for the reproductive effort, or the scent of flowers and honey that attracts pollinating insects?

Can any of these baits help the individual in a situation of crisis? Can the sex drive offer flow experiences when everything is already lost? We'll be taking a closer look at this in the section on Eros and Thanatos below. But first we'll examine another destructive effect of the combined flow experiences of many people. Where have we been brought by our technology, this brilliant result of nature's challenge which we've met with our creative ability? No one has a sharper eye for this than the poet.

THE POET AND NEW YORK

György Faludy, at the age of eighty-four, is a living classic in today's Hungarian literature. My generation grew up with his translations or rather transfigurations of the ballads of the French medieval poet

---

*M. Csikzentimihályi and I. S. Csikzentimihályi, eds., *Optimal Experience* (New York: Cambridge University Press, 1988).

François Villon. We knew that the poems were more Faludy than Villon, but this didn't lessen their influence, which mainly emanated from the evocative power of their words. They were recited and quoted in wide circles, especially by the young. The best actors competed for the privilege of reading them at evening recitals, they were whispered by couples in love, and they were shouted out in political debates with the angry conviction that can only be generated by the struggle against oppression. Faludy was our Villon, and Villon our Faludy.

Faludy's own poetry was quite extensive but not as well known. It enjoyed a good reputation among connoisseurs of lyric poetry but wasn't considered equal to the greatest Hungarian poetry of the period. Practically all of the foremost contemporary poets belonged to Faludy's closest circle of friends and acquaintances.

During the Nazi period Faludy left Hungary and fought as a soldier on the Allied side. Immediately after the end of World War II, when Hungary seemed on its way toward democracy, he returned to Budapest and assumed his given place among the country's leading cultural personalities. During the Stalinist Rákosi period he was jailed and later moved to a work camp, where he preserved his own sanity and that of his fellow prisoners by writing sonnets. He defied the prohibition against writing by "storing" the spoken poems in the brains of his fellow prisoners. Every prisoner learned one or a few sonnets by heart, and then wrote them down after being released. They've recently been collected and published under the title *Sonnets from Recsk*.

After several years of Stalinist imprisonment Faludy was freed in connection with the political thaw which preceded the Hungarian uprising of 1956. When the rebellion was put down, he again left Hungary and settled in Canada. He continued to write poetry and prose while teaching history at the University of Toronto and regularly lecturing in New York. In the fall of 1969 he described one of his many flights in a poem called "On My Way to New York." Armed with a volume of Plato as protection against unwelcome conversations, the poet boards the plane. The plane takes off through the "crowded and whirling horseherds of the rainclouds." It drills its way straight into the "snaking, loose bowels of the gray mares" until it reaches the blinding sunlight and casts its sharply cut shadow on the continent of clouds below.

The poet's lips are like dry brick tiles, his tongue feels like broken glass. In vain he caresses the volume of Plato in his hand. He had already shuddered on the ground when the non-music music began pouring forth from the plane's speakers. Now he looked around at his fellow passengers. Always the same clothes, the same greetings, movements, and attaché cases. Only the faces can be told apart, but not by much. Most are businessmen or engineers. One of them stares passively, while others peruse company reports, then lay them aside, thumb through magazines, then cast them aside. There are also a few men who are better preserved in cosmetic terms but less well dressed, and a few beefy yet still spry and sporty men. These are the managers who've run our menagerie ever since leading us from the meadow of scarcity to the trash heap of excess. They're called executives since they execute the death sentences that technology has brought on us.

Two pretty stewardesses serve nonsmoked smoked ham suffocating in cellophane, doughy bread, and tasteless coffee. In the old days we consumed in order to live—now we live to consume. Others decide for us what we should eat and drink; we've been turned into sausages that they stuff at their whim. The bread tastes bad, but the poet wouldn't be upset by his stomach and intestinal tract having become their sewer, if it wasn't that the houses, the streets, and the cities had also become their sewers, and if their TV, their newspapers, and books—everything already belongs to them—wouldn't do their best to transform our ears and heads to sewers, and if they could refrain from hollering about progress when our species has actually already given up.

We're flying in blinding sunlight, the poet continues. Our plane is pushed forward by many more horse powers than was ever spent by the army of Alexander the Great on its military campaign in India. I would have preferred to have taken a train, but the service has been terminated. I'm forced to drink gasoline like everyone else and support their manic acceleration with my twice-weekly tickets. Two engineers are talking behind me; it feels as if a dentist were about to drill in my ear.

My fellow passenger yawns and begins to cast sideway glances in my direction. I hide in my Greek book. If he addresses me I won't be able to
understand English or else I'll begin wailing in a falsetto voice. . . . Was
it in order to live among these people that you slipped me down on the
spider's thread of your sperm, Father? You couldn't have known in 1910
that a generation was approaching which detests the earth and which
will scrape the fetus out of the womb of the future. They'll hold the wide
horn of prosperity in their hands while vomiting deathly rays, indestructible plastic, and all kinds of junk. You didn't know, Father, that
wherever you'd slip me down, I'd find myself among either shrewd ban-
dits or helpless idiots. Inspiration has died everywhere: the poet stutters
in bad prose, the sculptor's chisel has been dulled, music has turned
into a mechanical racket. The bankers' neo-Babylonian mausoleums
rise skyward everywhere. Those who are cultivated have long since retired, the teachers shrug their shoulders, and where is the science that
can save us from science?

The plane is descending. The poet sees the mountains of trash, the
headlit ribbons of highways that shriek day and night, the fields of nature that have been skinned alive. Car chases car, and the concrete puddles have multiplied in all directions. A vast and cacophonous tivoli is
stuffed between the flag-filled gas-stations, dancing its dance of death
from Boston to Washington while craving to reach all the way to the Pa-
cific Ocean. Is this the smoky forest of chimneys which is envied by the
enemies of America and imitated by the entire world? Karl Marx's realized dream of the great city where unrestricted commercial trade has
swept everything else away lies immersed in its own fumes. It's run by
fat mafiosi and is vandalized by armed youths while left-leaning sons of
millionaires cruise around in their luxury cars. The police have been
bribed, the unions are led by gangsters, the robbers are demonstrating
for their rights.

The poet cannot understand this spoiled, uneducated, and victorious rabble that lives off of the social body like a parasite. They exist
without traditions, taste, harmony, and humility, but not without super-
stition. *They know not the gooseflesh-rousing physical pleasure of*

thinking. They die without ever having glimpsed the daisy-like nipple of shameless heavenly love. They don't even know the meadow-flowering joy of earthly love. They fantasize about crimson vaginas and biceps-thick penises in their glossy magazines and during their disconsolate copulations. They've wrung the neck of history, they gasp hysterically after the seconds on the clock, they seek the permanent in the temporary. In the place of harmony, and to the oily and persistent accompanying chorus of advertisers, they pursue conflict. They're building a Sahara of plastic, a Mount Everest of refrigerators, buildings, and cars. They accomplish everything, but their products turn into repulsive trash while they're hunting for new rubbish.

A while later the poet stands pensive at the foot of a skyscraper, enshrouded in lead-colored fog. Why does man become inferior and more cowardly when he's well off? Why does he start waging war against nature? How can we withstand the noisy hammer-blows against our heads? How can we endure our hunted and anxiety-ridden existence that doesn't give us any pause to think? Why have we let ourselves be recruited into the great march toward technocracy's automatized tyranny? Why do we have to ask science to provide tranquilizers against the discoveries of science? The Devil has dangled the sausage of prosperity in front of our noses until we've lost our sanity and like Faust have sold him our souls. Weren't some people always driven by an ancient instinct to paint lovely gazelles on the walls of caves, write poetry, search for the truth, and build cities and cultures? Are some of us even now driven by an equally strong instinct to smash everything that we've created and built?

The poem ends on a note of calm resignation. What can the poet's thread-thin voice accomplish when not even the shouts of Jeremiah would reach us above the din? "I'll have to be content that the sky remains blue, that I have many friends, books, and memories, and that my head is filled with the beauty of the world. I've persevered thus far, despite all the blows that life has dealt me. I can now rest my feet and hum to myself while keeping watch with one eye now and then in order to see these idiots who don't even know that they're in the process of destroying everything."

EROS AND THANATOS (A KALEIDOSCOPE)

Image 1. I see you, you unknown. You're on the subway in a city alien to me. You're alone in the crowd of people, as am I.

I look at you. I want you to look back. You look at me! Now my eyes won't let you go. You won't let me go either.

You're not letting me go.

I want my gaze to penetrate your eyes, reach the depths of their wells. You're not averting your eyes. You accept.

The crowds and the subway recede. I'm no longer on my way somewhere. Your gaze and mine have merged on the axis of eternity.

You get off. I know that I'll never see you again. But my day's gray dullness has vanished. I no longer feel mediocre, temporary, irrelevant like I did before. I remember. I feel strong and omnipotent. I am happy.

Image 2. He is nineteen, she is twenty. They're seated beside each other in her parental home. People are running back and forth. The war is raging outside. The gangs of the Arrow Cross are celebrating their last murderous orgies against Budapest's Jews. He and she are each wearing a yellow star. They're aware that their days, if not their hours, may be numbered. There's no risk that they'll forget this; there are constant reminders from her uncles who are rushing in and out. But they ignore all news. The experience of having been allowed to take her home after shyly having asked her after a first, short conversation overpowers everything else at this moment. Time has stopped. The cannons in the distance and the murderous threat nearby seem as insignificant as the buzzing of the flies.

Does he dare to touch her? How far are you allowed to go with a "family girl"? He knows nothing about women. He's been with prostitutes but experienced it as a form of masturbation with a completely uninterested stranger and a condom. Was that what everyone had so much to say about?

But this is something completely different. He collects himself. He asks if he may address her in the familiar form—an expression of great intimacy in the Hungarian language in 1944, and not at all a given between boys and girls their age.

You may, she says.

The room is empty for a second, while someone is already clutching the doorknob outside, talking.

He kisses her while trembling all over. Will she slap him in return?

No, she didn't slap him. Her soft, warm lips meet his.

How far does he dare to venture? What if she'll slap him after all! Outside the war is raging. Tomorrow we might both be dead.

An aunt enters. There curfew begins at six o'clock, and the tram is no longer running. He knows that he must get back home, on foot, and he has only five minutes.

The aunt leaves.

He kisses her again. Carefully, cautiously, as if he were approaching an electrical wire, he places a hand upon her knee. He feels her knee through her skirt. Suddenly he notices that she pulls up her skirt an inch with an subtle motion of her hand. His hand is now on her naked knee.

Nothing more happens, not that day. But when he's on his way home, alone, in the long, bloody summer night, well aware that he might be shot at any moment, he knows that her almost imperceptible, seemingly accidental yet without doubt deliberate hand motion will remain among his most precious memories for as long as he lives—if he survives. He's ready to open his shirt to the rifles now. Nothing more can happen in life that exceeds this moment. The motion of her hand has obliterated the institutionalized meaninglessness of the whorehouse. It has nullified the lonesome longing of many years. But it's also removed the immediate threat of death, at least for a short but timeless moment. It's created an untouchable island in the middle of the sea of death.

Image 3. One of the Hungarian war stories of the post-war years describes a lovely summer evening in a large park. Many people were on a field when they were suddenly surprised by an air-raid. The nearest shelter was too far away and everyone threw themselves to the ground. It was fairly dark. Only the light from the bomb explosions lit up the field.

Their rapid and seemingly unreal flashes were accompanied by ear-shattering and very real detonations. The narrator pressed close to the ground and held his breath. In vain he tried to view the explosions as a kind of fireworks display, a spectacle which didn't concern him. Then suddenly, in the rapid bursts of light he saw that a middle-age couple next to him had begun making love. They were fully visible to everyone huddling around them and did nothing to conceal what they were doing. Strangely enough none of the people nearby reacted, even though they ordinarily would have found such a public act immoral and insulting and surely would have summoned the police. But now it was almost the opposite. When he'd overcome his first astonishment and while waiting for the next round of explosions, the narrator noticed, with a certain surprise, that his own reaction was rather positive. He felt as if he was witnessing the triumph of life over death, the individual victorious against the machinery of murder, the revolt of biology against tyranny.

When death is so blind and rampant, the act of love takes on a deeply symbolic meaning, as does love in general. *"Alle Lust will Ewigkeit"* (all lust strives for eternity) according to Nietzsche's Zarathustra. The spellbound amorous couple in the rain of explosives which could take their lives at any moment had chosen a more meaningful activity. Neither the pathetic hopelessness of the situation nor the reactions of others could stop them from this ultimate protest.

The biologist wonders, well aware of the fragility of thought: has this behavior been fixed by our evolution, like the many reserve mechanisms of our bodies that increase our individual chances of survival and those of our species in heat, cold, during droughts or through many months of starvation? Is it comparable to nature's incredible wastefulness which discards trillions of perfect spermatozoa—each one with the complete DNA text of the species—for each successful fertilization? Is the sexual act protected by a psychological mechanism that can countermand the acute fear of death?

Image 4. Rudolf Vrba and his friend Wetzler escaped from Auschwitz in the spring of 1944 as the first survivors, and shortly thereafter Vrba provided history's first eyewitness report from the death camp. His two years in the center of the planet of hell have been described in a book.* Like other Jews, Vrba was on principle condemned to death, but since he was a registrar he was allowed a certain liberty of movement within the camp during his last six months there. Because of this he also came in contact with the small but well-organized resistance movement made up of non-Jewish prisoners.

In September 1943, 4,000 prisoners from the Nazi's "display-ghetto" in Theresienstadt were suddenly transferred to Auschwitz. According to the Auschwitz routine families were always separated on the platform as soon as they had gotten off the train. Children and old people were sent directly to the gas chambers, while able men and women were taken to separate slave work camps. The prisoners from Theresienstadt were greeted in a different way: they were allowed to stay together for six months in a so-called family camp. The regular prisoners could hardly believe their eyes when they saw the children behind the family camp's barbed wire. They hadn't seen children in a long time; everyone knew that they were gassed immediately after their arrival. But now they could see children running and playing. Sometimes smiling SS-men played with them and gave them sweets.

Thanks to his position as registrar Vrba happened to see the instructions for the family camp. It contained the sentence: "Six months of quarantine; then special treatment." The term "special treatment" was the code name for extermination. He also found out that the prisoners at the family camp were told to write letters and postcards to their relatives still in Theresienstadt, which was regularly visited by the international Red Cross. Vrba immediately realized that this was a deception which among other things would simplify the undisturbed transfer of the remaining Jews to Auschwitz.

At this time Vrba had regular meetings with Freddy Hirsch, the chil-

---

*Rudolf Vrba and A. Bestic, *Escape from Auschwitz* (New York: Grove Press, 1986). See also my essay about Vrba, "The Ultimate Fear of the Traveler Returning from Hell" in *Pietà*.

dren's physician in the family camp. They met by the barbed wire which separated the family camp from the regular camp. Freddy was very popular with the children and organized all their activities. One day Vrba noticed that Hirsch was accompanied by one of his assistants, a beautiful twenty-two-year-old Czech girl.

Vrba was nineteen. He was very shy with girls. A few furtive kisses at a dance were his only previous experience. A shy but warm contact eventually developed between Vrba and the girl, whose name was Alice. They would engage in increasingly longer and more personal conversations through the barbed wire.

"We saw nothing of the surrounding world, only each other," writes Vrba in his book. "Auschwitz with its barbed wire, walls, guard towers and horrifying death factory sank from view. We experienced a previously unknown sense of joy."

Despite the barbed wire between them.

"We talked about the future, as if there would be a future, while I intentionally turned so that the crematory's chimneys were beyond my line of sight."

Vrba was constantly aware of the planned fate of the family camp. Still, he tried to lead his and Alice's thoughts away from Auschwitz. He was completely overcome by his first love and could hardly think about anything else.

In December 1943 another 4,000 people from Theresienstadt arrived. They were brought to the family camp, but there were no increases in the food rations. Most importantly, time was running out. The resistance organization was asking Vrba to make contacts within the family camp. With Alice's help Vrba contacted thirty-three people who were ready to act. His daily courtship at the barbed wire now became a forum for this contact. However, Vrba did not yet pass on the information that the "special treatment" had been scheduled to take place on March 7.

The resistance group continued to collect information from their contacts within the main camp. Everything pointed to the crematory, Vrba drily observed. Against all reason he kept hoping that the resistance movement would save the Czechs and Alice along with them.

On March 3 the family camp inhabitants were ordered to write post-cards to their relatives and tell them how well they were. All postcards were to be be antedated by a month for reasons of "censorship and trans-portation." On the same day Vrba heard from the Sonderkommando, meaning the condemned Jews who worked at the crematories during a set period after which they were executed and replaced by another crew, that they'd been ordered to prepare the ovens for 4,000 corpses that would be burned on the night before March 7. The SS-men spoke about the im-portant and intense workday that lay ahead of them.

On March 4 the resistance movement's liaison ordered Vrba to warn the camp that they had only two days to live. He went to the barbed wire where Alice and two of her girlfriends were waiting for him. The three girls were full of confidence. They'd just been told that they'd be moved from Auschwitz to a much better camp. They preferred to believe this instead of listening to Vrba's unbearable warning.

In the morning of March 5 the barbed wire was suddenly gone. The inhabitants of the family camp were told to get ready to leave. The re-sistance liaison confirmed to Vrba that everyone within the family camp would certainly be dead within two days.

In the evening Alice and her two girlfriends were in Vrba's private room. As a registrar he held the privilege of living alone in a small hovel. They spoke about the horror that awaited them. This time they couldn't help but believe what Vrba had recounted. Their last hope was Freddy Hirsch, who'd been urged by the resistance movement to orga-nize a rebellion. Something within them still refused to believe that all the children would be killed. Hadn't the SS-men played, laughed, and joked with them?

After a while Alice's two girlfriends said, "We're leaving now. You have other things to talk about."

Vrba, who'd never before been alone with a girl, felt very embar-rassed after the two girls left. He continued to talk about what would happen the next day. But Alice pulled him close and asked him to stop talking. Vbra writes:

No more words were spoken. Suddenly Auschwitz didn't matter. It ceased to exist. The guard towers and the guns and the dogs, the mud, the death, the high and evil chimney had disappeared. They were erased by a spell that neither one of us had experienced before.*

The next day was the day of death, as expected. In the film *Shoah*, where I first saw Vrba, he and Philip Müller, the sole survivor from the Jewish Sonderkommando that worked with the crematory ovens, recounted the course of events for Claude Lanzmann. The plans to organize a revolt within the family camp with the moral support of the resistance movement couldn't be realized since Freddy Hirsch had taken his own life in Vrba's room. Hirsch couldn't bring himself to start an uprising which would immediately have led to the death of the children, even though he knew that they'd die a few hours later anyway.

When it was clear that an uprising was unthinkable, Vrba went back to Alice. They walked arm in arm during the early afternoon and spoke about the the future which didn't exist; a home, children, life and light. That was when they first heard the terrible sound of the trucks. These arrived full of new SS-soldiers that hadn't served in that particular part of the camp and knew neither the children nor any other prisoners. They began their task with a brutality unusual even for Auschwitz. For the first time thousands of people were gassed who'd been in Auschwitz for six months and who knew what fate awaited them. This situation differed from the regular "transports" when the confused and deceived people were taken to the gas chambers directly from the train. Some of the victims resisted in the dressing rooms or at the entrance to the gas chamber, but they were ruthlessly beaten with sticks and forced to get inside.

It was time to say farewell for Alice and Vrba. People were being brutalized all around them. Children were bludgeoned with rifle butts, infants crushed against rocks, while their mothers were pushed forward in a screaming, bleeding, formless mass. Vrba's clothes identified him

---

*Vrba and Bestic, *Escape from Auschwitz*.

as an administrative employee. Someone yelled at him that he too would be taken away if he didn't leave the area.

Alice let go of her embrace. Her face was pale, but she didn't cry. Go now, she said. Then she ran toward the trucks that took the condemned to the gas chambers. While running she was struck by an SS-soldier, fell, got up and continued running.

Vrba barely made it out of the area. He heard the empty trucks returning. But suddenly a song rose above the rumble of the motors. It was the Czech national anthem. It was sung by the condemned while they thronged at the entrance to the dressing room by the gas chamber. They continued with the Hebrew song "*Hatikva*" (hope), which later became Israel's national anthem.

Image 5. In his key novel *Árnyjáték* (Game of Shadows),* the Hungarian author György Somlyó describes the illness and death of a close friend. The names in the novel are fictitious, but the writer later admitted that the protagonist is based on Gábor Devecseri, a poet, author, and classicist who was known to the general public especially through his beautiful translations of Homer. A tall, dark, emotional, intellectual, and charismatic man, Devecseri was always admired and loved by both men and women, but especially by women. Devecseri loved and worshiped Woman, viewing Her as one of his most important sources of poetic inspiration.

Somlyó's book is about the serious illness and death of his friend. He was suffering from rapidly growing abdominal sarcoma, one of the most malignant of all cancerous tumors. It was inoperable and eventually grew to monstrous size. Even the hospital staff could hardly bear looking at his diseased belly. But the poet denied that he was ill. He willingly accepted the transparent lie which blamed his condition on a temporary loss of local circulation.

People interested in art and literature had always flocked around Devecseri. Many were women whom he had complimented, kissed, or embraced. But his most intimate confidantes were the words, the jewels of the poet. He continued writing while in the hospital and played with

---

*György Somlyó, *Árnyjáték* (Budapest: Magvetö, 1977).

his recently acquired "magno"—an early version of a dictaphone employing a magnetized steel wire. He was as fond of his "enchanting cart" as a child is of his new toy. Many of Devecseri's friends came to visit. Young, beautiful women would begin with the obligatory round of kisses: first their mouth, then their cheeks, and finally, after raising their skirt, one on each buttock. Then the same question was put to every visitor, regardless of age or sex: "I've written a few lines. Do you want to listen?" And everyone would listen, eagerly, with curiosity turning into enchantment. No one ever regretted having listened, despite the slightly troubling awareness that people didn't really mean much to him as individuals. Devecseri did love them, but mainly as a listening part of nature. If the listener would break out in praise or applause after the reading, he would smile shyly and say something like "Wasn't that tasteful!" or "That sounded pretty good." It wasn't a sign of false modesty. He was already on his way toward new poems, new enchanted carts. It had always been that way, and that was the way it was this time too, as he struggled with death while pretending to ignore it.

In the middle of this end phase of his life the incredible happened. A passioned and erotically consummated love affair flowered between the monstrously deformed yet still divine poet and a beautiful young female physician who on her own had decided to give the patient injections at five in the morning. Neither one tried to hide the affair from their friends—quite the contrary. It seemed that they wished that others would know about their love, but not because they wanted to boast or shock or be admired. They instead behaved like a young couple newly in love wanting to manifest their happiness to their friends.

Somlyó finished his *roman à clef* by referring to a short-story by Elias Canetti.* The narrator of the short story is in Marrakesch in North Africa. Late one night he encounters a crowd of people in a large square surrounding a man who is beating his donkey with a large stick. It is a poor, emaciated creature with colorless, thinned-out hair, a "skeleton in a skin bag" who can hardly stand on its own four legs. The man tries to

---

*Elias Canetti, "*Die Lust des Esels*" (The Donkey's Desire), in *Die Stimmen von Marrakesch* (Frankfurt, 1980).

force it to move, but without success. The narrator has never seen a more pitiful creature, and is consoled only by the thought that the animal probably doesn't have long to live. Perhaps his suffering will end that very evening. But when he passes the next morning the donkey is still there in the exact same spot. Has it been there all night? In the sunlight it appears even more worn and pathetic. The narrator turns away, discouraged and depressed. After a minute or so he looks at the donkey again. A completely unexpected sight meets his eyes:

> The donkey was in the same spot, but it was no longer the same donkey. Between his two hind legs an enormous male organ was now erect, stronger and larger than the stick with which the donkey had been beaten the previous night. During the moment I had looked away an overwhelming change must have occurred in the animal. I don't know what it had seen or heard, or which smell it might have smelled. I don't know what had happened in the mind of the animal. But this pathetically weak, old donkey who was hardly able to stand on its legs and whose only remaining strength was to refuse to move from his spot, this animal who had to endure more than other tormented donkeys in Marrakesch, this being who hardly ranked among the lowest on the ladder of the living and who'd been robbed of his muscles, fatty tissue, fur, and strength, had retained so much desire that seeing it made me forget the donkey's horrible predicament. I often think about this animal. I wish that every suffering person should be able to experience the same desire, right in the middle of his worst degradation.

Canetti's final words surprise me. Is this really what one should wish for suffering people? Desire, without the slightest possibility of experiencing anything else than sheer longing itself? An unfulfilled desire which cannot be satisfied by any feeling of togetherness or even an illusion, hardly better than when the erect phallus of the dead Osiris broke through the mummified god's funereal bandages—is this really what we should wish for one another when death approaches, rather than a state of enlightened serenity?

But who knows? Who understands the millions of reactive patterns and protective mechanisms that have been created by our evolution and that have developed through our confrontation with the manifold manifestations of the world? Does a desperate desire to propagate the species arise when the individual is facing his own annihilation? Or perhaps it doesn't have anything to do with reproduction, but rather with the hope that Beatrice will spirit away the confused from the mountain of Purgatory?

Do I really want to think about the donkey's desire? Would I want to experience it in my penultimate moment, the way Canetti recommends? Does this really have anything to do with Eros and Thanatos, perhaps our two strongest and most moving archetypes? It's doubtful, to say the least. Wouldn't it be wiser to discard the entire episode from this essay?

I've hardly faced this thought before I become aware of a few notes from the musical channel which is constantly switched on. It creates a pleasant background music while I work—if it becomes unpleasant, I turn it off—but also a certain sense of shame that I use meteors as street lamps, to paraphrase Zoltán Kodály's statement in reaction to the Hungarian Communist regime's fantasies about Bartók's planned role in Hungary had he lived. But this time my psyche's hardened protective wall is pierced by an unexpected signal; the antennas are turned outward, a stronger commando has taken over. But it isn't a meteor that shoots across my sky, nor a masterpiece that makes me listen. It's a synthetic, rather kitschy hybrid between a Bach prelude and an Ave Maria by Gounod. The prelude from Bach's *Das Wohltemperierte Klavier* carries Gounod's tenor voice on its shoulders. It can be rather beautiful if sung by Gigli or a comparably great tenor. This time it's performed by a hoarse alto of considerably lesser class. She's about to sing a few words that will lift my soul for many hours. I know it even before she's sung them: *Ora pro nobis, nobis peccatoribus.*

Pray for us, for us sinners. Mary! Oh Virgin Mary!

Pray for us . . .

Why do we want a holy woman whom we can implore to pray for us? Why must she be both a virgin and a mother to be able to intervene? What kind of archetypes are moving about in our subconscious? Why am I always so deeply touched by these words?—I, who don't believe in prayers nor a god nor a holy mother—not to mention a virgin birth, which can only bring indecent associations to my mind?

Archetypes? Yes, what could they otherwise be? One jetlagged morning in London I heard an intense debate on the BBC about virgin birth. I could hardly believe my ears. Several decades after the sexual revolution, at a time when it's become socially acceptable—with some reservations—that single women have children, a storm of protests have been raised against a woman who has never had, and wishes never to have, sexual relations with men, but who nevertheless wants a child. Bishops, priests, and other "respectable" personalities spoke up against this abominable thought. They especially stressed the drawbacks of growing up without a father. But similar protests have not been raised against single women who've had children the natural way.

What's the difference? Should such an insignificant anatomical detail as a hymen provoke the men of the church to react so strongly? Which holy taboo has been disturbed? The religious myth of the virgin birth? Do they want to protect their own inner Ave Maria? Will she no longer pray for us, *pro nobis peccatoribus,* if the virgin birth is realized and trivialized by modern medicine? Do they want to retain some "preferred status" in their relation to the holy, immaculate mother?

What is really meant by "immaculate"? Is a woman who has conceived a child the natural way stained, defiled, impure? Is my mother and your mother, sister, and daughter stained? Can this nonsense be accepted nowadays; should it be allowed to remain as a linguistic fossil despite its indecent meaning?

The thought that the act which has created each and every one of us is impure runs counter to the very idea of life. Have religious men branded our mothers impure in order to retain the "holy virgin" to pray for us? What logic! We must pray to her so that she can pray for us. She should be a virgin in order to be able to pray. What devil of a god must be appeased in this way? Why is he angry, really—why must he be appeased? Is this the same kind of god who's demanded bloody animal and human sacrifices in other cultures? Are these the kinds of gods that our archetypes create for us? Isn't it spineless servility to call him "good God"?

Fortunately our biology refuses to obey. Our DNA knows what it wants. If Thanatos has lowered his torch, Eros raises his, more unconcerned and self-assured than ever. Here is our victory, the road to our survival.

EPILOGUE

The Rilke quote at the start of this essay is the entry to *"Das Stundenbuch."* The hour bends down and moves the poet with its clear, metallic stroke. His senses tremble: he knows that he *can.* He seizes the "pliable day." He knows that he is creating a world through his way of seeing. He creates it from scratch. Nothing was complete until he had seen it. His message is like a bride—each one gets what he wants. In the last stanza he clarifies this: nothing is too small for the poet, he loves it still, he paints it large on a golden background, holds it up high *"und ich weiss nicht wem löst es die Seele los"* (and I know not whose soul it releases).

In *"Stundenbuch's"* concluding poem the poet knows that he has succeeded. He doesn't say that he's speaking about himself, but the reader—or at least this reader—is at poetic liberty to read this into these unforgettable lines:

> Denn er war keiner von den immer Müdern,
> die freudeloser werden nach und nach,
> mit kleinen Blumen wie mit kleinen Brüdern
> ging er den Wiesenrand entlang und sprach.
> Und sprach von sich und wie er sich verwende
> so dass es allem eine Freude sei;
> und seines hellen Herzens war kein Ende,
> und kein Geringes ging daran vorbei.
>
> Er kam aus Licht zu immer tieferm Lichte,
> und seine Zelle stand in Heiterkeit.
> Das Lächeln wuchs auf seinem Angesichte
> und hatte seine Kindheit und Geschichte
> und wurde reif wie eine Mädchenzeit.

Und wenn er sang, so kehrte selbst das Gestern
und das Vergessene zurück und kam;
und eine Stille wurde in den Nestern
und nur die Herzen schrieen in den Schwestern,
die er berührte wie ein Bräutigam.

Dann aber lösten seines Liedes Pollen
sich leise los aus seinem roten Mund
und trieben träumend zu den Liebevollen
und fielen in die offenen Corollen
und sanken langsam auf den Blütengrund.

Und sie empfingen ihn, den Makellosen,
in ihrem Leib, der ihre Seele war.
Und ihre Augen schlossen sich wie Rosen
und voller Liebesnächte war ihr Haar.

Und ihn empfing das Grosse und Geringe.
Zu vielen Tieren kamen Cherubim
zu sagen, dass ihr Weibchen Früchte bringe,—
und waren wunderschöne Schmetterlinge:
denn ihn erkannten alle Dinge
und hatten Fruchtbarkeit aus ihm.

Und als er starb, so leicht wie ohne Namen,
da war er ausgeteilt: sein Samen rann
in Bächen, in den Bäumen sang sein Samen
und sah ihn ruhig aus den Blumen an.
Er lag und sang. Und als die Schwestern kamen,
da weinten sie um ihren lieben Mann.

For he was quite unlike those weary others
who keep on growing ever joylesser;
with little flowers as with little brothers
he paced along the meadows to confer.
Spoke of himself and of his application
of that self to provide a joy for each;
and his heart's brightness knew no limitation,
that heart that nothing was too small to reach.

From light to ever more illumination
he passed; his cell was bathed in cheerfulness.
That smile of his began its germination
and had its childhood and initiation
and ripened like a young girl's youthfulness.
And when he sang, the long relinquished yester
and all-forgotten came and re-occurred;
and silence grew and grew in every nester
save that the crying hearts were manifester
in sisters whom his bride-groom touch bestirred.
Then, though, the pollen of his song was lifted
out of his red mouth inconspicuously,
and dreamingly to those that loved him drifted,
and through their open calyxes was sifted
in slow descendence to the ovary.
And him, the all-unblemished, each encloses,
like her own soul, within her body there.
And their closed eyelids were like leaves of roses,
and filled with nights of loving was their hair.
And him both great and little were receiving.
To many creatures there came cherubim,
as butterflies of brilliance past believing,
to tell them that their mates would be conceiving:
for he was clear to all perceiving,
and all had fruitfulness from him.
And when, so nameless-lightly he lay dying,
he was distributed; his seed ran free
in brooks; in trees his seed was psalmodying
and gazed at him from flowers tranquilly.
He lay and sang. And left the sisters crying
round their beloved consort bitterly.

(Translation by J. B. Leishman)

The feeling of "I can," the assurance that we're ready to meet a challenge or master an important task, stimulates us to focus our mental activity. The sense that we "can do it" can create a euphoric feeling of hap-

piness. The third component in this experience is the timelessness, the opposite of the "hour's stroke." The joyous feeling of timelessness born from the "I can" experience can only arise from the cruel desert landscape of time. That's the only place where the oasis can cool and refreshen, not in the middle of a rain forest.

My feet march mechanically on. My body which has lived through nineteen springs drags itself strenuously onward amidst the gray mass of forced slave laborers. We're on our way to nowhere. My mouth is dry, my mind empty, my emotions dulled, my hopes swept away, my prospects nonexistent. Only my feet mark time. They've been transformed into a clock ticking in an empty room. There are no living auditory organs that can perceive sound, our ears have been extinguished, our centers of hearing are as dead as old rolls of wax.

Then suddenly it happens. I see the mighty break of day, I hear the cock crowing after the night of time:

> Du bist die Zukunft, grosses Morgenrot
> über den Ebenen der Ewigkeit.
> Du bist der Hahnschrei nach der Nacht der Zeit,
> der Tau, die Morgenmette und die Maid
> der fremde Mann, die Mutter und der Tod.
>
> Rainer Maria Rilke, "Das Stundenbuch"

> You are the future, mighty break of day
> above the plainlands of eternity,
> cock crow to chase the night of time away.
> You are the dew, the matins and the She,
> the strange man, mother, and final decay.
>
> (Translation by Peter Zollman)

The mighty break of day after the night of time? In the middle of the book of hours? From which night of time must we escape? The clock of enzyme reactions and protein synthesis that counts milliseconds; the clock of cell divisions that shows the hours and the days; the clock of physical growth, sexual maturity, and learning with its many months and years; the long wave clock of aging with its decades; the clock of the generations with its half and whole centuries; the millennia of history; evolutionary time with its millions of years—they tick and tick, small clocks and large clocks; quick, fussy seconds that hurry round and round; the clock of large predatory cats which according to my grandchildren run quicker than any other animal; the clock of snails during their mating season in springtime; the iguana's clock when it sits on its dry branch and blinks once a day. All clocks can be placed on a continuum, they continue to tick discontinuously. You can place them on an instructive diagram in the same way that you can draw the relative size of animals, from an amoeba's dot to the massive corporality of an elephant or a whale.

Our soul is not on this continuum. Don't try to find it; you're searching in vain.

Some prominent nineteenth-century pathologist supposedly quipped that he didn't succeed in finding the soul during his many thousand autopsies. When my first boss, Torbjörn Caspersson, who was one of the pioneers of cellular chemistry, had given a lecture in Ohio during the 1950s, a local Christian paper wrote: "Dr. Caspersson says: The soul is only chemistry." One of the leading molecular biologists of our time recently wrote me that poetry, psychology, philosophy, and a few additional humanist subjects will become worthless junk when molecular biology has succeeded in providing a full chemical description of the function of the nerve cells. Such a description will offer a "unified, pragmatic solution" concerning humans and their functions.

I share my colleague's delight in the evolution of molecular biology and above all its great precision and objectivity. The hereditary code which is written in every person's DNA can only be read in one way. Scientists in different labs pronounce the same "words" when they read the same DNA. My colleague's excessive faith in the possibilities of molecular biology probably stems from this precision. But to read a text is not the same as to understand its full functional meaning—even if I don't want to go as far as Professor Leibowitz. When I ran into his roadblock with my discussion on flow as described earlier in this essay, I asked his opinion on the development of molecular biology. "It's the greatest scientific advance of our century," he answered without hesitation. "Still, no molecular biologist will ever be able to explain why this strand of hair on my head points to the right and not to the left."

"But, Professor Leibowitz," I replied; "I've just been to California where I've met a scientist who has isolated a gene in the fruit fly which determines the exact direction of the hair. He's managed to determine the sequence of the entire gene (i.e., read its full text). When he inserts it into another fruit fly, it changes the direction of the hair."

"This is no explanation," Leibowitz said. "It's possible to read the text of the gene, and to describe the composition of the protein it encodes. Still, no one will ever be able to explain why my hair points to the right and not to the left."

That was as far as we got. My own perception of molecular reality lies somewhere halfway between the standpoint of Professor Leibowitz and that of my molecular biologist colleague. The function of the gene is codified in its text (DNA sequence in technical language). The relationship between a DNA sequence and its protein product is similar to the relationship between the letters CHAIR and a real chair. But the genetic instruction does not define *any* chair like its etymological metaphor but all the details of a given chair and therefore its precise function. But it doesn't say anything about the relationship between the chair and the rest of the furniture or about the sensations of the person who sits on it. Other objects, including the person and his condition, are governed by other instructions. Each instruction is amenable, at least in principle, to definition and reading in its own right. But the total interplay between the furniture and the biological creatures who use it is more than the sum of all parts. This "more" is also dependent upon many coincidences in the very interplay itself. These cannot be predicted exactly, since each component is not only influenced by its instructive text but also by the coincidences of the interactions.

Yes, the pathologist is correct. There's no special organ for the soul. It's also correct to say that all psychological processes stem from the

chemistry of the brain cells. But my molecular colleague is still wrong
in his optimistic extrapolation. Even if a complete description of the
chemical processes of the brain was ever possible, which is doubtful, it
wouldn't abolish all poetry and all psychology. Poetry and psychology
will continue to live on their own levels and according to their own laws.
Knowledge of molecular biology can increase our possibilities to understand and influence these realms. But the belief that molecular biology
will replace them is as preposterous as it would be to claim that the eval-
uation of a sound oscillogram can be compared to or even surpass the
pleasure derived from listening to the Mozart symphony that the oscillogram has codified.

One of the subjective experiences of the soul that is at variance with
its chemical definition is its relative time- and agelessness. When my
sixty-five-year-old self ascended the same stairway as I used to climb at
the age of five, the same self and the same consciousness moved now as
it did then. But my consciousness was incomprehensibly linked to a certain body that is always at a certain place, at a certain time, and speaks
a certain language. In view of the timelessness of the soul it is equally
inexplicable why a certain moment is identified as "now."* Has the
Rilke poem transferred me from the deadly monotony of the meaningless march to the innate timelessness of my soul where I could feel at
home? Was it there Proust was taken when the taste of a madeleine cake
and a cup of tea inspired him to enter the immense building of memory
(*l'édifice immense du souvenir*)? Listen to his voice:

> No sooner had the warm liquid mixed with the crumbs touched my
> palate than a shudder ran through me and I stopped, intent upon the
> extraordinary thing that was happening to me. An exquisite pleasure
> had invaded my senses, something isolated, detached, with no sug-
> gestion of its origin. And at once the vicissitudes of life had become
> indifferent to me, its disasters innocuous, its brevity illusory—this
> new sensation having had on me the effect which love has of filling me

---

*For a closer treatment of this question, see Thomas Nagel, *A View from Nowhere*
(Oxford: Oxford University Press, 1986).

with a precious essence; or rather this essence was not in me, it *was* me. I had ceased now to feel mediocre, contingent, mortal.*

Many of us can be moved to tears, laugh out loud, or feel the incurable pangs of nostalgia when we're confronted with the smells, tastes, or sights of our childhood, or with the people whom we knew then. But we're seldom or never granted the privilege of experiencing Proust's flow. Most of us lack the will or the ability to use memory's steam to drive a creative power plant such as his. We cannot experience it as a challenge; it doesn't put our abilities to the test since most of us lack Proust's genius.

"De la même façon qu'opère l'amour"—love works the same way, says Proust. Falling passionately in love can also make time stop. The sense of mediocrity, mortality, and the ephemeral nature of time may disappear for a while, but as we all know, time stops only for a moment. Time then resumes its relentless chase and the flow-addicted time-hater must continue his pursuit of ever new love objects and/or other challenges.

---

*Marcel Proust:, *Swann's Way*, translated by C. K. Scott Moncrieff and Terence Kilmartin (New York: Vintage Books, 1989).

DEMCO